AF522229

Vocational Guide to Yoga and Health

Vocational Guide to Yoga and Health

Hari Narayan

RANDOM PUBLICATIONS
NEW DELHI (INDIA)

Vocational Guide to Yoga and Health

ISBN 978-93-5111-235-8

Published in 2014 in India by

RANDOM PUBLICATIONS

4376-A/4B, Gali Murari Lal, Ansari Road
New Delhi-110 002
Phone : +91-11-43580356, +91-11-23289044
e-mail: randomexports@gmail.com, sales@randompublications.com, info@randompublications.com

Type Setting by : Keystoneprintads, Delhi-110051
Digitally Printed at: Replika Press Pvt. Ltd.

Preface

The popularity of Yoga as a modality of health and wellbeing has steadily grown in recent years. With this growth comes the demand for suitably qualified teachers to guide people safely and effectively.

Yoga is an integral part of our lifestyle. It removes the impurities from the level of mind and unites everything with the spirit. For instance, insomnia could be connected to stress, anxiety or depression. You have to address that issue instead of merely taking medication. This way, you have a wider perception of your own mind, body, thoughts and emotions and there's more clarity and you are able to guide your prana (life force) in a positive way to progress in life.

Yoga is beneficial for the health in ways that modern science is just beginning to understand. Even though it has been applied with therapeutic intention for thousand of years, Yoga Therapy is only just now emerging as a discipline in itself. More health care practitioners are starting to include yogic techniques in their approach to healing and more yoga teachers give a therapeutic intention to their teaching. People who have never tried yoga before are starting to consider including Yoga in their treatment plan.

Most physical exercises develop the muscles or aid in the circulation of blood. Yoga asanas are "inner-sizes" in that, in addition to working on the muscles and circulation, they also have a profound affect on endocrine glands and nerves. Yoga asanas were developed over a period of thousands of years. At first yogis watched the postures of different animals and then imitated them. For example, the peacock is a bird with a powerful digestive system; it can digest a poisonous snake. Similarly there is a posture in which the yogi imitates the position of the peacock. The posture helps develop the glands and organs responsible for digestion and can prevent or cure many diseases that originate in this area of the body.

Physical Education, Exercise Science, Recreation, and the many related programs provide a number of varied and unique opportunities for students today. In the past, a degree in Physical Education meant that an individual would most likely become a gym teacher. However, with the increased attention to health, fitness, and leisure, as well as rehabilitation and therapy, physical education now encompasses many different areas.

I thank all members of my team who have helped in the preparation of the book. My special thanks go to "Random Publications" who have published the book.

*– **Hari Narayan***

Contents

1

The Origin of Yoga

The basic problem of every living creature is survival in a hostile world. Countless generations ago, from the teeming human masses of the East, where man lived in ever-present dread of famine, disease, flood, invasion and vengeance of the gods, Yoga, a system or method of attaining physical and mental serenity under adverse and even horrible conditions, was introduced.

Man, in his essence, has changed little in the course of historic time. The philosophy of Yoga and its practice, which enabled the Indo-Aryan to survive the stresses of his time, can also enable people of the modern Western world to achieve contentment and security in the face of the cold war, the hydrogen bomb, missile, counter-missile and counter-counter-missile and other perils in a rapidly changing world.

Scholars who have attempted to trace the beginnings of the practice of Yoga have found that its principles were well established as far back as the time when the written word was new. There are many "books" of Yoga among the oldest scripts in Sanskrit, the ancient sacred language of India. Even these refer to a distant past in which the secrets of Yoga were passed on from generation to generation by word of mouth. Only the Indian form of Yoga is well known in America and Europe, but there is strong evidence that Yoga principles were known to the Egyptians and Chinese and that there were monastic societies among the Hebrew Essenes who were, from reliable historical evidence, groups of Yoga practitioners. Perhaps the recent discovery of the Dead Sea Scrolls will reveal some of the secrets of this philosophy that have been lost in the shadows of the years.

The purpose of yoga (meaning to bind) was called the 'raising of Mother Kundalini'(the life force at the base of the spine). Yoga had its origins in India in the Sat Yuga, the Age of Gold, over 26,000 years ago. This was a long peaceful age of abudance in which humans had plenty of time to search within.

The yoga of the raising of the Kundalini at this time blossomed organically, out of the intuition and spontaneity of the practitioner. The goal of the yogi was to ascend into the immortal realms of pure spirit, to imbibe the intuitional nectar of enlightenment, irradicate disease and find liberation from suffering. This was called Samadhi.

In 600 B.C., during the dark age of Kali Yug, signified by Iron, these practices were written down for the first time by Patanjali in India and thus gained a structure that evolved into various systems given out by contemporary Gurus. This structure was called the Eight Limbs of Patañjali's Yoga. Ultimately, the students of yoga were to gain enough systematic knowledge of yoga techniques, that they could tap into the original or primal yoga of spontaneity, intuition, and creative freedom, a condition that modern yogic practitioners might refer to as Super-mind. The seed mantra of yoga is AUM or OM. It is the sound of the Cosmos and is the sound that constitutes the Akashic Realms (the non-material etheric plane), the source of Samadhi. This universal tone of pure resonance is produced elegantly by the disc-shaped instrument called the Ancient Gong.

WHAT IS YOGA?

The word "Yoga" cannot be translated into English. In the Sanskrit, it derives from the root "Yuja," which is to join or weld together. Just as two pieces of metal are welded together to become one, so in the philosophy of Yoga, the embodied spirit of the individual becomes one with the Universal Spirit through the regular practice of certain physical and mental exercises. In another definition, Yoga is the art of life and its philosophy is meant to furnish the principles that justify and explain that art.

One of the Sanskrit texts, the Bhagwad-Gita, describes Yoga as equanimity of mind which results in efficiency of action. For those to whom Yoga represents a religion as well as a way of life, Yoga means the union or linking together of man with God, or the disunion or separation of man from the objects of physical sensation in the material world. It is the science or skill which leads the initiate by easy steps to the pinnacle of self-realization.

There are many common misconceptions which stand between the truths of Yoga and those who live in the Western world. Many Americans have heard more about Yogis, or those who practice Yoga, than about Yoga itself. They picture the Yogi as an Indian fakir, swathed in rags, who spends his life on a bed of nails or sits motionless underneath a tree until birds build nests in his hair. Their knowledge of Yoga is gained from supposedly esoteric literature or from side-show performers billed as "Swamis" or "Yogis" who stick pins through their flesh or permit themselves to be buried alive. More charitably, they may think of the Yoga convert as some mildly eccentric individual who enjoys standing on his head before breakfast.

Nevertheless, the true spirit and practice of Yoga has already spread to this country and has achieved what might be called a high degree of respectability. A number of colleges and universities, including such institutions as the University of Southern California, offer courses in Yoga.

Also, such prominent athletes as Parry O'Brien, long-time holder of the world's shot-put record, have studied and practiced Yoga. It has spread even to the halls of our national Congress where Representative Francis P. Bolton's practice of Yoga has received nationwide press coverage. Stripping the "magic" from Yoga reveals that it is a practice that effectively enables its user to meet the stresses of modern life, and offers relaxation that may stand between its adherents and the stomach ulcers or psychiatrist's couch that are so common today. You need not retire to an "Ashram," or Yoga retreat, to acquire the benefits of this system; rather, you can attain the serenity and relaxation that it affords through the information in this volume. Practicing Yoga takes but a few moments a day, although Yoga itself gradually fills the entire day of the person who pursues it with faith and belief.

Yoga Is Not a Religion

Although the Original Yoga System presents detailed information and techniques regarding the 'soul', Yoga is not a religion. Yoga is a spiritual science. By learning this science, an individual understands the fundamentals of all religions. Yoga is a universal development system. Yoga develops a human on the subjects of consciousness and soul, yet it is not a religion based on theology and rituals. There is no hierarchy or worshiping of a leader or a deity in the Original Yoga System. Yoga is a source of spiritual information. By acquiring this information, an individual comprehends the basic principles of all religions. Yoga is a cultural and spiritual branch of knowledge that is open to all humans without regard of class, faith, color, race, gender and age. Perhaps the only essential quality necessary to begin Yoga is to accept the existence of the secret potentials of the human consciousness and to have the will to reach the summit of consciousness by practicing Yoga techniques. The factor that differentiates Yoga from religions is its perspective on the body, mind and emotions. Religions perceive the body, mind and emotions as an obstruction on the path to enlightenment and as a means of sin. Whereas the Original Yoga System teaches that the body, mind and emotions are a part of the universal truth and how it can be used for humankind to develop, become enlightened and ascend.

When the body, mind and emotions are cleaned and filled with positive energy by means of Yoga techniques, the individual is naturally freed of negative desires, thoughts and actions. By using one's free will in a positive manner and enhancing one's self-confidence, a person takes on the responsibility of his/her destiny and is emancipated from the slavery of destiny. An individual thus draws up his/her own destiny on the path to improving positiveness and unison without waiting for the mercy of others.

YOGA HISTORY

Yoga is more than mastering postures and increasing your flexibility and strength. "The traditional purpose of Yoga, however, has always been to bring about a profound transformation in the person through the transcendence of the ego," In Hinduism, Buddhism and Jainism the word yoga means "spiritual discipline". People often associate yoga with the postures and stances that make up the physical activity of the exercise, but after closer inspection it becomes clear that there are many more aspects of yoga. It is an activity that has been practiced for thousands of years, and it is something that has evolved and changed overtime. Different factions of yoga have developed since its conception.

The exact history and origins of yoga is uncertain; however, there are pieces that have been connected and allow us to make some conclusions. It is known that yoga originated from the East. The earliest signs of yoga appear in ancient Shamanism. Evidence of yoga postures were found on artifacts that date back to 3000 B.C. Evidence of yoga is found in the oldest-existing text, Rig-Veda. Rig-Veda is a composition of hymns. Topics of the Rig-Veda include prayer, divine harmony, and greater being.

"The primary goal of shamanism was to heal members of the community and act as religious mediators," Yoga originally focused on applying and understanding the world. Its focus later changed to the self. Self-enlightenment became the ultimate goal. It was not until the sixth century B.C. that the poses and meditation became a critical element. They were implimented by Buddhist teachings.

The history of Yoga can conveniently be divided into the following four broad categories:

- Vedic Yoga
- Preclassical Yoga
- Classical Yoga
- Postclassical Yoga

These categories are like static snapshots of something that is in actuality in continuous motion—the "march of history."

[SH]Vedic Yoga

Now we are entering somewhat more technical territory, and I will have to use and explain a number of Sanskrit terms. The yogic teachings found in the above-mentioned Rig-Veda and the other three ancient hymnodies are known as Vedic Yoga. The Sanskrit word veda means "knowledge," while the Sanskrit term rig (from ric) means "praise." Thus the sacred Rig-Veda is the collection of hymns that are in praise of a higher power. This collection is in fact the fountainhead of Hinduism, which has around one billion adherents today. You could say that the Rig-Veda is to Hinduism what the Book of Genesis is to Christianity.

The other three Vedic hymnodies are the Yajur-Veda ("Knowledge of Sacrifice"), Sama-Veda ("Knowledge of Chants"), and Atharva-Veda

("Knowledge of Atharvan"). The first collection contains the sacrificial formulas used by the Vedic priests. The second text contains the chants accompanying the sacrifices. The third hymnody is filled with magical incantations for all occasions but also includes a number of very powerful philosophical hymns. It is connected with Atharvan, a famous fire priest who is remembered as having been a master of magical rituals. These hymnodies can be compared to the various books of the Old Testament. It is clear from what has been said thus far that Vedic Yoga—which could also be called Archaic Yoga—was intimately connected with the ritual life of the ancient Indians. It revolved around the idea of sacrifice as a means of joining the material world with the invisible world of the spirit. In order to perform the exacting rituals successfully, the sacrificers had to be able to focus their mind for a prolonged period of time. Such inner focusing for the sake of transcending the limitations of the ordinary mind is the root of Yoga.

When successful, the Vedic yogi was graced with a "vision" or experience of the transcendental reality. A great master of Vedic Yoga was called a "seer"—in Sanskrit rishi. The Vedic seers were able to see the very fabric of existence, and their hymns speak of their marvelous intuitions, which can still inspire us today.

Preclassical Yoga

This category covers an extensive period of approximately 2,000 years until the second century A.D. Preclassical Yoga comes in various forms and guises. The earliest manifestations were still closely associated with the Vedic sacrificial culture, as developed in the Brâhmanas and Âranyakas. The Brâhmanas are Sanskrit texts explaining the Vedic hymns and the rituals behind them. The Âranyakas are ritual texts specific to those who chose to live in seclusion in a forest hermitage. Yoga came into its own with the Upanishads, which are gnostic texts expounding the hidden teaching about the ultimate unity of all things. There are over 200 of these scriptures, though only a handful of them were composed in the period prior to Gautama the Buddha (fifth century B.C.). These works can be likened to the New Testament, which rests on the Old Testament but at the same time goes beyond it. One of the most remarkable Yoga scriptures is the Bhagavad-Gîtâ ("Lord's Song"), of which the great social reformer Mahatma Gandhi spoke as follows:

When disappointment stares me in the face and all alone I see not one ray of light, I go back to the Bhagavad-Gita. I find a verse here and a verse there and I immediately begin to smile in the midst of overwhelming tragedies—and my life has been full of external tragedies—and if they have left no visible, no indelible scar on me, I owe it all to the teachings of the Bhagavad-Gita. In its significance, this work of only 700 verses perhaps is to Hindus what Jesus' Sermon on the Mount is to Christians. Its message, however, is not to turn the other cheek but to actively oppose evil in the world.

In its present form, the Bhagavad-Gîtâ (Gîtâ for short) was composed around 500 B.C. and since then has been a daily inspiration to millions of Hindus. Its central teaching is to the point: To be alive means to be active and, if we want to avoid difficulties for ourselves and others, our actions must be benign and also go beyond the grip of the ego. A simple matter, really, but how difficult to accomplish in daily life!

Preclassical Yoga also comprises the many schools whose teachings can be found in India's two great national epics, the Râmâyana and the Mahâbhârata (in which the Bhagavad-Gîtâ is embedded and which is seven times the size of the Iliad and Odyssey combined). These various preclassical schools developed all kinds of techniques for achieving deep meditation through which yogis and yoginis can transcend the body and mind and discover their true nature.

Classical Yoga

This label applies to the eightfold Yoga—also known as Râja-Yoga—taught by Patanjali in his Yoga-Sûtra. This Sanskrit text is composed of just under 200 aphoristic statements, which have been commented on over and over again through the centuries. Sooner or later all serious Yoga students discover this work and have to grapple with its terse statements. The word sûtra (which is related to Latin suture) means literally "thread." Here it conveys a thread of memory, an aid to memorization for students eager to retain Patanjali's knowledge and wisdom.

The Yoga-Sûtra was probably written some time in the second century A.D. The earliest available Sanskrit commentary on it is the Yoga-Bhâshya ("Speech on Yoga") attributed to Vyâsa. It was authored in the fifth century A.D. and furnishes fundamental explanations of Patanjali's often cryptic statements. Beyond a few legends nothing is known about either Patanjali or Vyâsa. This is a problem with most ancient Yoga adepts and even with many more recent ones. Often all we have are their teachings, but this is of course more important than any historical information we could dig up about their personal lives.

Patanjali, who is by the way often wrongly called the "father of Yoga," believed that each individual is a composite of matter (prakriti) and spirit (purusha). He understood the process of Yoga to bring about their separation, thereby restoring the spirit in its absolute purity. His formulation is generally characterized as philosophical dualism. This is an important point, because most of India's philosophical systems favor one or the other kind of nondualism: The countless aspects or forms of the empirical world are in the last analysis the same "thing"—pure formless but conscious existence.

Postclassical Yoga

This is again a very comprehensive category, which refers to all those many types and schools of Yoga that have sprung up in the period after Patanjali's Yoga-Sûtra and that are independent of this seminal work. In contrast to classical Yoga, postclassical Yoga affirms the ultimate unity of everything. This is the core teaching of Vedânta, the philosophical system based on the teachings of the Upanishads.

In a way, the dualism of classical Yoga can be seen as a brief but powerful interlude in a stream of nondualist teachings going back to ancient Vedic times. According to these teachings, you, we, and everyone or everything else is an aspect or expression of one and the same reality. In Sanskrit that singular reality is called brahman (meaning "that which has grown expansive") or âtman (the transcendental Self as opposed to the limited ego-self). A few centuries after Patanjali, the evolution of Yoga took an interesting turn. Now some great adepts were beginning to probe the hidden potential of the body. Previous generations of yogis and yoginis had paid no particular attention to the body. They had been more interested in contemplation to the point where they could exit the body consciously. Their goal had been to leave the world behind and merge with the formless reality, the spirit.

Under the influence of alchemy—the spiritual forerunner of chemistry—the new breed of Yoga masters created a system of practices designed to rejuvenate the body and prolong its life. They regarded the body as a temple of the immortal spirit, not merely as a container to be discarded at the first opportunity. They even explored through advanced yogic techniques the possibility of energizing the physical body to such a degree that its biochemistry is changed and even its basic matter is reorganized to render it immortal. This preoccupation of theirs led to the creation of Hatha-Yoga, an amateur version of which is today widely practiced throughout the world. It also led to the various branches and schools of Tantra-Yoga, of which Hatha-Yoga is just one approach.

Modern Yoga

The history of modern Yoga is widely thought to begin with the Parliament of Religions held in Chicago in 1893. It was at that congress that the young Swami Vivekananda—swami (svâmin) means "master"—made a big and lasting impression on the American public. At the behest of his teacher, the saintly Ramakrishna, he had found his way to the States where he didn't know a soul. Thanks to some well-wishers who recognized the inner greatness of this adept of Jnâna-Yoga (the Yoga of discernment), he was invited to the Parliament and ended up being its most popular diplomat. In the following years, he traveled widely attracting many students to Yoga and Vedânta. His various books on Yoga are still useful and enjoyable to read. Before Swami Vivekananda a few other Yoga masters had crossed the ocean to visit Europe, but their influence had remained local and ephemeral. Vivekananda's immense success opened a sluice gate for other adepts from India, and the stream of Eastern gurus has not ceased. After Swami Vivekananda, the most popular teacher in the early years of the Western Yoga movement was Paramahansa Yogananda, who arrived in Boston in 1920. Five years later, he established the Self-Realizaton Fellowship, which still has its headquarters in Los Angeles. Although he left his body (as yogins call it) in 1952 at the age of fifty-nine, he continues to have a worldwide following. His Autobiography of a Yogi makes for fascinating reading, but be prepared to suspend any materialistic bias you may have! As with some other yogis and Christian or Muslim saints, after his death Yogananda's body showed no signs of decay for a full twenty days.

Of more limited appeal was Swami Rama Tirtha, a former mathematics teacher who preferred spiritual life to academia and who came to the United States in 1902 and founded a retreat center on Mount Shasta in California. He stayed for only two years and drowned in the Ganges (Ganga) River in 1906 at the young age of thirty-three. Some of his inspirational talks were gathered into the five volumes of In Woods of God-Realization, which are still worth dipping into.

In 1919, Yogendra Mastamani arrived in Long Island and for nearly three years demonstrated to astounded Americans the power and elegance of Hatha Yoga. Before returning to India, he founded the American branch of Kaivalyadhama, an Indian organization created by the late Swami Kuvalayananda, which has contributed greatly to the scientific study of Yoga.

A very popular figure for several decades after the 1920s was Ramacharaka, whose books can still be found in used bookstores. What few readers know, however, is that this Ramacharaka was apparently not an actual person. The name was the pseudonym of two people—William Walker Atkinson, who had left his law practice in Chicago to practice Yoga, and his teacher Baba Bharata.

Paul Brunton, a former journalist and editor, burst on the scene of Yoga in 1934 with his book A Search in Secret India, which introduced the great sage Ramana Maharshi to Western seekers. Many more works flowed from his pen over the following eighteen years, until the publication of The Spiritual Crisis of Man. Then, in the 1980s, his notebooks were published posthumously in sixteen volumes—a treasure-trove for serious Yoga students.

Since the early 1930s until his death in 1986, Jiddu Krishnamurti delighted or perplexed thousands of philosophically minded Westerners with his eloquent talks. He had been groomed by the Theosophical Society as the coming world leader but had rejected this mission, which surely is too big and burdensome for any one person, however great. He demonstrated the wisdom of Jnana-Yoga (the Yoga of discernment), and drew large crowds of listeners and readers. Among his close circle of friends were the likes of Aldous Huxley, Christopher Isherwood, Charles Chaplin, and Greta Garbo. Bernard Shaw described Krishnamurti as the most beautiful human being he ever saw.

Yoga, in the form of Hatha-Yoga, entered mainstream America when the Russian-born yoginî Indra Devi, who has been called the "First Lady of Yoga," opened her Yoga studio in Hollywood in 1947. She taught stars like Gloria Swanson, Jennifer Jones, and Robert Ryan, and trained hundreds of teachers. Now in her nineties and living in Buenos Aires, she is still an influential voice for Yoga.

In the 1950s, one of the most prominent Yoga teacher was Selvarajan Yesudian whose book Sport and Yoga has been translated into fourteen or so languages, with more than 500,000 copies sold. Today, as we mentioned before, many athletes have adopted yogic exercises into their training program because... it works. Among them are the Chicago Bulls. Just picture these champion basket ball players stretching out on extra-long Yoga mats under the watchful eye of Yoga teacher Paula Kout! In the early 1950s, Shri Yogendra of the Yoga Institute of Santa Cruz in India, visited the United States. He pioneered medical research on Yoga as early as 1918, and his son Jayadev Yogendra is continuing his valuable work, which demonstrates the efficacy of Yoga as a therapeutic tool.

In 1961, Richard Hittleman brought Hatha-Yoga to American television, and his book The Twenty-Eight-Day Yoga Plan sold millions of copies. In the mid-1960s, the Western Yoga movement received a big boost through Maharishi Mahesh Yogi, largely because of his brief association with the Beatles. He popularized yogic contemplation in the form of Transcendental Meditation (TM), which still has tens of thousands of practitioners around the world. TM practitioners also introduced meditation and Yoga into the corporate world. It, moreover, stimulated medical research on Yoga at various American universities.

In 1965, the then sixty-nine-year-old Shrila Prabhupada arrived in New York with a suitcase full of books and $8.00 in his pockets. Six years later he founded the International Society for Krishna Consciousness (ISKCON), and by the time of his death in 1977, he had created a worldwide spiritual movement based on Bhakti Yoga (the Yoga of devotion).

Also in the 1960s and 1970s, many swamis trained by the Himalayan master Swami Sivananda, a former physician who became a doctor of the soul, opened their schools in Europe and the two Americas. Most of them are still active today, and among them are Swami Vishnudevananda (author of the widely read Complete Illustrated Book of Yoga), Swami Satchitananda (well-known to Woodstock participants), Swami Sivananda Radha (a woman-swami who pioneered the link between Yoga spirituality and psychology), Swami Satyananda (about whom we will say more shortly), and Swami Chidananda (a saintly figure who directed the Sivananda Ashram in Rishikesh, India). The last-mentioned master's best known American student is the gentle Lilias Folan, made famous by her PBS television series Lilias, Yoga & You, broadcast between 1970 and 1979. In 1969, Yogi Bhajan caused an uproar among the traditional Sikh community (an offshoot of Hinduism) when he broke with tradition and began to teach Kundalini Yoga to his Western students. Today his Healthy, Happy, Holy Organization—better known as 3HO—has more than 200 centers around the world.

A more controversial but wildly popular guru in the 1970 and 1980s was Bhagavan Rajneesh (now known as Osho), whose followers constantly made the headlines for their sexual orgies and other excesses. Rajneesh, a former philosophy professor, drew his teachings from authentic Yoga sources, mixed with his own personal experiences. His numerous books line the shelves of many second-hand bookstores. Rajneesh allowed his students to act out their repressed fantasies, notably of the sexual variety, in the hope that this would free them up for the deeper processes of Yoga. Many of them, however, got trapped in a mystically tinged hedonism, which proves the common-sense rule that too much of a good thing can be bad for you. Even though many of his disciples felt bitterly disappointed by him and the sad events surrounding his organization in the years immediately preceding his death in 1990, just as many still regard him as a genuine Yoga master. His life illustrates that Yoga adepts come in all shapes and sizes and that, to coin a phrase, one person's guru is another person's uru. (The Sanskrit word uru denotes "empty space.") Another maxim that applies here is caveat emptor, "buyer beware."

Other renowned modern Yoga adepts of Indian origin are Sri Aurobindo (the father of Integral Yoga), Ramana Maharshi (an unparalleled master of Jnana-Yoga), Papa Ramdas (who lived and breathed Mantra-Yoga, the Yoga of transformative sound), Swami Nityananda (a miracle-working master of Siddha-Yoga), and his disciple Swami Muktananda (a powerful yogi who put Siddha-Yoga, which is a Tantric Yoga, on the map for Western seekers). All these teachers are no longer among us.

The great exponent in modern times of Hatha-Yoga was Sri Krishnamacharya, who died in 1989 at the ripe old age of 101. He practiced and taught the Viniyoga system of Hatha-Yoga until his last days. His son T. K. V. Desikachar continues his saintly father's teachings and taught Yoga, among others, to the famous Jiddu Krishnamurti. Another well-known student of Sri Krishnamacharya and a master in his own right is Desikachar's uncle B. K. S. Iyengar, who has taught tens of thousands of students, including the world-famous violinist Jehudi Menuhin.

Mention must also be made of Pattabhi Jois and Indra Devi, both of whom studied with Krishnamacharya in their early years and have since then inspired thousands of Westerners. Of living Yoga masters from India, I can mention Sri Chinmoy and Swami Satyananda (a Tantra master who established the well-known Bihar School of Yoga, has authored numerous books, and has disciples around the world). There are of course many other great Yoga adepts, both well known and more hidden, who represent Yoga in one form or another, but I leave it up to you to discover them.

Until modern times, the overwhelming majority of Yoga practitioners have been men, yogins. But there have also always been great female adepts, yoginîs. Happily, in recent years, a few woman saints—representing Bhakti-Yoga (Yoga of devotion)—have come to the West to bring their gospel of love to open-hearted seekers. Yoga embraces so many diverse approaches that anyone can find a home in it. An exceptional woman teacher from India who fits none of the yogic stereotypes is Meera Ma ("Mother Meera"). She doesn't teach in words but communicates in silence through her simple presence. Of all places, she has made her home in the middle of a quaint German village in the Black Forest, and every year is attracting thousands of people from all over the world.

Since Yoga is not restricted to Hinduism, we may also mention here the Dalai Lama, champion of nonviolence and winner of the Nobel Peace Prize. He is unquestionably one of the truly great yogis of modern Tibet, who, above all, demonstrates that the principles of Yoga can fruitfully be brought not only into a busy daily life but also into the arena of politics. Today Tibetan Buddhism (which is a form of Tantra-Yoga) is extremely popular among Westerners, and there are many lamas (spiritual teacher) who are willing to share with sincere seekers the secrets of their hitherto well-guarded tradition.

If you are curious about Westerners who have made a name for themselves as teachers in the modern Yoga movement (understood in the broadest terms), you may want to consult the encyclopedic work The Book of Enlightened Masters by Andrew Rawlinson. His book includes both genuine masters (like the Bulgarian teacher Omraam Mikhaël Aïvanhov on whom I have written a book—The Mystery of Light) and a galaxy of would-be masters.

WHY DO WE DO YOGA?

We begin to do yoga with a motive. That motive may be for health, or for making a career, or enjoyment of worldly pleasures, or for emancipation. It is only after we continue practicing yoga that it dawns on us that we do not do yoga for health, or for enjoyment, or for emancipation. Then, why do we do yoga? In his treatise, the Yoga sutras, Patanjali explains in the very beginning that mind, intelligence, consciousness, and the very core of our being gets involved with thought waves making us forget for that moment their true element of nature. This conjunction of mind, intelligence, and consciousness with the thoughts of the objects seen, perceived, or conceived create desires. These desires make one to act at once without using the discriminative faculty the extra sense given to man and one becomes a victim of his own thoughts and deeds. Lord Krishna says in the Bhagvad Gita that each one of us remains unmanifest in the beginning, gets manifested and at the end dissolves into the unmanifested state. The cycle of our life is in these three forms; from the unmanifested form towards manifestation and from manifestation to unite back into the unmanifested state. Along with this cycle, our wheel of desires, fulfillments and frustrations get recycled as subliminal impressions.

These subliminal impressions act as seeds in our lives. These subliminal impressions, which are formed on account of our actions and accumulated merits and demerits of our past lives, become the cause of pleasures and pains of this life. The cultivation of modes and moods of this life becomes a springboard for the next life. Hence, Patanjali's expositions come handy to minimize these impressions so that the practitioner of yoga can build up free will and make his own destiny. He resolves to face and accept the fruits of his past actions and passively undergoes the merits and demerits without being caught in that web.

Life is eternal like nature which is eternal. As nature revolves as past, present, and future, so life too revolves between birth, death, and rebirth.

Uninterrupted practice of Yoga done with devotion, as propounded by Patanjali or Svatmarama, keeps the practitioner free from motivation, desire, and reward and he develops discriminative intelligence. This discriminative intelligence which develops in the practitioner of Yoga keeps his mind free from contact of the tempting objects and yokes it to the soul which is unmoving, unrotating, but ever in the state of present.

Yoking the mind, intelligence, and consciousness to the Soul or the Self is possible only through the Yogic disciplines which keeps the body firm and pure, mind stable, and intelligence clear. Precisely this is what the practice of Yoga does. Patanjali does emphatically say in Sutra II.28 that, "Through reverential practice of Yoga, the fire which emanates from the practice burns out the impurities of body, mind, and intelligence and bestows the consciousness with the crown of wisdom for it rest on the lap of the Self". From then on the never changing intuitive light of the Self radiates and frees the practitioner from the actions which are filled with afflictions.

Therefore practice of yoga is meant only to eradicate such actions which may not afflict the practitioner. Then emancipation is in his hands. Like the nine planets of the Zodiac which as the servants of god maintain a rhythmic universal order, we have nine gates in our body two eyes, ears, nostrils, and a mouth, anus and generative organ. By the regular practice of yoga these nine gates which cause nine afflictions, disease, sluggishness, doubt, carelessness, idleness, sense of gratification, living in the world of illusion, not being able to hold on to what has been undertaken and inability to maintain the progress achieved, are controlled and then the energy is channeled towards self realization.

As one installs a device in the form of a metallic rod on the top of the house to absorb the impact of lightening and prevent it from striking the building; practice of Yoga protects the practitioner by minimizing the onslaught of the effects of the past and present actions and frees him from bondage.

Thus, the main reason for us to stick to Yoga is to free ourselves from the fluctuations and afflictions. The practice of Yoga guards the doer from the recurrence of mixed sorrows and pleasures and thus dualities are minimized. That is why I continue with my practice daily. My advice to all of you is to practice with intensity daily, so that one can reach that state of emancipation that is free from the afflictions of sorrows.

That is why Yoga is done!!

CONTROL OF THE BRAIN AND NERVOUS SYSTEM

The nervous system is the network of nerves that control all the organs and illicit responses from the body. It is the nerves that allow the senses to work and the brain to coordinate the mechanisms of the entire body.

Since they have so many functions, it can be very easy for the nerves to get damaged, which in turn could cease the functioning of vital organs. Today, with so many of us under a lot of stress and leading lifestyles that are constantly on the go, our nerves have to take on a lot of stress and pressure just to keep the body functional. The good news is that several studies show that yoga has a direct beneficial effect on the nervous system. Not only does yoga help with relieving stress, it also helps with keeping the mind clear and sharp, delaying the onset of some nervous system disorders/diseases.

To attain a condition in which the fullest relaxation is possible, it is essential to control the brain and the nervous system. In old Sanskrit tracts we find the statement: "When the nervous system is relieved of all its impurities, there appears the perceptible signs of success...the glowing color of health."

While speaking of the "brain," we must, to some extent, drop the Western traditional concept of the brain as the sole seat of consciousness. As far back as 2,500 years ago, the Yogins were in conflict with the accepted Hindu medical science of the time. These ancient medical men held, as did the ancient Greeks, that the heart was the seat of consciousness. The Yogins, on the other hand, stated that the brain, with its highly involved nervous system, was one unit which represented the true physical medium of human mental activity. There is an interwoven cerebro-spinal system and an autonomic nervous system. In the Yoga system of histology, the cerebro-spinal system is said to consist of the sahasradala, the brain, and the susumna, the spinal cord, which are enclosed within the cavities of the cranium and the spinal cord or vertebrae. Linked together in the autonomic nervous system is a double chain of ganglia which are situated on each side of the spine and which extend from the base of the skull to the tip of the coccyx.

There are seventy-two thousand nadis, or nerves, which form a countless number of nerve endings. Of the nadis, about a dozen have been thoroughly studied by the Yogins. Three have been found to be of primary importance: The ida, or left nostril, the pingala, or right nostril, and the susumna, the spinal cord. These are believed to exercise control over voluntary and automatic responses of the human body and can be brought under control by Yogic methods. Centuries before the recognition of electrical force by scientists, the Yogins had evolved a theory of nerve-impulse transmission which has won acceptance from Western medical investigators in this century. If we substitute the word prana for electrical impulse, we find that the oldest Yoga principles of neurology are now endorsed in the modern theory of nerve action. We can now understand that the Yogins anticipated the principles of electrical phenomena by discovering the positive and negative animal-magnetic currents which are the nerve impulses and which may be controlled and adjusted by Yoga practice.

The physical and mental well-being of every individual depends on the fine adjustment of the nervous system which controls even the secreting glands. One of the benefits of a Yoga regime is the control or restraint of the various modifications which may take place in the nervous system. In addition to the beneficial effects of the physical aspects of Yoga on the gross and finer muscles and tissues, it also establishes, through the postures and attitudes and psycho-physiological practices, complete control over the nervous system. Only when the nerve impulses can pass in harmony through the spinal cord may samadhi, a state of suspended sensation, be reached.

NERVOUS AILMENTS

It is now fashionable to attribute many forms of disease to "nerves," which is a symptom, not a disease. Since the nervous system is in direct and intimate relationship with every part of the body, the slightest disorder in any organ registers upon the nervous system. Conversely, any serious nerve disorder will cause functional distress, and it is often impossible to disassociate the cause from the effect.

What we term "nervous weakness" is actually the response of a neglected or abused nervous system. The conditions that we lump together under the heading of "nerves" are merely the call of the nervous system for better care. Purification of the nervous system is possible through an improved mental attitude, rest, relaxation and recreation and the benefits of postures, or asanas, which adjust the tone of the spine and its components.

SOME AIDS TO MENTAL HYGIENE

Freedom from emotion is one of the tenets of Yoga. Early modern psychologists discovered a strong relationship between the emotions and the body in terms of increased or reduced ductless gland secretion, respiration, circulation and blood pressure. Yoga medical investigators have attributed diabetes, arteriosclerosis, nephritis and other diseases to the effects of emotion on the glandular system and thence on the body organs. Samatva, or absolute freedom from emotions, has been set as one of the prime essentials for the health of the nerves and brain. Even a minor emotional flare-up or a long period of subdued anxiety will affect the body.

Concentration

A method of avoiding emotions and anxieties is to train or habituate the mind to concentrate on a chosen object. This concentration is called dharana. Without purposeful concentration, the mind diffuses its energies in varied directions, while with strong concentration, the mind can be freed of distractions and can approach a state of detachment or non-awareness of extraneous matters. This is the essence of concentration. The habit of concentration is known to produce a sedative effect, similar to that induced by deep breathing, with manifold benefits to the health of the nervous system.

THE NEED FOR RECREATION

In India, a troubled individual is often able to retire for a while to an Ashram, or retreat, where he can live under the best possible conditions for the practice of Yoga and self-realization. (Note the use of the "retreat" by the Roman Catholic and other religions as a means to attain spiritual relaxation.)

One of the most depressing factors in the Western world is the monotony of occupation and the hectic pace required in almost every occupation or profession. In many cases, a change of occupation has effected radical cures in instances of nervous disorder, but this is not always feasible. However, any change in mental or physical occupation—and the change must be mental as well as physical—will add substantially to the health and tone of the nervous system. Persons of sedentary habits will find relief in outdoor sports, such as mountain climbing, hiking, swimming, in addition to the practice of the Yoga exercises. For mental relaxation, the Yogins, whose troubled times were yet more calm than life is today, found their recreation in a mental state—in study and love of nature. By seeking unison with nature, they found that their entire beings were called into delightful activity with almost no effort of the will. They learned that the mind which lost itself in the love of nature found its nervous system refreshed, its vital forces renewed.

EFFECTS OF PRANAYAMA ON THE BRAIN

Pranayama, or expansion of the prana or vital energy, occurs through the practices of prana nigraha, or control of the prana (1). This paper examines various prana nigraha practices which contribute initially to changing the physiological state of the brain and are said to awaken prana in the realm of the chakras, or psychic centres, within the human body. A comment is made on the effect that prana nigraha practices have had on the writer. A review of a medical examination of a yogic adept is included, which confirms the ability of pranayama to influence an indivdual's brain activity. The conclusion is drawn that extensive prana nigraha practices leading into pranayama can significantly influence the physical, pranic, mental and psychic aspects of the human brain.

Swami Niranjanananda Saraswati defines prana or vital energy as: "The essence of all created, manifest forms whether animate or inanimate, the force which determines the existence of matter and the elements"(2). Prana nigraha is the manipulation of the breath to control prana. When practised regularly, prana nigraha leads to pranayama or expansion of the vital energy.

Pranayama is the control of the upa pranas (sub pranas) which achieves harmonization of the physiological body and leads to awakening of prana in the chakras or psychic body. Once the prana is awakened in the chakras, pranayama begins. The culmination is the merging of apana, prana and samana forces at manipura chakra which, in turn, leads to the activation of udana and vyana pranas. When the five pranas are operating simultaneously, the kundalini (spiritual energy or evolutionary potential) (3) is awakened and the process of self-realization begins.

Pranayama is divided into three stages: (i) awareness of prana, (ii) prana nigraha, and (iii) expansion of prana. Prana itself has two aspects. One is prana shakti, which is the vital force and consists of the five minor pranas (5). The other is manas or chit shakti, the mental or conscious force, centred in the brain. Without prana, the body and mind are dead. Modern science states that there are ten areas of the brain of which we are using only one at our present stage of evolution. To use the other 90 per cent involves the distribution of prana to awaken these areas. The subconscious mind and its relationship to the conscious mind are dealt with in pranayama by the establishment of an interface between the conscious and the subconscious minds in the area of the brain called the reticular activating system (RAS) (6).

The RAS is the trigger for other parts of the brain. Man is able to affect the RAS through the breath only. No other function of the autonomic nervous system can be controlled by conscious human activity. Control of the brain through the RAS by means of conscious breathing is a method by which other functions of the body may be controlled, for example, heart rate, blood pressure, digestion, excretion and absorption. Therefore, control of the subconscious is achieved through conscious activity of prana nigraha and then pranayama (7). Four pranayama practices are examined for their effects on the brain or other parts of the human body. These practices are selected on the basis of their importance in the practice of yoga and their stated influence on the physiological and psychic bodies.

Kapalbhati

Van Lysbeth states that kapalbhati influences the circulation of blood within the brain. Kapalbhati changes the volume of the brain according to the respiratory rhythm and, therefore, increases the irrigation of the brain matter. Normal respiration consists of 12-18 massages per minute, whereas kaplbhati can involve up to 120 massages per minute, which leads to a significant increase in blood volume throughout and thereby improves irrigation of the brain.

The capillaries are opened up and the brain cells related to the pineal and pituitary glands receive significant stimulation (8). It is logical to conclude that increased brain irrigation with blood is accompanied by elevated pranic levels and ensures even and harmonious distribution of prana throughout the body.

Van Lysbeth supports this conclusion as follows: "Together with the acceleration of the blood circulation in the whole body, this stimulation of the brain and thereby of the central nervous system produces the special 'relation' of the body that invigorates and tonifies each cell" (9).

Kapalbhati reduces the ratio of the outward breath to the inward breath in kundalini yoga to one quarter. This in turn increases the breath control, stretching it to the limit, and dramatically effects the carbon dioxide, chemical, acid and alkalis in the blood (10). Carbon dioxide is the trigger for inhalation of breath into the lungs and the body and, therefore, the body is very sensitive to carbon dioxide levels.

Kumbhaka

In the practice of kumbhaka, or breath retention, which may be antar (internal) or bahir (external), tolerance to starvation of oxygen and buildup of carbon dioxide is achieved. Kumbhaka, practised over a duration of time, will allow the body to retain carbon dioxide and become accustomed to reduced oxygen levels to achieve hypometabolism, that is, a slowing down of the metabolic rate. The production rate of carbon dioxide is thereby reduced which causes a subtle effect to take place with conscious control of breathing. This effect influences the brain and body chemistry and reduces the need to breathe when carbon dioxide buildup is experienced (11).

External kumbhaka also affects the body physiologically by causing the mental process to stop, because of the vacuum created inside the body. This action is very useful in the practice of pratyahara, sense withdrawl, and dharana, concen-tration, as a prerequisite to achieve the state of meditation.

Kumbhaka stops vital body rhythms and affects the brain waves. Control of the brain waves is the key to conrolling all brain rhythms (12). While the effects of bahir kumbhaka are many, in broad terms, the body and mind learn to stay calm under stress.

Nadi Shodhana

Kumbhaka is used in the practice of nadi shodhana or alternate nostril breathing. Nadi shodhana is the 'perfect balancing practice' (13) which stimulates equally the left and right sides of the brain and body. Ida and pingala, the major nadis, or pranic channels, are balanced which, in turn, modifies the human thinking process to balance introversion and extroversion. The ancient yogis have recorded that once ida and pingala are balanced and purified, the central nadi, sushumna, begins to flow, leading to increased awareness and the state of meditation (14).

Nadi shodhana imposes a rhythm on the brain and the nadis, over the irregular state that normally exists. Modern living has removed the regular rhythms of nature from the human body and nadi shodhana assists in bringing the body, prana and mental activity into balance. Research has shown that nadi shodhana affects the brainwaves by superimposing a regular sine wave over the normal irregular brain activity, imposing a discipline on the irregularities of the mental process and, eventually, the autonomous body rhythms.

Kumbhaka in nadi shodhana places a momentary block on the body rhythms, changing the usual carbon dioxide/oxygen relationship, thereby affecting the whole system. Antar kumbhaka emphasizes the oxygen content and bahir kumbhaka emphasizes the carbon dioxide phase (15).

Ujjayi

Ujjayi, or the psychic breath, produced by a slight contraction of the throat, has a subtle effect on brain activity via four processes:

- Ujjayi increases the pressure of air in the lungs and expands the effective use of the lungs. This ensures transfer of oxygen to each cell within the lungs, rather than a significantly smaller percentage used during normal respiration.
- Increased oxygen transfer in the lungs enhances blood flow throughout the body, while the body is in a relaxed state. The effect is similar to that achieved when the body is physically active, with the advantage of the whole body being in a relaxed state (16).
- Conscious awareness is transferred into the unconscious mind which affects the nervous system governing respiration. A smooth rhythm is exerted on the nervous system that has a profound effect at the psychic level of the mind.
- The contraction of the throat caused by ujjayi affects the carotid sinuses which regulate blood pressure in the arteries. Ujjayi exerts a slight pressure on the carotid sinuses which, over time, lowers the blood pressure, which leads to reduced tension and slows the thought processes of the mind (17).

Examination of a Yogic Ddept

The effect of the practices of prana nigraha outlined above have been substantiated in part through work carried out at the 5th annual convention of the International Association for Religion and Parapsychology in 1977. The research revealed that Ramananda Yogi, who had practised pranayama for many years, had the abilty to control the heart muscle itself and was, therefore, able to control his heart function. During pranayama, Ramananda Yogi was able to reduce his pulse rate from 100 per minute to 65-80 per minute, although such changes would be dangerous for persons who had not practised pranayama (18).

It was also concluded at the confer-ence through biological tests that Ramananda Yogi was able to control his basal metabolic rate through pranayama. The effects of pranayama on the brain as detailed by Swami Niranjanananda, and the results of clinical trials carried out by the International Association for Research for Religion and Parapsychology, substantiate the profound effects of pranayama on the physical and mental human body.

Experiences of the Writer

While extensive pranayama leads to significant control over the brain, prana nigraha practices carried out by the writer have affected subtle changes in ability to control both the breath and energy within the body. It is more difficult to detect any major effects on body physiology, but there has been a definite change in the state of one-pointedness and calmness of the mind over the past two years as result of the practices of kapalbhati, nadi shodhana, bhastrika and ujjayi breathing.

The ancient yogic texts speak of the ability of pranayama to control the mind. The Hatha Yoga Pradipika by Yogi Swatmarama states that pranic constraint can control the mind: "When prana moves, chitta (the mental force) moves; when prana is without movement, chitta is without movement. By this (steadiness of prana), the yogi attains steadiness of mind and this restrains the vayu (air)".

REGULATE YOUR BREATH TO CONTROL BODY AND MIND

In conclusion, current writings by recognized yogis and research into the effects of the practices of pranayama support the ancient yogic view that pranayama exerts profound effects on the human brain. The limited experience of the writer also supports the view that the practices of pranayama can have subtle effects on the brain, human well-being and influence the individual's level of spirituality. Simon Borg-Olivier doing Pranayama in Kandasana. The ultimate state of pranayama (yogic breath-control) and meditation is a state where breathing is reduced as much as possible without force. However this is a process that can for most people take a life time. In order to work towards the mastery of yoga it is sometimes useful to breathe more than normal (hyperventilation) but eventually the aim to be able to comfortable live and practice while breathing less than normal (hypoventilation).

In yoga and life breathing may guided or controlled for five main reasons. These are:

- Physical
- Neurological
- Mental
- Emotional
- Cardiovascular
- Physiological

Pranayama (yogic breath-control) is the art of learning how to breathe less than normal (hypoventilation). Although sometimes fast, deep and/or complete breaths have benefits, the less you breathe overall the better your mental capacity is and the greater is the blood flow to nourish the brain and the heart.

The haemoglobin also transfers oxygen more efficiently to all the cells of the body (the Bohr effect). Many studies on meditation have shown that focus and concentration are better when you breathe less! Additionally, the nervous system is much calmer when you breathe less and this is reflected in a reduced desire to eat.

Breath-control is also useful on a mental level. Any type of focus on your breathing can help you concentrate but the nervous system works best if you breathe less than normal. Breath-control works on the cardiovascular and circulatory system. You can enhance the movement of energy and information through your subtle channels and enhance the movement of blood and heat through your blood vessels by breathing differentially from your abdomen (diaphragmatic breathing) or from your chest (thoracic breathing). You can also bring more blood and oxygen to the brain and heart and less blood and oxygen to the arms and legs by breathing less than normal (hypoventilation). Conversely, you can bring less blood and oxygen to brain and heart and more blood and oxygen to the arms and legs by breathing more than normal (hyperventilation). A brief summary of the the different possible effects of breathing is shown.

1. Physical
   - Mobilising the spine
     - deep inhalation tends to cause spinal flexion (bends your spine more forward) while deep exhalation tends to cause spinal extension (bends your spine more backwards)
   - Stabilising the spine o the muscles of breathing out (especially from the chest) can make your spine more stable
   - Strengthening the spine and body othe diaphragm (the main muscle of inhalation) can be used as powerful strength muscle
2. Neurological
   - Control of the autonomic (automatic) nervous system via the diaphragm which can be controlled either by the conscious mind (somatic) or unconscious mind (autonomic)
   - Reciprocal relaxation of the muscles of abdominal exhalation (which include many of the muscles that can tend to over-tense and contribute to lower back pain) by the main muscle of inhalation (the diaphragm)
3. Mental
   - Focus on any type of breathing can help with concentration
   - Reduced breathing (hypoventilation) leaves the body slightly more acidic (with carbonic acid), which gives the physiological effect of calming the nervous system and the mind in general
4. Emotional
   - Slow abdominal (diaphragmatic) breathing tends to enhance parasympathetic control of relaxation response with ahimsa (non-violence) and/or love and peace and happiness as dominant emotions
   - Faster chest (thoracic) breathing tends to enhance sympathetic control of 'flight or fight' response with tapas (passion to do your best) and/or fear anger and aggression as dominant emotions
5. Cardiovascular
   - Deep breathing with the abdomen relax (which can be diaphragmatic and/or thoracic provided the abdomen is relaxed) causes an increase in blood flow
   - With this type of breathing heart rate increases on inhalation as does blood pressure
   - Heart rate decreases and blood pressure decreases on exhalation
   - This type of breathing causes increased pressure into the abdomen on inhalation and decreased pressure on exhalation that increases blood flow and nervous system stimulation to the abdominal organs

6. Physiological
   - Reduced breathing (hypoventilation) for
     - Calmer nerves
     - Increased oxygenation and blood flow to brain and heart
     - Reduced hunger
   - Increased breathing (hyperventilation) for
     - Stimulation of nerves
     - Decreased oxygenation and blood flow to brain and heart
     - Increased hunger

THE EIGHT PRINCIPLES OF RAJA YOGA

We will concern ourselves mainly with Raja Yoga, a system which has been found to be most applicable to the mental and physical conditions in which we live. Raja Yoga has eight principles. These are: (1) Yama—non-killing, truthfulness, non-stealing, continence, and non-receiving of any gifts; (2) Niyama—cleanliness, contentment, mortification, study and self-surrender to good; (3) Asana—posture; (4) Pranayama—control of vital body forces; (5) Pratyahara—introspection; (6) Dharana—concentration; (7) Dhyana—meditation; (8) Samadhi—super-consciousness.

Yama and Niyama constitute the moral training without which no practice of Yoga will succeed. As this moral code becomes established, the practice of Yoga will begin to be fruitful. The Yogi must not think of injuring either man or animal through thought, word or deed. However, this should not be extended to the limits to which the Jains of India carry it. Their creed forbids them to kill even an insect, and many never bathe lest by placing their bodies in water they may drown some creature living upon them. Yoga is logical. Its principles are not rules of magic that must be followed without deviation, but general principles that expand to cover the exigencies of any situation. Before continuing with our discussion of Raja Yoga, we should make a distinction between that school of thought and another, called Hatha Yoga.

Hatha Yoga deals entirely with the body. The sole aim of that school of Yoga is to make the body physically strong. For a strong body, however, you can achieve almost the same effects as those given by Hatha Yoga by enrolling in a gymnasium course at any muscle-building establishment. The exercises of Hatha Yoga are difficult and demand years of steady endeavor. Through this system, it is claimed that a Yogi can establish perfect control over every part of his body. The heart can be made to stop or go at his bidding and can control the flow of blood and the sensations of his nervous system.

The result of this part of Yoga is to make men stronger and to prolong their lives; good health is its one goal. From the point of view of the Raja Yogi, the person who perfects himself in Hatha Yoga is merely a healthy animal. This system does not lead to spiritual growth or give man the help to meet his need for relaxation which is found in Raja Yoga. However, certain aspects of Hatha Yoga have become part of the regime of Raja Yoga. These include some of its exercises, dietary aspects, and disease preventives, which provide the physical state of well-being which enables the proper pursuit of Yoga.

The exercises, or postures, are called asanas. These are a series of exercises which should be practiced daily until certain higher states are reached. They constitute the next stage in Yoga. At first, a posture should be adopted which can be held comfortably for a fairly long time. It has become necessary to adapt the traditional Yoga postures to meet the needs of Western man. While there is no evidence of any physical or physiological difference between the people of the East and West, there are certain acquired differences.

Ours is a civilization in which much time, both at leisure and at work, is spent in a sitting position. In the East, the great mass of people are unfamiliar with the chair in its different forms. Theirs is what might be called a "squatting" culture. Hence muscular development from childhood on is along different lines. Postures in which the Indian naturally relaxes would be torture for the Westerner. The position which is easiest is the proper one to use.

You will discover later that in the carrying out of these physiological matters there will be a good deal of action going on in the body. Nerve currents will have to be displaced and given new channels. New vibrations will begin and the constitution will in effect be remodeled. The main part of the action will lie along the spinal column, so that it is necessary to hold the spinal column free by sitting erect and holding the chest, head and neck in a straight line. Let the whole weight of the body be supported by the ribs and in an easy natural posture with the spine straight. You will find that you cannot think high thoughts with the chest in. Such is the effect on the body of what we call the mind.

After you have learned to have a firm, erect seat, you should perform a practice called the purification of the nerves. In the words of one of the ancient scriptures, or Upanishads, "the mind whose dross has been cleared away by pranayama becomes fixed in the path of Yoga...first the nerves are to be purified, then comes the power to practice pranayama." The technique for this is as follows: stopping the right nostril with the thumb, with the left nostril inhale according to your capacity. Without pausing, exhale through the right nostril, while closing the left one. Now, inhale through the right nostril and exhale through the left. Practice this three or five times at four intervals of the day—on awaking, at midday, in the evening and before going to sleep. Within fifteen days to a month, purity is attained; then begins pranayama.

Practice is absolutely necessary. You may read about Yoga by the hour, but without practice, you will not make progress. We never understand without experience. You will have to see and feel this yourself, as explanations and theories will not do. There are several obstructions to practice. The first is an unhealthy body. You must keep your body in good health. Be careful of what you eat and drink and what you do. Always use a mental effort to keep the body strong. Keep in mind that health is but a means to an end.

The second obstruction is doubt. We always are skeptical about things we cannot see. You will naturally have doubts as to whether there is any truth in this philosophy. With practice, however, even within a few days, the first glimpse will come, giving encouragement and hope. A widely-quoted commentator on Yoga has written: "When one proof is realized, however little that may be, that will give us faith in the whole teachings of Yoga." If you should concentrate on the tip of your nose, in a few days you will begin to smell the most beautiful fragrance. That will be enough to show that there are certain mental perceptions that can be made without contact with physical objects. Remember, too, that these are only the means. The aim, the goal, the end of this training is the liberation of the soul and freedom from tension and fear. You must be master of your surroundings. Nature or the world about you must not rule you. Never forget that the body is yours, you do not belong to the body.

Now, we may consider pranayama, or breath control. What has this to do with concentrating the powers of the mind? Breath is like the flywheel of your living machine. In a big engine you will find that the flywheel moves first and that motion is conveyed to finer and finer machinery until the most delicate and finest mechanism in the machine is set in motion. Breath is like that flywheel, supplying and regulating the motive power to everything in the body.

Consider that we know very little about our own bodies. We cannot know. Our attention is not discriminating enough to catch the very fine movements that are going on within. We can know of them only as our minds enter our bodies and become more subtle. To get that subtle perception, we must begin with the grosser perceptions, thus reaching the mysterious something which is setting the whole engine in motion. That is prana, the most obvious manifestation of which is the breath. Along with the breath, we slowly enter the body, which enables us to discover the subtle forces and how the nerve currents are moving throughout the body. When we perceive and learn to feel these forces, we begin to get control over them and the body. The mind is also set in motion by the different nerve currents, bringing us to a state in which we have perfect control over body and mind, making both our servants. Knowledge is power, and to get this power we must begin at the beginning, the pranayamarestraining the prana. As you follow this text, you will see the reasons for each exercise and learn which forces in the body are set in motion. You must practice at least twice a day, preferably in the early morning and toward evening. When night passes into day and day passes into night, there is a state of relative calmness. At those times, your body will also have a tendency to become calm. Take advantage of these natural conditions and practice then. Make it a rule not to smoke or eat until you have practiced. If you do this, the sheer force of hunger will prevent any tendency to laziness.

If possible, it is best to have a room devoted to your practice of Yoga and to no other purpose. Do not sleep in that room; you must keep it holy. You must not enter the room until you have bathed and are perfectly clean in body and mind. Place flowers and pleasing pictures in the room. Have no quarreling, or anger or unholy thought there. Allow only those persons to enter who are of the same thought as you are. Eventually, an aura of holiness will pervade that space, and when you are sorrowful, doubtful or disturbed, entrance into that room will make you calm. If you cannot afford a room, set aside a corner; if you cannot do that, then find a place inside your house or out where you can be alone and where the prospect is pleasing.

Sit in a straight posture. The first thing to do is to send a current of holy thought to all creation. Mentally repeat, "Let all things be happy; let all things be peaceful; let all things be blissful." Do so to the East, South, North and West. The more you do, the better you will feel. You will find that the easiest way to make yourself healthy is to see that others are healthy, and the easiest way to make yourself happy is to see that others are happy. Afterwards, if you believe in God, pray. Do not pray for money, or health, or heaven, but for knowledge and light; every other prayer is selfish. The next thing to do is to think of your own body and see that it is strong and healthy. Your body is the best instrument you have. Think of it as being adamant. Like a strong ship, it will help you to cross this ocean of life. Freedom is never reached by the weak. Throw away all weakness. Tell your body it is strong; tell your mind so. Have unbounded faith and hope in yourself. By following the instructions above, you will open your mind to the Yogic forces. Another important aspect of Yoga, the postures, will be discussed in a later section.

THE SECRET OF PRANA

Pranayama may seem at first to be totally involved with breathing. However, breathing is only one of the many exercises through which we get to the real pranayama, or control of the prana. According to old Indian philosophers, the universe is composed of two materials, one of which is called akasa, the omnipresent, all-penetrating existence. Everything that has form, or that is made up of compounds, evolves from the akasa. The akasa becomes air, liquids, solids, the sun, moon, stars and comets. It is the akasa that forms animal and plant life. It is everything we see, all that can be sensed and everything that exists. It cannot be perceived, as it is so subtle that it is beyond all human perception. It can be seen only when it has become gross and taken form. At the beginning of creation there was only this akasa, at the end of the cycle, solids, liquids and gases melt into the akasa again, and the next creation evolves from the akasa.The akasa is manufactured into our universe by the power of prana. Just as akasa is the infinite omnipresent material of our universe, so is prana the infinite, omnipresent power of this universe. At the beginning and at the end of a cycle everything becomes akasa and all the forces that are in the universe resolve back into the prana. In the next cycle, out of this prana is evolved everything that we call energy or force. It is the prana that is manifested as motion, the power of gravity and magnetism. The prana is manifested as the actions of the body, nerve currents and thought. All thought and all physical motion are manifestations of prana. The sum total of all force in the universe, mental or physical, when resolved back to its original state, is called prana. The knowledge and control of this prana is really what is meant bypranayama.

This opens the door to almost unlimited power. Suppose, for instance, one understood the prana perfectly and could control it. What power on earth could there be that would not be his? Many believe he would be able to move the sun and stars out of their places, to control everything in the universe from the atoms to the biggest suns because he would control the vital force of the universe, theprana. When the Yogi becomes perfect, there might be nothing in nature not under his control. All the forces of nature might obey him as his slaves. But let us not reach beyond the stars! The control of the prana is the one goal of pranayama. This is the purpose of the training and exercises. Each man must begin where he stands, must learn how to control the things that are nearest to him. Your body is the nearest thing to you, nearer than anything else in the universe, and your mind is the nearest of all. The power which controls this mind and body is the nearest to you of all the pranain the universe. Thus, the little wave of prana which represents your own mental and physical energies is the nearest wave of all that infinite ocean of prana. You must first learn to control that little wave of prana within you. If you will analyze the many schools of thought in this country, such as faith-healers, spiritualists, Christian Scientists, hypnotists, therapists and many psychologists and psychiatrists, you may find that each attempts to control the prana. Following different paths, they stumbled on the discovery of a force whose nature they do not know, but they unconsciously use the same powers which the Yogi uses and which come from prana.

This prana is the vital force in every being and the finest and highest action of prana is thought. There are several planes of thought. Instinctive thought has been called "conditioned reflex" by Western scholars. If a mosquito bites you, your hand will strike it automatically. All reflex actions belong to this plane of thought. There is also a higher plane of thought, the conscious. You reason, judge, think, see pros and cons of certain situations. Reason, however, is limited; its sphere is very small. We are constantly confronted with facts which penetrate our consciousness from the outside, facts which are ordinarily beyond the powers of the reason. The Yogi believes the mind can exist on this higher plane, the superconscious. When the mind has attained to that state which is called samadhi—perfect concentration or superconsciousness—it goes beyond the limits of reason, and comes face to face with facts which instinct or reason can never know. Manipulation of the subtle forces of the body, which are different manifestations of prana, if trained, stimulates the mind, which progresses to the plane of the superconscious.

Let us repeat that pranayama has little to do with breathing, except insofar as breathing is an exercise which helps you attain control of the vital forces. The most obvious manifestation of prana in the human body, therefore, is the motion of the lungs. If that stops, all the other manifestations of force in the body will also stop. This is considered to be the principal gross motion of the body. To reach the more subtle, we must utilize the grosser and so travel toward the most subtle. Breath does not produce the motion of the lungs. On the contrary, the motion of the lungs produces breath. Prana moves the lungs, and the motion of the lungs draws in air.

From the explanation above, it can be seen that pranayama is not breathing, but controlling that muscular power which moves the lungs. Muscular power which travels through the nerves to the muscles and from those to the lungs, making them move in a certain manner, is the prana. Once this prana is controlled, we find that other actions of the prana in the body slowly come under control. If we have control over certain muscles, why not obtain control over every muscle and nerve? What stands in the way? At present, control is lost, and the motion has become automatic. We cannot move our ears at will, but we know that animals can. We do not have that power because we do not exercise it. This is what is called atavism.

We know that physical agility which has been lost can be brought back to manifestation. It has been shown, moreover, that by sincere work and practice, it is not only possible, but even probable that every part of the body can be brought under perfect control.

THE EIGHT LEVELS OF RAJA YOGA

The real power of Martial Arts and Yoga as a systems of transformation lies in linking physical training to meditation practices. Many adepts in the arts practice breathing and concentration exercises, most of them receiving encouraging results for their efforts. However, very few have an opportunity to participate in what could be defined as a complete system of meditation.

Like Yoga students, Buddhists, and other esoteric aspirants, many martial artists learn techniques that increase awareness and energy development. Regrettably, even the most serious and diligent practitioners of all these sacred arts never achieve the higher levels, levels that are well within their reach.

The problem is in a lack of understanding of how their physical practice, or "Asana", relates to their breathing exercises and concentration techniques. Once this understanding is clear, all levels of training can accelerate. One complete Yoga system reknowned as the "Royal Yoga", Raja Yoga, breaks down the process into eight levels, which are referred to as "The Eight Limbs of Raja Yoga." These eight levels are traditionally pursued after a sound basis in Hatha Yoga is established. The sort of meditation that is talked about in Raja Yoga is done in lotus position, or some other meditation posture that is equally as challenging, for hours at a time. It must be pain-free and energized by perfect concentration of the mind. To have this sort of capacity, the a practitioner's body has to undergo a rigorous regime of preparatory practices, i.e. Hatha Yoga.

Likewise, the mind has to be naturally inclined to follow the philosophical principles that will guide the practitioner's behavior and psychological growth. This sort of change of lifestyle in favor of simple, healthy, and spiritual living does happen over night. A gradual change in attitude and understanding can take place during the time of preparatory practices. The eight levels of Raja Yoga, clearly spelled out, are as follows:

Self-Restraint/ "Yama"

Self restraint can be best defined as the codes of behavior that keep the aspirant at peace with the world he lives in, as well as with himself. By engaging in such "self-restraint," the aspirant is freed from the negative Karma that unwholesome behavior will generate. Typically, this level of practice in all of the esoteric traditions is to instill a sense of righteous behavior in the aspirant. What many fail to realize is that an absence of past indiscretions also frees the mind in the present. Thus, a mind free from these concerns is at peace and free to focus on meditation. The Hindus have five precepts for self-restraint, which are very similar to the Buddhists five. The traditional prayer greeting of the Buddhists and Hindus is considered a conscious recognition of these five principles, one for each finger, by the exchangers of the sign. The precepts are:

- Non-killing/ "Ahimsa"
- Truthfulness/ "Satya"
- Non-stealing/ "Asteya"
- Sexual Continence/ "Brahmacharya"
- Non-covetousness/ "parigraha"

Observance/ "Niyama"

Observances build on the concepts of self-restraint, putting those principles into action in daily life. Such natural extensions comprise this second level.

- Purity of action
- Contentment
- Austerity
- Study of self-development through classic treatises
- Physical discipline

- The honoring of a guru
- Surrender of ego to the ultimate universal power

Much or most of this is not possible for modern society without having heightened awareness and psychological growth that could only come through some sort of preparatory practice like Hatha Yoga.

Physical Practice/ "Asana"

For all practical purposes, this is the level where most Martial Art and Yoga practitioners start and end their practice. Although "physical practice" is considered an absolute necessity to open up and develop the muscular and central nervous systems in all of the traditions, it is not enough. "Physical practice" overdone creates an artificially low learning curve plateau in the aspirant. This tends to be the norm in America. In the Yoga tradition, physical practice is most recognizable as the Yoga postures and exercises practiced in a typical studio, everthing from Sun Salutations to headstands. The majority of these exercises are stretching in character, but many "Asanas" build incredible strength. The Buddhist and Taoist traditions have used martial arts and various qigongs that are marked by intense, physical exertion that provide the body a foundation for sitting meditation. In the truest understanding of Raja Yoga, though, asana relates to the sitting meditation postures of padmasana/lotus pose, siddhasana/accomplished pose for men, and siddha yoni asana/accomplished pose for women. To be able to sit in these poses for hours at a time comfortably with perfect concentration necessitates a high level of accomplishment in the asana practice of Hatha Yoga.

Breathing Exercise/ "Pranayama"

Breathing exercises develop the connection between the cultivation of energy/"Prana" and the breath of the aspirant. Various techniques are used in Yoga, from alternating nostrils to forced exhalations to timed inhalations and exhalations. It is at this point where the production of "Prana"/ "Chi" really accelerates and where the luckier aspirants of Martial Arts and Yoga typically end their exploration. An advanced aspirant learns breathing techniques, some which trace the sensation of the breath up and down certain limbs or energy lines. Energy develops, and the aspirant presupposes that, in the energy felt, the ultimate goal of his exploration into meditation has been realized- the ability to feel energy travel through limbs or spine.

The usual goal of such aspirants in Martial Arts is the ability to execute more powerful martial techniques, and the sensation of energy moving through the body provides for them verification that the ultimate goal has been achieved. Punches, kicks, and throws all improve dramatically, and the diligent martial artist surpasses the normal person in strength and fighting skill. The irony of this is that the sincere aspirant misses out on further development because of a preoccupation with these first gains.

Sense Withdrawal/ "Prathyahara"

Sense withdrawal is the pulling of the five senses back into the mind and the detaching from the various sense stimuli that the surrounding environment is generating. This level is considered to be the last level of the foundation necessary to be successful in the pursuit of a true a spiritual experience in meditation.

"The excited senses of even a wise man, though he may be strong, impetuously carry away his mind. The practice demands considerable patience and perseverance. It is a trying discipline of the senses." -Swami Sivananda, "Fourteen Lessons on Raja Yoga" Prathyahara is also where the techniques of Hatha Yoga end and the techniques of the more advanced Yogas begin.

Concentration/ "Dharana"

Concentration is possible once sense withdrawal has begun. The refocusing of the senses on a single concentration point continues the inward turning of the mind. In the practice of Trataka, seeing an image with the eyes closed at the eyebrow center is one example of such a concentration technique. When one focuses the mind like this, it is akin to all of the light being generated by a light bulb condensing into one point- a light bulb can light a room, whereas a laser can cut through metal. You are training your mind to be like a laser. Raja Yoga has it that if one can inwardly focus on such a point in this way for 12 seconds without interruption, it is considered a "Dharana." This is much harder than it sounds. Most people's minds will interrupt such an endeavor almost immediately.

Most often, aspirants' minds are interrupted from this task by either physical or emotional considerations. Worldly matters force their way into the mind just as a "Dharana" is achieved, necessitating a restart in Pratayahara. Re-examining one's "Yama" and "Niyama" practices is a continuing process for anyone pushing forward to "Dhyana".

Meditation/ "Dhyana"

Meditation is the unbroken flow of the mind on a single point for an extended period. In practice, it can be measured by counting the numbers of breaths in one's focus on a concentration point, with or without a mantra.

Each attempt, however successful, strengthens the aspirant. One teacher explained that it was like doing pushups. The first time you try, you can only do a couple and your muscles ache. Years down the road, if you practice hard, doing a couple hundred can be quite an invigorating round of exercise.

Superconsciousness / "Samadhi"

Superconciousness is the state of "union" that word Yoga directly refers to. The union achieved is described as.

"In Samadhi, the meditator loses his individuality and becomes identical with the Supreme Self. Just as the river joins the ocean, the individual soul joins the Supreme Soul, the ocean of absolute consciousness." Swami Sivananda, "Fourteen Lesson on Raja Yoga" It is at this level that the aspirant reaches a peak in his/her evolution. Very few aspirantst reach this level of development. It is really not worth talking about, since words fail to convey the experience adequately to any one who has not experienced this directly. All we can do is to continue our exploration with diligence and intelligence.

OBTAINING RELAXATION THROUGH YOGA

While the asanas or postures which will be described later are a basic part of the practice of Yoga, we should continue our study of Raja Yoga, the non-physical phases of this practice. Some readers may find they cannot follow the rigid discipline of a full Yogic life; others may be seeking an easier path to relaxation, and may feel that they are less concerned with their physical than their mental states.

Breath control is an essential first step in obtaining a state of relaxation. If you can, assume the Padmasana or Lotus Pose or place yourself in a comfortable sitting position. Taken directly from the ancient Sanskrit texts, the Hatha Yoga Pradipika of Swatmaram Swami, published in 1893, provides a specific guide for relaxation through breathing exercises.

There are three Yogic terms which you should know: "puraka" is the term for inhalation; "rechaka" for exhalation; "kumbhaka" for retention of breath. Yogic instructions are: the Yogi assuming the Lotus Pose should draw in the prana (breath) through the ida (left nostril), and, having retained it as long as he can, exhale it through the pingala (right nostril). Again, inhaling through the right nostril, he should hold his breath as long as possible and exhale slowly through the left nostril. He should inhale through the same nostril by which he exhaled and having restrained the breath to the utmost (until he is covered with perspiration, or until his body shakes) he should then exhale slowly, as exhaling forcefully would diminish the energy of the body.

These exercises should be performed four times a day—in the early morning, at midday, evening and midnight—slowly increasing the number from three, each time, to eighty. Their effects are described as "to render the mind and body slender and bright." Although in the direct translation from the Sanskrit, the ida is named as being the left nostril and the pingala as the right one, these words more properly designate the two supposed conduits which connect with the nostrils, and thence conduct throughout the entire body the vital air (the prana) that enters with the atmospheric air.

Before undertaking these exercises, persons of phlegmatic temperament are directed to go through the following course of preparation: (1) Cleanse the gullet with a strip of cloth, the width of four fingers, by swallowing it and then withdrawing it. Start gradually at the rate of one hand-span's length daily;

(2) Take daily enemas of water; (3) Cleanse the nostrils by putting up a thread and drawing it out by way of the mouth; (4) Look without winking at a minute object with concentrated mind until the tears come; (5) With head bent down, turn the viscera of the body to right and left; (6) Breathe in and out rapidly, like a bellows. Internal concentration, causing the stomach to empty itself by vomiting, is also recommended.

According to the Hindu system of physiology, there are seventy-two thousand nadis or channels leading from the throat to thekundali in the pelvic region. When these channels have been purified by proper breath control, the body is ready to absorb the fullest prana from the atmosphere. Then, according to the old tracts, "the body becomes lean, the speech eloquent, the inner sounds of the individual's body are distinctly heard, the eyes are clear and bright, the body is freed from all disease, the seminal fluid is concentrated, the digestive fire is increased and the nadis are purified."

LOOKING INWARD FOR RELAXATION

It is known that long and close concentration upon any given part of the body will induce sensations there and, sometimes, even movement. Control over unused muscles may be obtained in this way. While it is a basic claim for Hatha Yoga that the breathing exercises can lead to control over the mind by supplying arterialized blood to the brain, and thus control mental by physical action, it is also claimed that strong, persistent concentration of the mind will induce controlled breathing, thus directing physical action by mental.

A story is told of a student whose teacher made him sit meditating in silence for twelve years and at last commanded him to pronounce the sacred syllables A.U.M. This he did with the following results: "When the student came to the first syllable, rechaka, or the process by which the air in the lungs is pumped out, set in naturally. When he finished the second syllable, puraka, or the process of inhalation, set in. At the end of the third syllable, kumbhaka, or the process of retention, set in, and in a short time he had settled into the pure and elevated state of samadhi, which may be defined as perfect relaxation."

This story illustrates the largeness of the claim on behalf of Raja Yoga, or mental Yoga, that it brings physical Yoga with it, provided that the mental processes take the form of long-continued silent concentration. It also supports the claim that what it brings is important, since the pranayama of the student soon brought him into perfect absorption.

THE ASANAS

Though many asanas, or postures, are unsuited to people who habitually sit in chairs, those who practice Yoga often find themselves falling into these poses almost involuntarily. Many believe that the asanas are natural positions of relaxation into which the body falls when freed from the controls of the conscious mind and from the postures into which they have been trained in our so-called "civilized living." William Flagg, one of the first Westerners to probe the secrets of Yoga, once stated: "A leg has jerked itself upwards and pressed the sole of its foot against the other as high up as seemed possible; this has happened hundreds of times." The posture here imitated is sitting on a foot, and its efficacy is supposed to lie in the pressure upon the nerve centers in the foot, leg and region of the perineum.

Another asana resembling the "plant balance" of modern gymnastics is described thus: "Plant your hands firmly on the ground and support your body on your elbows, pressing against the sides of your loins. Raise your feet in the air stiff and straight on a level with the head." This position was attempted while the practitioner was seated in an easy chair, and failed to be completed only because the back of the chair kept the head from falling to the level of the feet. The legs were lifted from the floor and thrust out stiffly, while the weight of the body was made to rest on the elbows, which were resting on the arms of the chair. This was repeated not only once, but a great number of times. The elbows were pressed against the sides, forcefully and involuntarily hammering themselves violently and repeatedly against the sides, giving excellent massage to both liver and spleen.

The Shavasana, said to eliminate fatigue and induce calmness of mind, is described as lying on one's back at full length like a corpse. Often, when lying on his side, the practitioner has been turned over on his back as though by a power foreign to him, though apparently using his own muscles. This resulted in a curious sensation, which reproduced on the feet, ankles and seat of the body the compression which is obtainable by sitting on the feet, Eastern fashion. It was as if a foreign body were pressed against the person's sides with a force equal to what would be felt in the postures of Hatha Yoga. Sometimes several of the parts in question were acted upon simultaneously.

Another incident of a similar nature is described by Flagg in the practice of the mudras, or acts for putting the body in good condition. The Nauli Mudra is described: "With the head bent down, one should turn right and left the intestines of the stomach with the slow motion of a small eddy in the river." Something like this interior movement is produced by one process of the Swedish movement-cure. It consists of sitting on a stool, bending the body forward as far as possible and rotating the trunk of the body like the spoke of a horizontal wheel. The head represents the tire and the seat, the hub. It was just this movement that, in the case of two persons observed, was set up as often as kumbhaka, or the suspension of the breath, was practiced, neither of them having an idea of such a result. The Nauli Mudra is considered one of the most important of all Hatha exercises, and the body rotation is one of the most effective of the Swedish exercises.

CONCENTRATION

A Yoga technique for concentration is expressed as "looking fixedly at the spot between the eyebrows." Many have reported that while cleansing the mind of thought, the eyeballs would of themselves roll upward as far as they could go, and hold themselves there. The Shambhavi Mudra provides almost complete relaxation by dividing the conscious concentration. It consists of fixing the mind on some part of the body and the eyes rigidly and unwinkingly on an external object. Often while you are concentrating intently with your eyes closed, they will seem to open almost of themselves and fix on some object within range, always rigidly and without winking.

Another direction for the Yogi says: "Direct the pupils of the eyes toward the light by raising the eyebrows a little upward." Often while trying this, your eyebrows will raise themselves as if to get out of the way of the eyes. In the motions noted here and in others, it seems as though an intelligent power beyond conscious reach takes the Yoga adherent out of his own hands. This power appears to assume control of voluntary and involuntary muscles, working them independently of the person's will, though, it should be noted, never against it.

RELAXATION TECHNIQUES FOR STRESS RELIEF

For many of us, relaxation means zoning out in front of the TV at the end of a stressful day. But this does little to reduce the damaging effects of stress. To effectively combat stress, we need to activate the body's natural relaxation response. You can do this by practicing relaxation techniques such as deep breathing, meditation, rhythmic exercise, and yoga. Fitting these activities into your life can help reduce everyday stress and boost your energy and mood.

The relaxation response: Bringing your nervous system back into balance Stress is necessary for life. You need stress for creativity, learning, and your very survival. Stress is only harmful when it becomes overwhelming and interrupts the healthy state of equilibrium that your nervous system needs to remain in balance. Unfortunately, overwhelming stress has become an increasingly common characteristic of contemporary life. When stressors throw your nervous system out of balance, relaxation techniques can bring it back into a balanced state by producing the relaxation response, a state of deep calmness that is the polar opposite of the stress response.

When stress overwhelms your nervous system your body is flooded with chemicals that prepare you for "fight or flight". While the stress response can be lifesaving in emergency situations where you need to act quickly, it wears your body down when constantly activated by the stresses of everyday life. The relaxation response puts the brakes on this heightened state of readiness and brings your body and mind back into a state of equilibrium.

A variety of different relaxation techniques can help you bring your nervous system back into balance by producing the relaxation response. The relaxation response is not lying on the couch or sleeping but a mentally active process that leaves the body relaxed, calm, and focused. Learning the basics of these relaxation techniques isn't difficult, but it does take practice. Most stress experts recommend setting aside at least 10 to 20 minutes a day for your relaxation practice. If you'd like to get even more stress relief, aim for 30 minutes to an hour. If that sounds like a daunting commitment, remember that many of these techniques can be incorporated into your existing daily schedule—practiced at your desk over lunch or on the bus during your morning commute.

Finding the relaxation technique that's best for you

There is no single relaxation technique that is best for everyone. When choosing a relaxation technique, consider your specific needs, preferences, fitness level, and the way you tend to react to stress. The right relaxation technique is the one that resonates with you, fits your lifestyle, and is able to focus your mind and interrupt your everyday thoughts in order to elicit the relaxation response. In many cases, you may find that alternating or combining different techniques will keep you motivated and provide you with the best results.

YOGA RELAXATION TECHNIQUES

In yoga, relaxation refers to the loosening of bodily and mental tension. Keeping muscles in a constant alert state expends a great amount of your energy, which then is unavailable when your muscles are called upon to really function. Conscious relaxation trains your muscles to release their grip when you don't use them. This relaxation keeps the muscles responsive to the signals from your brain telling them to contract so that you can perform all the countless tasks of a busy day.

Tips for a Successful Yoga Relaxation Practice

Relaxation is a conscious endeavor that lies somewhere between effort and noneffort. To truly relax, you have to understand and practice the skill. Try the following:

- Practice in a quiet environment where you are unlikely to be disturbed by others or the telephone.
- Try placing a small pillow under your head and a large one under your knees for support and comfort in the supine, or lying, positions.
- Ensure that your body stays warm. If necessary, heat the room first or cover yourself with a blanket. Particularly avoid lying on a cold floor, which isn't good for your kidneys.
- Don't practice relaxation techniques on a full stomach.

Deep Relaxation in Yoga: The Corpse Posture

The simplest and yet the most difficult of all yoga postures is the corpse posture, also widely known as the dead pose. The corpse posture is an exercise in mind over matter. The only props you need are your body and mind.

Here is how you do the corpse pose:

- Lie flat on your back, with your arms stretched out and relaxed by your sides, palms up (or whatever feels most comfortable).
  Place a small pillow under your head if you need one and another large pillow under your knees for added comfort.
- Close your eyes.
- Form a clear intention to relax.
  Some people find it helpful to picture themselves lying in white sand on a sunny beach.
- Take a couple of deep breaths, lengthening exhalation.
- Contract the muscles in your feet for a couple of seconds and then consciously relax them.
  Do the same with the muscles in your calves, upper legs, buttocks, abdomen, chest, back, hands, forearms, upper arms, shoulders, neck, and face.
- Periodically scan all your muscles from your feet to your face to check that they are relaxed.
  You can often detect subtle tension around the eyes and the scalp muscles. Also relax your mouth and tongue.
- Focus on the growing bodily sensation of no tension and let your breath be free.
- At the end of the session, before opening your eyes, form the intention to keep the relaxed feeling for as long as possible.
- Open your eyes, stretch lazily, and get up slowly.

Use yoga for relaxation before sleep

If you want to enjoy deep sleep or are experiencing insomnia (but don't want to count sheep), the following exercise can help you. Many people don't make it to the end of this relaxation technique without falling asleep.

For this exercise, you need the following props: a bed or other comfortable place to sleep, two pillows, and one or two blankets. Allow five to ten minutes. Follow these steps:

- Prepare yourself for sleep and get into bed, lying on your back under the blankets.
  Your legs can be straight or bent at the knees with your feet flat on the mattress.
- Place one pillow under your head and have the other one close by.
- With your eyes closed, begin to breathe through the nose, making your exhalation twice as long as your inhalation.

Keep your breathing smooth and effortless. Also, don't try to direct your breath to any part of your body. Let the 1:2 breathing ratio be effortless, something you can keep up.

- Remain on your back for eight breaths, then roll over onto your right side and place the second pillow between your knees. Now use the same 1:2 ratio for 16 breaths.
- Finally, roll over on to your left side, with the second pillow still between your knees, and use the 1:2 ratio for 32 breaths.

RELAX YOUR MIND AND BODY WITH YOGA

Is stress wearing you down? Are your muscles tense and your posture less than perfect? Bringing yoga, a touch of Eastern culture, into your Western lifestyle may be the perfect answer to help you unwind both your body and mind. People of all ages and physical abilities have been practicing yoga for more than 5,000 years for general well-being. Today, an estimated 12 million Americans practice yoga for conditions as varied as addiction, fatigue and weight management.

De-stress and Lower Your Health Risks

Studies show that yoga, like many forms of physical activity, can actually help relieve stress. Emotional stress from daily life often contributes to physical stresses like muscle tension and constricted breathing. Because of its impact on the circulatory system, stress is also linked to cardiovascular disease. By alleviating physical and emotional stress, you may reduce your risk of heart disease and other illnesses. Some hospitals are making yoga and meditation classes available to cancer patients, and reductions in stress levels have been observed. It is yet unclear, however, whether stress reduction influences long-term prognosis for cancer. But studies show that stress relief helps bolster the immune system's ability to fight diseases, including cancer.

Yoga reduces stress by encouraging deep, rhythmic breathing. It also promotes relaxation by increasing the flow of blood and oxygen to each part of the body. Some forms of yoga include meditation or the repetition of a soothing sound or phrase. Because yoga also lengthens muscles, stretches joints and limbers ligaments, the exercises may actually help reverse some physical effects of aging like arthritis, stiff joints and general aches and pains. So, take a deep breath, and open your mind to this ancient form of exercise.

Pointers for Starting Yoga

- Be sure to check with your doctor before beginning a new exercise program.
- Find a yoga instructor in your area by asking other people or visiting websites such aswww.YogaJournal.com or www.YogaAlliance.org
- Start out with simple standing and sitting poses. Some forms can give you an intense workout. If in doubt, ask the instructor to clarify what will be taught.

- As a beginner, it is advisable to choose a gentle, slow form of yoga. Consider one of the following:
  - Hatha yoga is the most popular branch of yoga from which a lot of other styles originated. Because the practice can vary widely, students should find out exactly what a class offers.
  - In Iyengar yoga, students hold poses, especially standing postures, typically longer than in other forms.
  - Svaroopa is a consciousness-oriented yoga that promotes healing. Students often begin this form in comfortable chair poses that help the spine.
  - Integral focuses on integrating yoga teachings into everyday work and relationships.

CORRECTIVE POSES OF YOGA

The first section of this book discussed the mental, or psychological, approach to Yoga. As you apply the earlier lessons to mental relaxation, you must also bring your body to a state in which it will support your efforts to attain full contentment, relaxation and ease. Ancient teachers of scientific Yoga realized, as do modern physicians, that proper carriage of the body is essential for mental and physical health. You will note that on the following pages there is very little reference to the Sanskrit philosophy of Yoga, for here we put aside the mind and devote our attention to the body. As you assume these postures, however, keep in mind the eight principles of Raja Yoga. They will help you in dealing with both mind and body as you practice Yoga.

At first, spend only as much time on each exercise as you can without feeling fatigued. As the timbre of your body improves and as your mind takes fuller control of your body, you will find it possible to remain in any pose for longer and longer periods. One of the most prevalent causes of sluggishness and disturbance of the digestive organs is faulty carriage of the body, especially above the waist, involving the spinal and abdominal muscles. Practically all of us are victims of faulty posture and suffer from enteroptosis, a condition in which the stomach, intestines and very often the kidneys, liver and pelvic organs, are dragged downwards and remain permanently out of their correct anatomical positions.

Medical internists will verify the statement that poor carriage retards circulation of large blood vessels. An habitual slouching position causes the blood of the abdomen to stagnate in the liver, inducing a feeling of despondency and confusion, as well as headache, accompanied by coldness of the hands and feet, chronic fatigue and often constipation. The Yoga Institute in Bombay has traced varied disorders of the digestive and pelvic organs and even functional defects of the heart and lungs directly to poor posture habits. Persons who had been approaching invalidity as a result of posture habits are said to have been cured after a few weeks of training.

Persons in normal health have gained markedly, physically and mentally, from a short, but regular, corrective posture program.

The proper pose of the body imparts graceful curves to the female figure and an air of strength to the male. The proper posture, as imparted by Yoga, embodies in beauty the feelings of triumph and self-respect, whatever the age or condition of the practitioner. The common drooped and slouching position is both ugly and unhealthy, and invariably reflects a degenerated mental attitude.

Ancient Yogis were perhaps first to recognize the influence of carriage on health of the mind and body. The prime objective of posture in Yoga is not mystic, mysterious or magic, but the achievement of physical ease and poise. An erect posture is recommended to maintain free spinal circulation during prolonged sitting and concentration.

THE FIRST LESSON IN YOGA POSTURE

When beginning the practice of Yoga postures, start with the simple prayer pose in a standing position. Medical investigation shows that many corrective and therapeutic benefits stem from even these first simple poses. It is no longer known whether the ancient Yogins, the founders of Yoga, attached any special mystical significance to these first poses. However, they are excellent poses for prayer and meditation.

STITHA-PRARTHANASANA, OR PRAYER POSE

This pose helps to achieve steadiness through gradual control of voluntary muscular movements and offers, through steadiness, the best physical attitude for standing prayer; it permits normal standing posture by coordinating skeletal muscles and it corrects postural defects.

While standing, hold your body as tall as possible without actually rising on your toes. Keep your heels together, placing all your weight upon the balls of your feet. Throw your head and chest up, shoulder blades flat. The abdominal muscles should be deflated at their lower part, but not drawn inward, and fuller just below the ribs, while the pelvis should be tilted at such an angle as to prevent any exaggeration of the lumbar curve. Your knees must be straight but not stiff, with legs together touching at the knees. Fold your hands over the sternum; avoid tension. Relax your mind and fix your eyes on any pleasing object before you.

In this position, the thorax is full and round; the diaphragm is high; the abdomen at its greatest length. The stomach and intestinal viscera are held in proper place and the pelvic organs are relieved of pressures from above. There is a partial relaxation of the larger muscles and relief from tension. With the arms relaxed and let down at the sides, it is an ideal position for standing. Maintain this position for about one minute, breathing normally. Keep your mind free and observe complete silence. Turn slowly to either side, parallel to a wall or post, and notice whether you sway. Swaying is an indication of nervous disturbance which must be overcome.

Fig. Stitha-Prarthanasana, or Prayer Pose

If possible, practice opposite a mirror, where swaying motions can be noted. During the period of test and correction, keep your eyes half-closed, allowing just enough vision for observation, and concentrate on the parts of your body above the waist. Stand immobile as a statue, and as soon as you have a tendency to sway, check it by will power. After the first few weeks, try to sustain this motionless pose for two to three minutes, always breathing normally. This pose is best practiced in the morning, and should be followed daily until complete control has been achieved. Afterwards, it may be practiced once weekly.

EKAPADASANA, OR ONE-LEG POSE

Begin by assuming the Prayer Pose. Bend down, lift one leg with your hands and bring it up to the thigh. Keep your balance on the other leg. If you experience the fear of falling, stand and practice near a wall or window sill or other support. After you have attained sufficient steadiness on one leg, adjust the raised leg by pressing the heel tightly against the opposite groin, with the sole of the foot against the opposite thigh. Study the illustration for details of this pose. Steadiness, or nerve control and coordination between muscular and nervous systems, is one of the prime goals of Yoga physical education, and must be learned in slow stages. At first it may be necessary to use some support to maintain balance. Later you will be able to practice without support, maintaining this pose with your hands in the prayer posture. It may be difficult to keep this pose for more than a few seconds at the beginning, but you should gradually be able to extend the duration of time until you can keep the pose comfortably for two or three minutes. Do not overdo at first. Limit practice to one or two minutes mornings and evenings, alternating legs.

In addition to exercising and relaxing the muscles and nerves of alternate legs, this pose helps to develop the nerve control necessary for relaxation. When swaying is experienced during this exercise, the best corrective is to concentrate your mind on each of your movements. Become consciously aware of the most insignificant variations in steadiness, so that you will be able to secure control over all motion. Along with other Yoga measures—meditation, diet, etc.—this posture facilitates nerve control in the course of a few months.

Fig. Ekapadasana, or One-Leg Pose

PADMASANA, OR LOTUS POSE

The traditional meditative posture, the Padmasana, or Lotus Pose, is essential for posture training, body-free meditation and preserving normal elasticity of the muscles connected with the pelvis and lower extremities. As noted previously, those who have been raised in the Western culture are stiff and lack flexibility in their legs and lower bodies. This must be corrected in order to restore natural suppleness of the limbs. The Lotus Pose may at first be a bit difficult, but with regular practice, massage of the limbs and determination, it can be achieved. Avoid undue strain and do not force yourself into this by violent jerks or tension of your legs. When you are ready for it, your body will fall naturally into the desired posture. Now that you have begun the sitting and the lying-down exercises, you should avoid the use of a bare floor. If the room in which you are practicing is not carpeted, provide yourself with a soft mat at least 6 x 3 feet, and spread a clean sheet over the area where you will sit or lie.

Fig. Padmasana, or Lotus Pose

Fig. Ardha-Padmasana, or Semi-Lotus Pose

ARDHA-PADMASANA, OR SEMI-LOTUS POSE

Beginning with the Lotus Pose, sit on the floor with your legs stretched out. Bend the right leg slowly and fold it upon itself. Using your hands, place the right heel at the root of the thigh so that its sole is turned upwards and your foot is stretched over the left groin. Similarly, bend the left leg and fold it upon itself with your hands, placing the left heel over the root of the right thigh. Your ankles should cross each other, while your heel-ends touch closely. The left foot with its upturned sole should lie fully stretched over the right groin. Keep your knees pressed to the ground, feet tight against the thighs, and press your heels firmly against the upper front margin of the pubic bone slightly above the sex organs.

To complete this pose, hold your body erect, with neck straight, chest thrown forward and abdomen drawn moderately inwards. Fix your eyes on any object in front of you, then close them. Spread your left hand with its back touching both heels, palm upwards. Place your right hand over the left in the same manner. The ancient texts associate this pose with peace. Although many find it easier to achieve the pose by folding the left leg first, you may alternate the position of your legs.

A highly effective meditative posture, the Semi-Lotus Pose offers many corrective and cultural benefits. It results in either extension, flexion or relaxation to almost all the important muscles, ligaments and tendons of the lower limbs. It also induces increased blood circulation in the abdominal and genital areas by blocking the flow in some areas and drawing a larger supply of blood from the bifurcation of the abdominal aorta. Restraint of the general circulation caused by the pressure of the heels provides an increased supply of blood to the sex organs and also helps to tone the various nerve centers located in the pelvic region, such as the chain of coccygeal and sacral nerves.

Respiration is improved as a result of the chest being thrown forward and the abdomen being held in normal position. Muscle tone is increased in the internal organs, especially those of the intestinal tract. In this posture, it is important that the shoulders should not sag forward, crowding the chest, nor should the upper part of the body crowd down upon the stomach and the abdominal viscera. The Lotus Pose is suggested for the regulation of breath movements.

YASTIKASANA, OR STICK POSE

This is a recent addition to the traditional asanas, or poses. Developed in the 19th century by Yoga practitioners, it is believed to increase the height of the user. While this benefit may be questioned, the pose induces a state of complete relaxation. An all-body stretch which does not strain even the novice in Yoga, this pose is most easily held while lying down.

To take this pose, harmonize your breathing with your actions. Lie on your back on a comfortable mat or carpet, with your legs and arms fully extended. Fall into a relaxed position. Inhale for three seconds and, while retaining your breath, stretch your body slowly to full length. Your toes and fingers should point outwards, as if trying to reach an object beyond their grasp. Repeat this stretch position for three seconds and then release the tension of the stretch while exhaling. Any maximum stretching of the body should be attempted only while the breath is retained. Do not attempt to hold your breath for more than four or five seconds.

To simplify the explanation of the Yastikasana movements: (1) With body supine, arms and legs outstretched, inhale for three seconds; (2) while your body is outstretched, hold your breath for three seconds; (3) return to the starting position; exhale for three seconds. Repeat the entire exercise five times in one minute.

The primary object of this posture is to stretch the body fully. It serves to correct faulty postural habits and tenses the usually relaxed abdominal and pelvic muscles. According to the schools of Yoga which have utilized the Stick Pose, stretching aids height and its regular practice will at least halt the tendency of the aging to lose height. It may be done both in the morning and in the evening. Where it is used solely for relaxation, normal, rhythmic breathing should be maintained without any effort at stretching.

PARVATASANA, OR MOUNTAIN POSE

Overweight can bring both mental and physical problems. The posture known as Parvatasana, or the Mountain Pose, has been found in several Yoga institutes to be highly effective in maintaining slimness and in correcting minor postural defects of the spinal cord. Assuming the Semi-Lotus Pose, slowly raise your hands upward and above the head. Keep your palms pressed together. If it is easier, interlace your fingers. Finally, stretch upward as if to touch some object directly above your head. Keep your arms close to your ears, your head erect, your back straight, and pull your abdomen in. While inhaling, raise the upper part of your body to its maximum height. Make sure your elbows and wrists are in a straight line. Maintain this slightly stretched, upright position between breaths, since this is the point at which attempts at upward stretching are most successful. During this exercise, keep your eyes fixed on some object before you and keep your mind at ease.

This pose was named Parvatasana because it has the appearance of a mountain. For maximum benefits, the movements and breathing should be in harmony with actions as shown in the following instructions: (1) In a sitting pose, raise arms and inhale for three seconds; (2) maintain pose and try to retain breath for six seconds; (3) return to starting position, exhale for three seconds. Repeat this pose five times to a minute without pausing. This posture tenses and pulls all the abdominal and pelvic muscles, strengthens and straightens the muscles of the back and also stretches and exercises the usually inactive waist zone.

One of its most evident benefits will be the reduction of fat and flabby abdominal tissue. However, it must be followed consistently for one minute, both in the morning and evening.

VARIATIONS OF THE PARVATASANA POSE

There are four dynamic variations of this pose. They are: (1) Swaying forward; (2) leaning backward; (3) bending to the right; (4) bending to the left. These variations should be utilized during a six-second breathing pause. Instead of maintaining the perpendicular position while stretching, vary it by making the movements on the four sides and alternately. Gradually increase the retention of your breath to nine seconds, which will permit four movements to a minute. The purpose of the variations is to provide additional stretching of all sets of muscles in the trunk. They also massage the internal organs just below the ribs and the abdominal muscles.

TRIKONASANA, OR TRIANGLE POSE

The Trikonasana will enable you to reach a state of physical suppleness and elasticity that will have a relaxing effect on your mental state. It is more difficult at first than the earlier poses, as it calls upon ordinarily unexercised muscles. Because of the exceptionally straight and full-length adjustments of the bony structure of the spine, this pose will correct many of the ailments due to misplaced internal organs and poor body tonicity. The dynamic variations of this pose will enhance its benefits considerably.

Stand erect with your feet together and arms down at your sides. Slowly exhale while bending downward; keep your legs straight. Lower only the upper part of the body. Keep your legs perfectly straight and pressed backwards. Now, touch your toes with the tips of your fingers, keeping your arms straight, with spine and neck horizontal, abdomen in, head thrown forward, and your eyes fixed on the tip of your nose. Maintain this pose as illustrated on the next page, then return to the original position while inhaling. Your movements and timing should be as follows: (1) Touch toes and exhale for three seconds; (2) keep pose and hold breath for six seconds; (3) return to starting position and inhale for three seconds. Repeat five times in one minute without pausing. Do not become discouraged if you fail to touch your toes on the first attempt. Try each day until you can hold the pose comfortably. Work into this pose gradually, avoiding attempts to force your body into it by jerks or sudden pulling of muscles. Before working for other refinements of the pose, aim to touch your toes. If you should find yourself feeling muscle tenderness, try a warm massage to alleviate the discomfort.

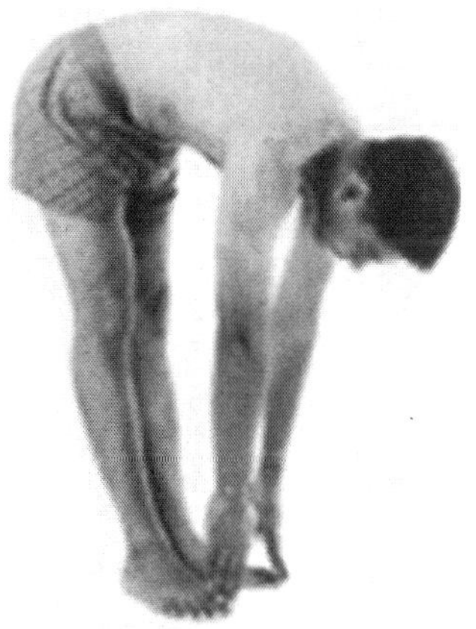

Fig. Trikonasana, or Triangle Pose

A dynamic variation of the Triangle Pose is fairly simple. Stand with your feet twenty-four inches apart and, while inhaling, raise one arm and bend it laterally on the opposite side, sliding the other arm lengthwise. When the complete lateral stretch is achieved, retain your breath and return to the original position. Repeat the lateral stretch on the other side.

Movements, breathing and timing should be as follows: (1) Bend sideward; inhale for three seconds; (2) keep pose and retain breath for six seconds; (3) return to normal position and exhale for three seconds. Repeat alternately, without pausing, ten times in two minutes. For best effects, the exercise should be practiced for at least one minute. However, persons with poor physical tone and those with a history of circulatory or respiratory ailments should try it only in moderation, for about ten seconds at one time.

GARUDASANA, OR EAGLE POSE

Another cause of both physical and mental tenseness is a lack of suppleness and elasticity in joints and extremities. Correctives for this are postures involving fairly simple body twists. The purposeful twisting of the extremities may be accomplished through the Garudasana. Stand erect as shown in the illustration. Lift either leg (the alternate use of each leg will follow), and twist the same leg both near the hip joint and the knee. Then twine one leg around the other. Adjust the twists very carefully without strain or muscle tension. Lock the ankle with the toe of the other twisted leg and hold it there as a safety against possible accidental release. Do this while exhaling. When you are balanced on one leg, make an effort to keep the body straight, and gradually increase the pressure of the toe-hold near the opposite ankle until the greatest possible twist is achieved.

At first, practice only the leg twist while retaining your breath. After the first week or so, when this becomes easier, try the arm and hand twists by twining one arm around the other (alternating arms). Twist the hands from the wrists and press the palms against each other. Try to keep the pose for several seconds and, while inhaling, return to the original position.

Do not force yourself into this pose until your limbs have gained sufficient suppleness. Then you should follow this time-plan: (1) Twist your body and exhale for five seconds; (2) maintain the pose as shown in the illustration and retain your breath for ten seconds (or you may with normal, rhythmic breathing hold the pose for not more than two minutes); (3) return to starting position and inhale for five seconds.

It is advised that this posture be repeated alternately three times on each side for a two-minute period, preferably in the morning. Note that in the Garudasana you should avoid straining while twisting. Practice it by gradual stages before attempting to follow the full exercise.

SPECIFIC POSTURES FOR RELAXATION

While the great majority of the asanas have a curative or therapeutic value, there are several which are purely for the purpose of relaxation. Relaxation should not be mistaken for inertia. It is not a state of lethargy; rather, it is rest after effort or, perhaps, conscious rest after conscious effort. One definition of relaxation is "a complete resignation of the body to the power of gravity, surrender of the mind to nature, and the whole body energy being transferred to a deep, dynamic breathing."

PHYSICAL RELAXATION

Complete relaxation of the voluntary muscles at once transfers energy to involuntary parts so that, strictly speaking, there can be no such thing as relaxation except in the voluntary muscles and brain. But this is quite sufficient! This transfer of energy by voluntary action and involuntary reaction produces the necessary equilibrium for the renewal of strength.

In many parts of the world, where human beings still transport heavy loads, it is amazing how far they can carry burdens that most individuals could not even lift from the ground. Observation of porters in many parts of the Orient and the Arabic world has shown that their endurance may be due to the ability to relax. During long, heavy hauls, they often stop and lie down in apparently semi-lifeless states for as long as an hour. Then they rise, refreshed, and resume their arduous journeys.

Proper, purposeful relaxation offers the greatest amount of renewed strength in the shortest length of time. After extended exertion or stress, perfect rest in the form of relaxation is the principle which revitalizes the nerve centers, collects the scattered forces of energy and invigorates the body. The three poses of Yoga for complete relaxation are Dradhasana, Shavasana and Adhvasana.

DRADHASANA, OR FIRM POSE

This is considered best for sleeping, as it is the most comfortable. To take the pose, lie relaxed with your right arm under your head, using it as a pillow. By lying passively on the right side, you favor emptying of the stomach and make breathing movements easier. In practice, it has been found that sleeping in this manner generally inhibits dreams and nocturnal emissions and improves digestion. A short period of sleep becomes the equivalent of a longer sleep for recuperative purposes. It is also recommended for short periods of waking relaxation.

SHAVASANA, OR CORPSE POSE

This is recommended for use when the student of Yoga experiences fatigue during any of his exercises. This pose is described in the tracts as "destroying fatigue of the body; quieting the agitation of the mind." Lie face up with your feet extended. Remain motionless with a sense or feeling of sinking down like a corpse. Gradually relax every muscle of the body by concentrating on each individually, from the tip of the toe to the end of the skull. Exercise absolute resignation of will by trying to forget the existence of your body and detaching yourself from it. Hold this posture until you feel restored. Medical authorities have confirmed that the Shavasana pose brings about a fall in the blood pressure and pulse rate and establishes an even rate of respiration. If this pose is kept for more than ten minutes, the deepened respiration and lowered circulation in the brain will probably bring about a tendency to sleep.

ADHAVASANA, OR RELAXED POSE

Lie down with your head on your folded arms, as if on a pillow, and concentrate as in Shavasana. Relax all your muscles. Then stretch your hands and legs out fully, and permit the power of gravity to take over the weight of your body as you relax every voluntary muscle.

MENTAL RELAXATION

Another group of asanas, or postures, specifically provides for the care of the nervous system. These exercises have been found to be especially helpful to persons of a neurasthenic condition. An individual in this state will be mentally vague, lack determination, and have continual feelings of inferiority, fatigue and distraction, accompanied by a state of anxiety. Lack of will power and other forms of nervous or mental debility are all indications of a lack of tonicity in the brain-nervous system.

In many ways, symptoms of the neurasthenic are similar to those of an older person who is approaching or has reached senility. Yoga investigators feel that the condition may be due to a degeneration of the nerve cells with resultant subnormal functions. While the Yoga process may not reverse the situation in the case of an aged person, it has resulted in relief for neurasthenics of young and middle age. In addition, the normal person who utilizes these asanas will find that he derives from them a new keenness of mind and an ability to utilize his nerve-energy to the utmost for whatever personal goals he may have set for himself.

BHUJANGASANA, OR SNAKE POSE

The anterior and posterior stretching offered by the Snake Pose are said to be ideal spinal exercises, preserving or restoring tonicity in the spinal column and nervous channels. Lie on your stomach, with your legs stretched and toes pointed outward. Keep your arms at your sides, with palms down, and your forehead on the floor. Then, slowly raise your head and neck upward and backward.

When your head and neck are slightly raised, plant your hands on both sides of the abdomen. Inhale, and gradually raise your thorax and the upper part of your abdomen by increasing the angle between your hands and rising shoulders. From the navel downward, your body should remain fixed to the ground. Only the upper portion of your body should be raised. In some texts, this pose is called the "Like a hooded cobra striking" pose. Work toward this pose gradually, avoiding muscular strain or "jerkiness" in your efforts to raise the upper part of your body. As you practice this pose, you will feel the pressure on your spinal column gradually working down the vertebrae until you feel a deep pressure at the coccyx.

At first, concentrate on the posture. Having achieved the correct pose, exhale and return to the starting position. Lower yourself slowly. In contrast to the pressure which you felt as you entered this posture, you will experience a feeling of relief along your spine as you lower yourself. This asana should not be utilized by women during menstruation or advanced pregnancy, or by men suffering from hernia. Persons with a weak physical structure should approach this asana slowly and drop it if they find it too arduous. It may be attempted later when the other muscle-tone asanas have shown their effects.

After the pose has been mastered, follow this procedure: (1) Raise thorax and inhale for three seconds; (2) maintain pose, retaining your breath for six seconds; (3) return to starting position, while exhaling for three seconds; (4)

repeat five times in a minute. It is suggested that the Snake Pose be practiced for at least a month, by which time its effects should be felt. Practice it daily, preferably in the evening before dinner.

HALASANA, OR PLOUGH POSE

The Snake Pose is actually the first of a linked pair of postures, the second being the Halasana, or Plough Pose. This pose should be undertaken when you are fully rested. To start, lie on the floor with your face upward and arms resting at your sides, palms downward. Then raise your legs together, slowly inhaling until your legs are brought at a right angle to the body. Next, while exhaling slowly, raise your hips and lower your legs beyond your head. Keep your legs together and straight. As you become practiced in this posture, stretch your toes further and further beyond your head. If you find this posture too difficult, keep your legs folded or bent and raise them as high as you can. Practice in the following manner: (1) Raise legs to a right angle with body and inhale for two seconds; (2) lower legs beyond head and exhale for two seconds; (3) maintain pose for four seconds while suspending breath; (4) return to starting position, while inhaling slowly for two seconds.

Do not overdo this posture. At first try it once daily, then, as it becomes easier, work toward the completion of six rounds in a minute. It may be easier at first in the evening, when the body is more supple. When perfected, it should be practiced in the morning on an empty stomach. Those who are extremely overweight may find this pose impossible, as will those with stiff muscles. Also, it is not recommended for those with any form of hernia. In addition to its cerebro-nervous system therapy, this pose is highly effective in ridding the body and nervous systems of toxic accumulations and its perfection and regular use will aid largely in achieving purification of the nervous-energy channels.

ULTRASANA, OR CAMEL POSE

This is the climactic pose of the series suggested for nerve-spinal adjustment. Generally it is impossible to achieve before the two previous poses have been perfected. Kneel and while supporting your body on your toes gradually lean backward, after fixing your arms behind you, with your palms to the ground, fingers pointed outward and thumbs toward your toes. Keeping your arms straight, slowly lift your hips while inhaling. Then, push your body above the waist slowly outward and upward, throwing your neck downward. As you come into this posture, you should feel the pressure traveling upward toward your shoulders and neck, finally reaching your neck and facial muscles. It is suggested that this pose be practiced in the morning, but not more than once daily. In timing, the body-lift should take three seconds with inhalation; retention, six seconds; return to kneeling position while exhaling, three seconds.

TIME SCHEDULE FOR PRACTICING THE ASANAS

The time schedule has been established to enable the person of ordinary muscular development to follow a routine of Yogic exercises. After reading the text and gradually taking the step-by-step procedure for the postures and exercises, you should make a copy of this chart and place it on the wall of the room in which you practice the asanas. Do not overdo, as the Yoga exercises are designed for a gradual program of improvement. This is not an easy, one-day course. Those who have been reading popular articles on Yoga may notice that there are no standing-on-head asanas recommended. Those, and the other drastic asanas, may actually be harmful unless they are preceded by a full program of physical preparation under a competent teacher of Yoga. The sequence recommended here goes from easy to difficult movements, and will exercise alternate sets of muscles. Where breathing routines are shown with the asana, it is of utmost importance that they be followed closely for maximum benefits. In a few months the benefits of this program will be evident and the exercises, diet and mental therapy suggested in this book should be made a lifetime project.

	Asanas	Time
1.	Stitha-Prarthanasana (Prayer Pose)	1 Minute
2.	Padmasana (Lotus Pose)	1 Minute
3.	Yastikasana (Stick Pose)	1 Minute
4.	Parvatasana (Mountain Pose)	2 Minutes
5.	Trikonasana and Variant (Triangle Pose)	2 Minutes
6.	Garudasana (Eagle Pose)	2 Minutes
7.	Hastapadangustasana (Toe-Finger Pose)	1 Minute
8.	Hastapadasana (Hand-Leg Pose)	1 Minute
9.	Ekapadasana (One-Leg Pose)	1 Minute
	Total Daily Exercise	12 Minutes

Please note that a woman in advanced pregnancy should avoid all but the first two exercises. Men and women who are suffering from serious arthritis, colic, sciatica or kidney ailments, should also limit themselves to the first two asanas.

YOGA POSES & EXERCISES

Yoga is a very old Indian practice that goes back to over 5000 years. The term 'yoga' comes from a Sanskrit word 'yuj', which actually means to bring oneself to a disciplined way of life. There are many types of yoga but Raja and Hatha yoga are most popular in the West. It is believed by ancient yogis that for man to harmonize with the environment and himself, he has to unite the spirit, mind and body, and for all of it to be united, there must be balance in the physical, emotional and spiritual aspect of life. The way to maintain and achieve this balance is through meditation, breathing, and yoga postures.

Thus, both the body and the mind are used when practicing yoga exercises, as it requires perseverance and willpower to be able to perform each of the yoga asanas. Regular practice of the yoga positions can result in plenty of benefits, including stimulation of the internal organs and improving blood circulation. Yoga stretches provide benefits to the mind and body and bring about balanced energy flow. This is especially helpful for women who are in the menopause transition or currently in menopause.

Types

The different types of yoga poses serve various purposes and include levels of difficulty in different ranges. Some of the yoga poses provide more benefits than others.

- Arm balance Poses: Arm balance poses help strengthen the core and arms. These poses will involve either supporting your whole body with your arms or just your upper body. Some of the arm balance poses include Dandasana(Plank Pose), Chaturanga Dandasana or the Four-Limbed staff Pose, Vasisthasana (Side Plank Pose), Bakasana (Crane Pose), Astavakrasana (Eight Crooked Limb Pose), and Pincha Mayurasana (Feathered Peacock Pose).
- Backbend Poses: There are many ways in which the backbend poses can be practiced. Poses like Dhanurasana (Bow Pose) begin with the student on the stomach and builds back flexibility and leg strength. Students perform Natarajasana (Lord of the Dance Pose) from a standing position to improve balance as well as flexibility. Some other backbends include Setu Bandha Sarvangasana (Bridge Pose), Bhujangasana (Cobra Pose), Ardha Bhekasana (Half Frog Pose), Kapotasana translated into the King Pigeon Pose and Urdhva Dhanurasana (Upward Bow or Wheel Pose).
- Bandha Poses: While there are many yoga bandha poses, the most common ones are Jalandhara Bandha(Net-Bearer Bond), Uddiyana Bandha (Upward Abdominal Lock), and Mula Bandha (Root Bond). Each bandha is considered a lock, which closes a certain part inside the body. These locks are made use of in various asanas and pranayamas to energize, cleanse and stimulate the organs. When all the three locks or the three bhandas are simultaneously activated, it is known as the great lock or maha bandha.
- Core Poses: Core poses are yoga poses that strengthen your abs and core. Some of the core poses include Marjaryasana (Cat Pose), Bakasana (Crane Pose), Ananda Balasana (Happy Baby Pose), Bhujapidasana (Shoulder-Pressing Pose), Anantasana (Side-Reclining Leg Lift) and Paripurna Navasana (Full Boat Pose).
- Forward Bend Poses: Forward bend poses help strengthen the organs of the abdomen and stretch the hamstrings and back muscles. Some of the forward bend poses include Adho Mukha Svanasana

(Downward Facing Dog), Uttana Shishosana (Extended Puppy Pose), Parsvottonasana (Intense Side Stretch Pose) Marichyasana I (Pose Dedicated to the Sage Marichi, I), Ardha Uttanasana (Standing Half Forward Bend) and Prasarita Padottanasana (Wide-Legged Forward Bend).

- Inversion Poses: Inversions are known to be effective in cleaning the circulatory system, stimulating the glands, and reducing fatigue. In a full inversion, you will need to bring your feet over your head like in Sirsasana (Headstand) and Sarvangasana (Shoulder stand). These inversions help build core strength and endurance. Yoga poses like Uttanasana (Standing Forward Fold) and Setu Bandha Sarvangasana (Bridge Pose) are half inversions.
- Meditation Poses: Using meditation poses for meditation is considered to be better than lying down. This is because it reduces the chances of you going to sleep. Some of the meditation poses include Padmasana (Full Lotus Posture), Ardha Padmasana (Half Lotus Pose), Egyptian Pose, and Burmese Pose.
- Pranayama Poses: Pranayamas are effective in bringing about good health through the process of breathing. The pranayama exercises improve breathing technique from rapid and shallow breathing to a healthy duration of breathing. Some of the good pranayama poses you can practice the breathing exercises on are Sukhasana (Easy Pose), Ardha Padmasana (Half-Lotus Pose) and Padmasana (Lotus Pose).
- Restorative Poses: The aim of the restorative poses is to bring about relaxation. Some of the restorative poses are Balasana (Child's Pose), Viparita Karani (Legs-Up-the-Wall Pose), and Savasana (Corpse Pose).
- Seated & Twist Poses: Seated and twist poses are effective in increasing the flexibility of the spine. Deep twists are also known for their detoxifying and cleansing benefits. Some of the seated and twist poses are Bharadvajasana I (Bharadvaja's Twist), Gomukhasana (Cow Face Pose) and Agnistambhasana (Fire Log Pose).
- Standing Poses: Standing poses help increase flexibility and strength. They can also increase your awareness of body posture and energize your body. Some of the standing poses include Tadasana (Mountain Pose), Trikonasana (Triangle Pose) and Uttanasana (Standing Forward Bend).

What are the Seated Yoga Poses?

Seated poses can be extremely basic and extremely advanced as well. The easy pose as the name suggests is an example of yoga seated pose that is easy to achieve. Beginner seated yoga poses are used to improve posture and to encourage students to focus on breathing exercises. The collection of yoga seated poses marichyasana 1, 2 and 3 are variations of one of the advanced poses of yoga that involves a seating pose. This pose should only be attempted by someone who has a fair degree of flexibility as well as a good amount of control over his or her movements.

What is Benefits of Sarvangasana?

Sarvangasana (Shoulder Stand) is sometimes called the queen of poses and provides benefits to the mind, body and soul. The literal meaning of Sarvangasana is a 'posture for all body parts'. The working of these inverted postures is by causing the effects of gravity to become reversed on certain parts of the body. The benefits of Sarvangasana include improving the circulation of blood and improving the efficiency of the thyroid, heart, and lungs. Practicing Sarvangasana for weight loss can be effective as it helps in regulating the thyroid gland, which if defective, can bring about weight problems. However, women who are menstruating should avoid practicing this posture.

Why do I Need to do a Warm up before Starting Yoga?

Before starting your yoga routine or any exercise for that matter, it is important that you first perform some warm up exercises to loosen the muscles. Performing a warm up before your session will prepare you physically for the yoga poses you will need to perform. If you start directly with the exercise there is a possibility of incurring some injury. There are many warm up poses you can find on the Internet that can help loosen stiff muscles and reduce the chances of injury. For beginners, yoga poses that are taken should be easy to perform and not too strenuous. Following some yoga tips can help you get the most out of your session.

Which Yoga Asana will help for Premature Ejaculation?

Practicing yoga can be an effective method you can make use of to help with premature ejaculation. Some of the postures of yoga for premature ejaculation are Dhanurasana (Bow Pose), Halasana (Plow Pose), Mayurasana (Peacock Pose), and Bhujangasana (Cobra Pose). These postures also help in dealing with stress and anxiety, which are among the main contributors to premature ejaculation. Practicing yoga for diabetes can help reduce blood pressure and blood sugar levels. Some of the effective yoga asanasfor diabetes are Adho Mukha Svanasana (Downward Facing Dog), Trikonasana (Triangle Pose), and Matsyasana (Fish Pose). It is also important that you combine these postures with a proper diet.

What are the Most Advanced Yoga Poses and Sequences?

There are many postures in yoga, and although all of them are beneficial, some are more challenging than others. There are some easy poses that can be practiced by beginners, and there are advanced yoga poses that should be done by practitioners with enough experience. Before coming to the advanced yoga postures, it is important that you first perfect the beginner poses. Some of the most advanced yoga poses include Bakasana (Crow Pose), Garudasana (Eagle Pose), and Tittibhasana (Firefly Pose). It is recommended that you perform the advanced yoga sequence first in front of an instructor to get the proper technique.

SPECIFIC POSTURES FOR RELAXATION

While the great majority of the asanas have a curative or therapeutic value, there are several which are purely for the purpose of relaxation. Relaxation should not be mistaken for inertia. It is not a state of lethargy; rather, it is rest after effort or, perhaps, conscious rest after conscious effort. One definition of relaxation is "a complete resignation of the body to the power of gravity, surrender of the mind to nature, and the whole body energy being transferred to a deep, dynamic breathing."

PHYSICAL RELAXATION

Complete relaxation of the voluntary muscles at once transfers energy to involuntary parts so that, strictly speaking, there can be no such thing as relaxation except in the voluntary muscles and brain. But this is quite sufficient! This transfer of energy by voluntary action and involuntary reaction produces the necessary equilibrium for the renewal of strength.

In many parts of the world, where human beings still transport heavy loads, it is amazing how far they can carry burdens that most individuals could not even lift from the ground. Observation of porters in many parts of the Orient and the Arabic world has shown that their endurance may be due to the ability to relax. During long, heavy hauls, they often stop and lie down in apparently semi-lifeless states for as long as an hour. Then they rise, refreshed, and resume their arduous journeys.

Proper, purposeful relaxation offers the greatest amount of renewed strength in the shortest length of time. After extended exertion or stress, perfect rest in the form of relaxation is the principle which revitalizes the nerve centers, collects the scattered forces of energy and invigorates the body. The three poses of Yoga for complete relaxation are Dradhasana, Shavasana and Adhvasana.

DRADHASANA, OR FIRM POSE

This is considered best for sleeping, as it is the most comfortable. To take the pose, lie relaxed with your right arm under your head, using it as a pillow. By lying passively on the right side, you favor emptying of the stomach and make breathing movements easier. In practice, it has been found that sleeping in this manner generally inhibits dreams and nocturnal emissions and improves digestion. A short period of sleep becomes the equivalent of a longer sleep for recuperative purposes. It is also recommended for short periods of waking relaxation.

SHAVASANA, OR CORPSE POSE

This is recommended for use when the student of Yoga experiences fatigue during any of his exercises. This pose is described in the tracts as "destroying fatigue of the body; quieting the agitation of the mind." Lie face up with your feet extended. Remain motionless with a sense or feeling of sinking down like a corpse. Gradually relax every muscle of the body by concentrating on each individually, from the tip of the toe to the end of the skull. Exercise absolute resignation of will by trying to forget the existence of your body and detaching yourself from it. Hold this posture until you feel restored. Medical authorities have confirmed that the Shavasana pose brings about a fall in the blood pressure and pulse rate and establishes an even rate of respiration. If this pose is kept for more than ten minutes, the deepened respiration and lowered circulation in the brain will probably bring about a tendency to sleep.

ADHAVASANA, OR RELAXED POSE

Lie down with your head on your folded arms, as if on a pillow, and concentrate as in Shavasana. Relax all your muscles. Then stretch your hands and legs out fully, and permit the power of gravity to take over the weight of your body as you relax every voluntary muscle.

MENTAL RELAXATION

Another group of asanas, or postures, specifically provides for the care of the nervous system. These exercises have been found to be especially helpful to persons of a neurasthenic condition. An individual in this state will be mentally vague, lack determination, and have continual feelings of inferiority, fatigue and distraction, accompanied by a state of anxiety. Lack of will power and other forms of nervous or mental debility are all indications of a lack of tonicity in the brain-nervous system.

In many ways, symptoms of the neurasthenic are similar to those of an older person who is approaching or has reached senility. Yoga investigators feel that the condition may be due to a degeneration of the nerve cells with resultant subnormal functions. While the Yoga process may not reverse the situation in the case of an aged person, it has resulted in relief for neurasthenics of young and middle age. In addition, the normal person who utilizes these asanas will find that he derives from them a new keenness of mind and an ability to utilize his nerve-energy to the utmost for whatever personal goals he may have set for himself.

BHUJANGASANA, OR SNAKE POSE

The anterior and posterior stretching offered by the Snake Pose are said to be ideal spinal exercises, preserving or restoring tonicity in the spinal column and nervous channels. Lie on your stomach, with your legs stretched and toes pointed outward. Keep your arms at your sides, with palms down, and your forehead on the floor. Then, slowly raise your head and neck upward and backward.

When your head and neck are slightly raised, plant your hands on both sides of the abdomen. Inhale, and gradually raise your thorax and the upper part of your abdomen by increasing the angle between your hands and rising shoulders. From the navel downward, your body should remain fixed to the ground. Only the upper portion of your body should be raised. In some texts, this pose is called the "Like a hooded cobra striking" pose. Work toward this pose gradually, avoiding muscular strain or "jerkiness" in your efforts to raise the upper part of your body. As you practice this pose, you will feel the pressure on your spinal column gradually working down the vertebrae until you feel a deep pressure at the coccyx.

At first, concentrate on the posture. Having achieved the correct pose, exhale and return to the starting position. Lower yourself slowly. In contrast to the pressure which you felt as you entered this posture, you will experience a feeling of relief along your spine as you lower yourself. This asana should not be utilized by women during menstruation or advanced pregnancy, or by men suffering from hernia. Persons with a weak physical structure should approach this asana slowly and drop it if they find it too arduous. It may be attempted later when the other muscle-tone asanas have shown their effects.

After the pose has been mastered, follow this procedure: (1) Raise thorax and inhale for three seconds; (2) maintain pose, retaining your breath for six seconds; (3) return to starting position, while exhaling for three seconds; (4) repeat five times in a minute. It is suggested that the Snake Pose be practiced for at least a month, by which time its effects should be felt. Practice it daily, preferably in the evening before dinner.

HALASANA, OR PLOUGH POSE

The Snake Pose is actually the first of a linked pair of postures, the second being the Halasana, or Plough Pose. This pose should be undertaken when you are fully rested. To start, lie on the floor with your face upward and arms resting at your sides, palms downward. Then raise your legs together, slowly inhaling until your legs are brought at a right angle to the body. Next, while exhaling slowly, raise your hips and lower your legs beyond your head. Keep your legs together and straight. As you become practiced in this posture, stretch your toes further and further beyond your head. If you find this posture too difficult, keep your legs folded or bent and raise them as high as you can.

Practice in the following manner: (1) Raise legs to a right angle with body and inhale for two seconds; (2) lower legs beyond head and exhale for two seconds; (3) maintain pose for four seconds while suspending breath; (4) return to starting position, while inhaling slowly for two seconds.

Do not overdo this posture. At first try it once daily, then, as it becomes easier, work toward the completion of six rounds in a minute. It may be easier at first in the evening, when the body is more supple. When perfected, it should be practiced in the morning on an empty stomach. Those who are extremely overweight may find this pose impossible, as will those with stiff muscles. Also, it is not recommended for those with any form of hernia. In addition to its cerebro-nervous system therapy, this pose is highly effective in ridding the body and nervous systems of toxic accumulations and its perfection and regular use will aid largely in achieving purification of the nervous-energy channels.

ULTRASANA, OR CAMEL POSE

This is the climactic pose of the series suggested for nerve-spinal adjustment. Generally it is impossible to achieve before the two previous poses have been perfected. Kneel and while supporting your body on your toes gradually lean backward, after fixing your arms behind you, with your palms to the ground, fingers pointed outward and thumbs toward your toes. Keeping your arms straight, slowly lift your hips while inhaling. Then, push your body above the waist slowly outward and upward, throwing your neck downward. As you come into this posture, you should feel the pressure traveling upward toward your shoulders and neck, finally reaching your neck and facial muscles. It is suggested that this pose be practiced in the morning, but not more than once daily. In timing, the body-lift should take three seconds with inhalation; retention, six seconds; return to kneeling position while exhaling, three seconds.

TIME SCHEDULE FOR PRACTICING THE ASANAS

The time schedule has been established to enable the person of ordinary muscular development to follow a routine of Yogic exercises. After reading the text and gradually taking the step-by-step procedure for the postures and exercises, you should make a copy of this chart and place it on the wall of the room in which you practice the asanas. Do not overdo, as the Yoga exercises are designed for a gradual program of improvement. This is not an easy, one-day course. Those who have been reading popular articles on Yoga may notice that there are no standing-on-head asanas recommended. Those, and the other drastic asanas, may actually be harmful unless they are preceded by a full program of physical preparation under a competent teacher of Yoga. The sequence recommended here goes from easy to difficult movements, and will exercise alternate sets of muscles. Where breathing routines are shown with the asana, it is of utmost importance that they be followed closely for maximum benefits.

In a few months the benefits of this program will be evident and the exercises, diet and mental therapy suggested in this book should be made a lifetime project.

	Asanas	**Time**
1.	Stitha-Prarthanasana (Prayer Pose)	1 Minute
2.	Padmasana (Lotus Pose)	1 Minute
3.	Yastikasana (Stick Pose)	1 Minute
4.	Parvatasana (Mountain Pose)	2 Minutes
5.	Trikonasana and Variant (Triangle Pose)	2 Minutes
6.	Garudasana (Eagle Pose)	2 Minutes
7.	Hastapadangustasana (Toe-Finger Pose)	1 Minute
8.	Hastapadasana (Hand-Leg Pose)	1 Minute
9.	Ekapadasana (One-Leg Pose)	1 Minute
	Total Daily Exercise	12 Minutes

Please note that a woman in advanced pregnancy should avoid all but the first two exercises. Men and women who are suffering from serious arthritis, colic, sciatica or kidney ailments, should also limit themselves to the first two asanas.

2

The Benefits of Yoga

People have been doing Yoga for hundreds of thousands of years because Yoga is beneficial to them. In this chapter, we will give a short summary of the benefits of the Original Yoga System. You will be able to attain these benefits when you begin the Yoga system. What we will explain here are the benefits you will achieve from the Original Yoga System. Those so-called schools or kinds of 'yoga' that are currently widespread cannot yield these benefits. When one practices the principles known as Yama, positive inclinations will strengthen, positive energy and motivation will increase, and a person will feel that he/she is part of the universe.

When one practices the principles known as Niyama, negative inclinations are eliminated, bad habits are overcome, negative energy is expelled and a person will realize that he/she is a member of the family of all the living beings in the universe. The postures named Asana work on the spine and stretch it, make it suppler and healthier. The central nervous system is fed with oxygenized blood and is strengthened. The body exercises flex the joints, strengthen and lengthen the muscles, stimulate and invigorate the inner organs. The blocked energy is set free, the body becomes energetic and lively. The whole body, organs and muscles are purified with nutritional materials, oxygenated blood and bioenergy. Each and every cell is purified, renewed and enlivened. The respiratory, nervous, cardiovascular, circulatory, digestive and excretory systems become healthier and work more efficiently. Brain functions become more orderly, the mind becomes sharper, stress is expelled and fatigue is overcome. (For more detailed information, refer to the book titled Yoga: Asanas – Postures.)

Yoga postures develop and improve the blood and lymph circulation. The head down postures supply more blood to the brain and lungs. Consequently these organs are cleansed with oxygenated blood and are purified and revitalized, the toxins accumulated in the brain are expelled and brain functions improve. The legs are cleansed of accumulated blood which contains waste products and consequently rest. Since the effect of gravity is reversed, the heart is freed of its function of pumping blood to the brain and thus relaxes. The body relaxes as a result of the stimulation on the sympathetic nervous system, leading to a higher quality of sleep. The mood and outlook on life changes positively.

The exercises involving bending postures act as a natural massage on the body, and thus revitalize the muscles and inner organs, increase blood circulation, speed up the transfer of nutrients and expel the toxins. Problems related to the spine, waist, hips and groins are overcome. Toxins are expelled and the body is cleansed.

Postures which involve bending forward exert pressure on the inner organs of the abdomen, initiate their movements and purify them. The digestive and excretory systems are stimulated and begin to function more efficiently. The muscles on the back of the body and joints become more flexible. The kidneys and adrenal glands relax and fatigue is overcome, the urinary system works more efficiently, and energy is replenished. The mind becomes serene and awareness increases. When a person turns inwards, emotions calm down and anxiety decreases.

THE HEALTH BENEFITS THROUGH YOGA

Yoga has been practiced for more than 5,000 years, and currently, close to 11 million Americans are enjoying its health benefits. Yoga can hardly be called a trend. Most Westernized yoga classes focus on learning physical poses, which are called asanas. They also usually include some form of breathing technique and possibly ameditation technique as well. Some yoga classes are designed purely for relaxation. But there are styles of yoga that teach you how to move your body in new ways. Choosing one of these styles offers the greatest health benefits by enabling you to develop your flexibility, strength, and balance.

Before You Start: Staying Safe While Practicing Yoga

Even though for most healthy people yoga is a safe non-aerobic form of exercise, it is not without its risks. According to the American Academy of Orthopaedic Surgeons, the yoga injuries most commonly treated in emergency rooms involve overstretching and strain from repetition to the:

- Neck
- Shoulders
- Spine
- Legs
- Knees

Also, certain poses can increase your risk of injury if you have conditions such as:

- Severe osteoporosis
- High or low blood pressure

- Ear problems
- Problems with your spine
- Pregnancy (including risks to your unborn child)

Here are some tips to help you reduce your risk of injury from yoga:

If you are pregnant or have a pre-existing health condition: Consult your health care provider before starting a yoga program. Your health care provider can help you know how to judge what type and level of yoga exercise is safe for you.

Don't try learning yoga on your own. Work with an experienced and credentialed instructor to learn the proper way to perform the exercises and avoid injury. Yoga is not a substitute for medical care. Yoga offers many health benefits and may even be included as part of some treatment plans. But it's still important to work closely with your regular health care providers and get proper treatment when you need it.

Know your limits and stay within them. Before beginning any new type of yoga, ask about its physical demands. Find out how strenuous it is. Talk with the instructor and others who do that type of yoga to be sure it's suitable for you. Go slow. You're not in competition with anyone else in the class. Learn the basics, such as proper breathing and how to maintain balance, before you attempt the more ambitious stretches.

Warm up properly before every session. Cold muscles increase your chance of injury. Wear proper clothing. Wear clothes that allow you to move freely. Ask questions. If you don't understand an exercise, ask to see it again before you attempt it yourself, Stay hydrated. That's especially important if you are practicing what's called "hot" yoga, which is done in a very warm and humid room. Pay attention to what your body is telling you. Yoga isn't supposed to hurt. If you feel pain, stop. If the pain persists, see your health care provider. Stop immediately if you have chest pain, feel faint or overheated, or become dizzy. Get immediate medical help if the sensation continues after you stop.

Yoga and Flexibility

When some people think of yoga, they imagine having to stretch like a gymnast. That makes them worry that they're too old, unfit, or "tight" to do yoga. The truth is you're never too old to improve flexibility. The series of yoga poses called asanas work by safely stretching your muscles. This may release the lactic acid that builds up with muscle use, which may cause stiffness, tension, pain, and fatigue. In addition, yoga increases the range of motion in joints. It may also increase lubrication in the joints. The outcome is a sense of ease and fluidity throughout your body.

Yoga stretches not only your muscles but all of the soft tissues of your body. That includes ligaments, tendons, and the fascia sheath that surrounds your muscles. And no matter your level of yoga, you most likely will see benefits in a very short period of time. In one study, participants had up to 35 per cent improvement in flexibility after only eight weeks of yoga. The greatest gains were in shoulder and trunk flexibility.

Yoga and Strength

Some styles of yoga, such as ashtanga and power yoga, are more vigorous than others. Practicing one of these styles will help you improve muscle tone. But even less vigorous styles of yoga, such as Iyengar or hatha, which focuses on less movement and more precise alignment in poses, can provide strength and endurance benefits. Many of the poses, such as downward dog, upward dog, and the plank pose, build upper-body strength. This becomes crucial as people age. The standing poses, especially if you hold them for several long breaths, build strength in your hamstrings, quadriceps, and abdominal muscles. Poses that strengthen the lower back include upward dog and the chair pose. When practiced correctly, nearly all poses build core strength in the deep abdominal muscles.

Yoga Can Help Posture

With increased flexibility and strength comes better posture. Most standing and sitting poses develop core strength. That's because you're counting on your deep abdominals to support and maintain each pose. With a stronger core, you're more likely to sit and stand "tall." Another benefit of yoga is the increased body awareness. This heightened awareness tells you more quickly when you're slouching or slumping so you can adjust your posture.

Yoga Benefits Breathing

Because of the deep, mindful breathing that yoga involves, lung capacity often improves. This in turn can improve sports performance and endurance. But yoga typically isn't focused on aerobic fitness the way running or cycling are. Taking an intense power yoga class that gets you breathing hard in a heated room, however, can provide an aerobic benefit. Most forms of yoga emphasize deepening and lengthening your breath. This stimulates the relaxation response -- the opposite of the fight-or-flight adrenaline boost of the stress response.

Yoga Means Less Stress, More Calm

Even beginners tend to feel less stressed and more relaxed after their first class. Some yoga styles use specific meditation techniques to quiet the constant "mind chatter" that often underlies stress. Other yoga styles depend on deep breathing techniques to focus the mind on the breath. When this happens, the mind calms. Among yoga's anti-stress benefits are a host of biochemical responses. For example, there is a decrease in catecholamines, the hormones produced by the adrenal glands in response to stress. Lowering levels of hormone neurotransmitters -- dopamine, norepinephrine, and epinephrine -- creates a feeling of calm. Some research points to a boost in the hormone oxytocin. This is the so-called "trust" and "bonding" hormone that's associated with feeling relaxed and connected to others.

Yoga, Concentration, and Mood

Harder to pin down and research scientifically, concentration and the ability to focus mentally are common benefits you'll hear yoga students talk about. The same is true with mood. Nearly every yoga student will tell you they feel happier and more contented after class. Recently, researchers have begun exploring the effects of yoga on depression, a benefit that may result from yoga's boosting oxygen levels to the brain. Yoga is even being studied as an adjunct therapy to relieve symptoms of obsessive-compulsive disorder.

Yoga's Benefits the Heart

Perhaps one of the most studied areas of the health benefits of yoga is its effect onheart disease. Yoga has long been known to lower blood pressure and slow the heart rate. A slower heart rate can benefit people with high blood pressure, heart disease, and stroke. Yoga was a key component to the heart disease program designed by Dean Ornish, MD. This was the first program to partly reverse heart disease through lifestyle and diet rather than surgery. On a biochemical level, studies point to a possible anti-oxidant effect of yoga. And yoga has been associated with decreased cholesterol and triglyceride levels as well as a boost in immune system function.

Yoga's Effects on Other Medical Conditions

As yoga has become more popular in the West, medical researchers have begun studying the benefits of therapeutic yoga. This is also called integrative yoga therapy or IYT. It's used as an adjunct treatment for specific medical conditions, from clinical depression to heart disease. Yoga benefits other chronic medical conditions, relieving symptoms of asthma, back pain, and arthritis. Most worldwide clinical studies are happening outside of the U.S. But even the NIH has funded clinical trials on yoga and its health benefits for insomnia and multiple sclerosis.

Other Benefits of Yoga

Some studies have suggested that yoga may have a positive effect on learning and memory. Other researchers have been studying whether yoga can slow the aging process, increase a person's sense of self-acceptance, or improve energy levels. Some potential benefits of yoga may be hard to study scientifically. For instance, yoga has been said to increase spiritual awareness. Nevertheless, there is an abundance of anecdotal claims for what yoga can do. Go to any yoga studio and listen to students after class. Some will even tell you that yoga can help improve marriages and relationships at work.

THE HISTORY OF YOGA

In order to study the history of Yoga, we must view the history of the universe. Some souls become curious about a life independent from The Absolute Being and come from the spiritual universe to the material universe. Souls must incarnate so as to be able to realize their objectives in the material universe. While the incarnated soul pursues an imaginary freedom, he/she imitates God, changes many bodies and experiences adventures. Finally, after having repeatedly experienced temporary material happiness and agonies, he/she becomes bored with life in the material universe. Thus one day he/she awakens and begins to long for his/her true spiritual nature, wants to return to the spiritual universe and exerts effort to actualize this aim. The Yoga science and practice is a return ticket for the soul to pass from the material universe to the spiritual universe.

For this reason, when the material universe was created, first of all the science of Yoga was given to souls which were there. This is the most important science because souls can escape from the material world by means of this science and return to the spiritual universe. The material universe is created and destroyed in eternal cycles. When the material universe materializes anew, those souls which haven't been able to return to the spiritual universe incarnate and continue their education. The Original Yoga System exists so that souls can escape from these eternal cycles.

The earth is renewed around every 5 or 6 million years. These renewals have taken place in the form of floods. After the waters receded, life on land began again. Following the establishment of balances of all forms of life on earth, people came down from a higher planet system and brought Yoga and other knowledge with them. These people spoke the Sanskrit language and the knowledge was named Veda. Thus the first civilization on earth began. The name of this civilization was Ari Civilization. The word Ari means 'enlightened person'. The Aris mean enlightened people, Ari civilization means 'society of enlightened people'. The word Ari is not the name of a race or tribe. The people of the Ari civilization practiced the techniques of Yoga, mastered the body, mind and emotions, and were in continual contact with The Universal Consciousness without detaching themselves from nature.

The Aris' memories were so powerful that once they heard something, they never forgot it. That's why they had no need for written information, that is to say they did not need books. The science of Yoga was passed down orally from master to student for millions of years. In those days the continents were connected as one and the Ari civilization ruled the whole world. That is why there are Sanskrit words in all the languages in our world. When we study the ancient civilizations of our world, we can see that they have all come from the same origin. Yoga postures are engraved on relics found in excavations in different parts of the world.

TOP 10 YOGA BENEFITS

Weight loss, a strong and flexible body, glowing beautiful skin, peaceful mind, good health – whatever you may be looking for, yoga has it on offer. However, very often, yoga is only partially understood as being limited to asanas (yoga poses). As such, its benefits are only perceived to be at the body level and we fail to realize the immense benefits yoga offers in uniting the body, mind and breath. When you are in harmony, the journey through life is calmer, happier and more fulfilling.

With all this and much more to offer, the benefits of yoga are felt in a profound yet subtle manner. Here, we look at the top 10 benefits of regular yoga practice. All-round fitness. You are truly healthy when you are not just physically fit but also mentally and emotionally balanced. As Sri Sri Ravi Shankar puts it, "Health is not a mere absence of disease. It is a dynamic expression of life – in terms of how joyful, loving and enthusiastic you are." This is where yoga helps: postures, pranayama (breathing techniques) and meditation are a holistic fitness package.

Yoga – My personal fitness mantra
My weight-loss formula
My mind soother
My tool for better communication
My creativity machine
My doubt repeller
My time planner

- Weight loss: What many want! Yoga benefits here too. Sun Salutations and Kapal Bhati pranayama are some ways to help lose weight with yoga. Moreover, with regular practice of yoga, we tend to become more sensitive to the kind of food our body asks for and when. This can also help keep a check on weight.
- Stress relief: A few minutes of yoga during the day can be a great way to get rid of stress that accumulates daily - in both the body and mind. Yoga postures, pranayama and meditation are effective techniques to release stress. You can also experience how yoga helps de-tox the body and de-stress the mind at the Sri Sri Yoga Level 2 Course.
- Inner peace: We all love to visit peaceful, serene spots, rich in natural beauty. Little do we realize that peace can be found right within us and we can take a mini-vacation to experience this any time of the day! Benefit from a small holiday every day with yoga and meditation. Yoga is also one of the best ways to calm a disturbed mind.

- Improved immunity: Our system is a seamless blend of the body, mind and spirit. An irregularity in the body affects the mind and similarly unpleasantness or restlessness in the mind can manifest as an ailment in the body. Yoga poses massage organs and stregthen muscles; breathing techniques and meditation release stress and improve immunity.
- Living with greater awareness: The mind is constantly involved in activity – swinging from the past to the future – but never staying in the present. By simply being aware of this tendency of the mind, we can actually save ourselves from getting stressed or worked up and relax the mind. Yoga and pranayama help create that awareness and bring the mind back to the present moment, where it can stay happy and focused.
- Better relationships: Yoga can even help improve your relationship with your spouse, parents, friends or loved ones! A mind that is relaxed, happy and contented is better able to deal with sensitive relationship matters. Yoga and meditation work on keeping the mind happy and peaceful; benefit from the strengthened special bond you share with people close to you.
- Increased energy: Do you feel completely drained out by the end of the day? Shuttling between multiple tasks through the day can sometimes be quite exhausting. A few minutes of yoga everyday provides the secret to feeling fresh and energetic even after a long day. A 10-minute online guided meditation benefits you immensely, leaving you refreshed and recharged in the middle of a hectic day.
- Better flexibility & posture: You only need to include yoga in your daily routine to benefit from a body that is strong, supple and flexible. Regular yoga practice stretches and tones the body muscles and also makes them strong. It also helps improve your body posture when you stand, sit, sleep or walk. This would, in turn, help relieve you of body paindue to incorrect posture.
- Better intuition: Yoga and meditation have the power to improve your intuitive ability so that you effortlessly realize what needs to be done, when and how, to yield positive results. It works. You only need to experience it yourself.

Remember, yoga is a continuous process. So keep practicing! The deeper you move into your yoga practice, the more profound are its benefits.

SOURCES OF YOGA

The Yoga philosophy, having been passed on orally throughout innumerous generations since the creation of the universe, resembles a breathing, living organism preserving its integrity. At one time people had such powerful memories that a student would never forget what a teacher said. However as the Kali-Yuga period we are now living in approached, people's memories began to weaken. As mankind's memory weakened and his need for written information increased, the first books were written about 5–6 thousand years ago. These books were written in the Sanskrit language. The meaning of the word Sanskrit is 'learned' or 'noble'.

First of all the four Veda were written:

- Rig Veda
- Sama Veda
- Yajur Veda
- Atharva Veda

After these four Veda books were written, the subjects they covered were explained in detail in the subsequent books: Brahmana, Aranyaka, and Upanishada. Following these, the Purana books, which explained the history of the universe, and the Itihasa books, which described the earth, were written. Reference to Yoga can be seen in all of these books. Although Yoga is not dealt with under a separate title, information about Yoga is present in all of these books. In order to fully comprehend the science of Yoga, one must study all these books.

As time passed this became a difficult task; thus about two thousand years ago Patanjali wrote the book Yoga Sutra in which he concisely covered the Yoga philosophy. Patanjali summarized the Yoga science as it is in Veda literature. Patanjali has explained the Yoga system without going into detail in his book Yoga Sutra. Yoga was explained as Ashtanga in this book, that is to say as a path of eight steps.

The word Ashtanga is a combination of two words: Ashta and Anga. The word Ashta means eight; Anga means 'part', 'division', or 'branch'. Thus Yoga consists of eight divisions. Because Yoga develops a person and prepares him/her for ascending, the word Anga can also be interpreted as 'step'. Consequently Yoga is named as an eight step path. As a result of this, as time passed, the Original Yoga System has come to be known as Ashtanga Yoga, thus the name of the Original Yoga System became Ashtanga Yoga and this is the name of the true Yoga. However this is not the kind of "ashtanga yoga" of our present day that consists of many rigorous and strenuous exercises that lead to injuries. Some religious sects use the word yoga as a ruse and present themselves as "ashtanga yoga". One must be careful for religious sects who act under the name of Yoga.

YAMA – UNIVERSAL ACTION CONTROL

The first step of the Original Yoga System is named Yama. The Sanskrit word Yama means 'control'. Yama is the first stage of the process of developing controlling energy. This step is the foundation of the Original Yoga System. The principles of Yama are eternal and beyond race, time and space. In the Yama step, the individual practices the most important principles beyond religion, nation, age, gender, and time.

From a wide philosophical standpoint, the word Yama may be interpreted as 'purification from negatives'. By practicing Yama, a person controls his/her actions and thus escapes from negative or harmful influences. An individual must be cleansed of all negative ideas, words and actions so as to be able to develop and evolve spiritually. In order to do this, a person must first and foremost practice the Ahimsa (no violence) principle. The universal action aspect of a person's life is developed in the Yama stage.

This stage is based on 10 principles:

1. Ahimsa – (No violence) Violence control
2. Satya – (Honesty) Lie control
3. Asteya – (No Stealing) Possession control
4. Brahmacharya – Sexual energy control
5. Aparigraha – (No Accumulating) Accumulation control
6. Daya – (Compassion) Hate control
7. Kshama – (Forgiving) Anger control
8. Dhriti – (Endurance) Weakness control
9. Mitahara – (Mildness) Excessiveness control
10. Arjava – (Righteousness) Error control

Practicing these principles has a positive influence on a person's psychological state. An individual achieves four goals with these practices:

- Negative energy is expelled.
- Energy channels are purified.
- Energy builds up in the body.
- The accumulated energy leads to physical well-being and spiritual development.

If the individual does not abide by the Yama principles, his/her energy is dispersed and the energy channels are blocked. When these principles are practiced, the energy blocks are resolved, energy flows freely in the body, and the accumulated energy leads to personal development.

Yama principles are implemented in three levels:

- Baudhika: mental
- Vachika: verbal
- Sharirik: physical

Ahimsa (No violence)

The word Ahimsa is formed from the prefix A meaning 'not' and the word Himsa which means 'to kill' or 'violence', and is used in the sense of 'no violence'. The individual should refrain from all kinds of violence in his/her thoughts, speech and actions because violence has a negative effect on human intelligence and prevents development.

NIYAMA – PERSONAL ACTION CONTROL

The second step of the Original Yoga System is named Niyama. The prefix

Ni has been added to the word Yama which means 'control'. In Sanskrit, Ni means 'definiteness'. Consequently Niyama means 'definite control'. In the Niyama stage, a person develops the personal action aspect of his/her life.

This stage is based on 10 principles:

1. Shaucha – (Cleanliness) Dirtiness control
2. Santosha – (Sufficiency) Greediness control
3. Tapas – (Seclusion) Excess control
4. Svadhyaya – (Education) Ignorance control
5. Ishvara Pranidhana – (Perception of The Supreme Being) Perception control
6. Astikya – (Loyalty) Devotion control
7. Dana – (Charity) Selfishness control
8. Hri – (Modesty) Pride control
9. Mati – (Analysis) Thought control
10. Vrata – (Vow) Fluctuation control

The ten principles each of the Yama and Niyama steps are explained in the books: Darshana Upanishada, Gandharva Tantra, and Agni Purana. In these first two steps of the Yoga system, emotions, thoughts and actions are analyzed and taken under control. A person is no longer a slave of his/her emotions, thoughts and actions but becomes a master of them. This is the beginning of controlling destiny. The process of supervision and controlling develops naturally. The individual tries to control his/her emotions, thoughts and actions by only analyzing them without putting pressure on himself/herself.

From a wide philosophical viewpoint, the Niyama step may be interpreted as 'strengthening the positives'. The individual should get rid of negative qualities and strengthen positive qualities on the path of Yoga. Practice of the Yama principles is universal, while practice of the Niyama principles is personal.

By practicing the Niyama principles, the individual achieves the following skills:

- Collecting life energy from the cosmic source to the body
- Directing this energy to lower energy centers
- Using life energy to balance energy centers
- Elevating this energy to higher energy centers

The Niyama principles are personal practices involving the individual's own self. By means of these principles, the senses and sensory organs are controlled.

Shaucha (Cleanliness)

The first of the Niyama principles is the Shaucha principle. The Sanskrit word Shaucha means 'cleanliness'. Dirtiness is controlled by means of this principle. Cleaning is actualized in two levels: external and internal.

ASANA – BODY WORKING TECHNIQUES

The third step of the Original Yoga System is named Asana. The Sanskrit word Asana means 'stand', 'postures', or 'position'. To express it in general terms, Asana means the practice of a prolonged, comfortable, and relaxed special position. Asana is described in old texts as 'firm and pleasing'. Asana means the necessary life state for an individual to remain composed, calm, quiet, and relaxed. The Asana positions are practiced so that the individual can develop the skill of sitting comfortably for a prolonged duration in one position. This is to be utilized later in meditation practice. Moreover, the energy channels and centers in the body become active and work as a result of these specific body positions. Thus the individual's awareness increases and a firm foundation is established for discovering the body, mind and soul. Practicing the postures not only leads to physical control but also to achieving mind and energy control.

The Asanas are beneficial for: the bones; muscles; joints; glands; cardiovascular, nervous, digestive, circulatory, lymphatic, excretory systems; energy currents; mind and soul. The postures are psychosomatic practices which strengthen and balance the entire nervous system, and carry the mind to a state of harmony and peacefulness. The feeling of contentment, mental clarity, relaxation, inner freedom and peace of mind are some of the effects of these practices. Just as a house protects a person from the heat of the sun, the Asanas protect a person from the fever of illnesses. The postures lay a foundation for health. The important details of Asana techniques are kept secret so that worldly people will not be able to harm themselves and others.

Practicing the Asana techniques are effective for a proper posture, for healthiness and for the body to gain a feeling of lightness. The body's energy currents known as Ida and Pingala are balanced. A person is healthy when these energy currents are balanced and ill when they are out of balance. Practicing the postures leads to physical endurance and to direction of energy to every point in the body. The toxins in the body are expelled, the organism gains liveliness, and the nervous system develops. A person feels more energetic and relaxed at the same time. An individual who is rid of inner tensions finds it easier to cope with the increasing external tensions of modern life.

The Asanas create a harmony between the body and mind so that complete physical and mental relaxation can be achieved. Regular practice of Yoga positions rejuvenates the entire physiological system. The postures are truly important for the organism to develop its endurance against illnesses and protect human health. The Asanas mainly affect the endocrine and nervous systems. Since all the systems in the organism are interconnected to each other, positive effects on these two systems leads to the relaying of the same positive effects to the other systems.

PRANAYAMA – BREATHING AND BIOENERGY TECHNIQUES

The fourth step of the Original Yoga System is named Pranayama. Pranayama is a combination of two words: Prana and Ayama. The word Prana means 'energy', the word Ayama means 'control'. Consequently the word Pranayama means 'energy control'. In addition, the word Prana means 'breathing' or 'breath', the word Ayama means 'to hold'. Thus the word Pranayama also means 'to hold the breath'. Moreover, the word Prana also has the meanings 'life', 'liveliness', 'wind', and 'power'. The word Ayama also means 'to prolong', 'to widen', and 'to spread'. As can be understood from these explanations, all breathing functions are strengthened, prolonged and controlled during Pranayama.

Another meaning of the word Prana is 'cosmic energy' or 'life energy'. Prana is defined as 'cosmic energy'; this is an extremely fine kind of energy that is present everywhere throughout space. Prana is also defined as 'life energy' due to the fact that the body's life functions are dependent on this energy. Prana circulates within the body and supports all life functions of the organism; to speak in terms of modern terminology, it may be called 'bioenergy'.

Explaining the word Prana is as difficult as explaining the universe itself. Prana is the fundamental energy that is spread out throughout space and permeates into all the dimensions of the universe. Prana is present in the basis of physical, mental, intellectual and sexual energies. Prana is the source of all energy vibrations. Prana is the foundation of all physical energies: heat, light, gravity, magnetism and electricity.

The secret or potential energy that is present in all living beings and which emerges in just the right amount in times of danger is the energy known as Prana. Prana is the power that puts everything into motion. Prana is the cause of the actualization of creation, protection and destruction processes. Strength, faculties, power, vitality, and life emerge by means of Prana.

Prana energy is the nutrient liquid that nourishes the roots of the life tree. Prana is the life breath of all the living beings in the universe. Living beings are born by means of this energy, live by means of this energy and when the body dies, the individual energy unites with the cosmic energy. Prana is the center of the life wheel. Prana is the foundation of everything in the universe. Prana permeates into the sun, moon, earth, clouds, wind and all material forms.

PRATYAHARA – ASTRAL TECHNIQUES

The fifth step of the Original Yoga System is named Pratyahara. The Sanskrit word Pratyahara means 'withdrawal', 'removal', or 'leaving'. From a wider standpoint, the word Pratyahara means 'the withdrawing of senses from material objects'. When people's minds and intellects surrender to their senses and submit to them, their development is obstructed.

By means of certain techniques in the Pratyahara step, the individual withdraws his/her senses from material objects and takes control of the senses. Thus he/she becomes freed of being the slave of his/her senses. Senses are taken completely under control in the fifth step of the Yoga system.

Pratyahara practices lead to a natural directing of senses and reaching a state beyond them rather than covering, stopping, or suppressing them. This practice involves the calming down of senses so that the unfocused attention can be fixed and increased.

Pratyahara is actualized in four steps:

- Yatamana
- Vyatireka
- Eka Indriya
- Vashikara

The detailed explanation of the meanings of the Yatamana, Vyatireka, Eka Indriya, and Vashikara stages will be given in the book Yoga: Pratyahara – Astral Techniques. Pratyahara techniques protect the body from external effects and help the inner energy to flow without obstruction. By means of these techniques, the mind becomes serene, concentration becomes clearer, inner focus strengthens and the events in the outer world no longer disturb the individual. The sensory organs (tongue, nose, ears, eyes and skin) withdraw from the exterior towards the center to observe the inner world.

The sensory organs have antenna like extensions on an energetic level. These extensions roam out like the tentacles of an octopus to pursue material objects. This commotion disturbs the mind and leaves the individual unprotected against external influences. The energetic extensions of the sensory organs withdraw by means of Pratyahara techniques, the mind relaxes and the individual focuses on his/her inner world.

When Pratyahara is achieved, the individual is engaged in the thing he/she is focusing on to the extent that he/she cannot be aware of external stimuli and does not perceive any sound, vision or odor. The individual focuses on the inner influences of Yoga techniques and utilizes the body as an experimental laboratory. Thus the process of self discovery and evolution is experienced at a purer and more detailed level.

DHARANA – CONCENTRATION TECHNIQUES

When actions are taken under control by means of the Yama and Niyama principles, the body is strengthened by means of the Asana techniques, the mind is cleansed by means of Pranayama, the senses are taken under control by means of Pratyahara, the individual reaches the sixth step of the Yoga system. The sixth step of the Original Yoga System is known as Dharana.

Dharana is the first stage of mental control. The root of the Sanskrit word Dharana is the word Dhri. The word Dhri means 'to hold'. Consequently, Dharana is the process of holding the mind on an object. The mind should be kept on one object and prevented from jumping to another object. For this reason, Dharana is the process of concentrating the mind on one object. Mental concentration, namely Dharana, is beyond emotions, thoughts, wishes and behavior.

The Dharana techniques develop the skill of focusing without breaking one's concentration, and carry energy and concentration to the inner depth of an individual. Dharana is defined as the steady focusing of the mind on a single object for a particular time. According to the Yoga system, concentration is actualized when the mind focuses on an object without diverting attention for 12 seconds.

The individual studies mental functions and takes them under control by practicing concentration techniques in the Dharana step. In this stage, an individual learns how to focus completely on an object or an activity. The mind should attain silence in order to be able to achieve deep concentration.

Attaining Mental Silence

To attain mental silence, lay down face up on the floor in the Shavasana position (Picture 14). Be completely relaxed. Practice Pranayama and Pratyahara. Focus your mind on your breathing. Let yourself into natural breathlessness each time you exhale and listen to mental silence. If any thought enters your mind, don't hang on to it, just watch it and let it pass.

If flows of thought continue, just watch them and don't let your mind dwell on them. Be a silent observer. After a while, the flow of thoughts will end and different visions can be seen. Don't hang on to these visions, just watch them and let them pass.

This way your mind will begin to plunge into natural silence. You may fall asleep during this process. Don't fight against sleep, let yourself relax entirely. You may see dreams in your sleep; don't hang on to these dreams, let them pass by.

When you wake up, keep your mind on the border of sleep and awareness and continue to plunge into silence. When your mind reaches universal silence, you will no longer hear the sounds from outside. You will feel very relaxed, joyful and light. You may make a mental journey to any of the dimensions in the universe during this time.

DHYANA – MEDITATION TECHNIQUES

The seventh step of the Original Yoga System is named Dhyana. Dhyana is the second stage of mental control. The root of the Sanskrit word Dhyana is the word Dhyai. The word Dhyai means 'deep concentration' or 'meditation'. Hence Dhyana is the process of continued and uninterrupted holding of an image by the consciousness by means of deep concentration. Dhyana is achieved when concentration is deepened by keeping an image uninterruptedly and continually in the consciousness for a sufficient length of time. This continual and uninterrupted deep concentration is the explanation of the process of meditation. According to the Yoga system, if concentration lasts for 144 seconds without diversion of attention, meditation is actualized. Dhyana is the state of continual and uninterrupted deep concentration, that is meditation. In the Dharana (concentration) state, the mind still plunges into thoughts and diverges from concentration, whereas in the Dhyana (meditation) state, the mind is under control and does not divert from the object of concentration. Hence Dhyana or uninterrupted deep concentration or meditation continues nonstop for hours.

Dhyana (meditation) differs from the previous Dharana (concentration) step because the skill of focusing has been sharpened and developed. The focus is no longer on a single object but has spread to the entire conscious. The mind becomes silent during Dhyana, the flow of thoughts end and serenity is experienced. In general, the mind is fragmented and dispersed; it is simultaneously full of many thoughts and continually working. In this situation it seems impossible to concentrate on a single object. By means of the Dhyana techniques, it is possible to gather mental energy and direct it to one object.

The individual does not force his/her mind to concentrate during meditation; since the mind is under control and peaceful, it focuses on the chosen object and does not break off from it. Due to this reason, it is impossible to practice true meditation without first practicing the techniques given in the first six steps of the Yoga system. The so-called conjured up 'meditation' methods that are currently widespread have nothing to do with the true meditation called Dhyana.

Another important rule of meditation: For energy to be able to flow freely in the Sushumna Nadi channel and for the individual to not fall asleep, meditation should always be done in Padmasana (Picture 12), Siddhasana or other sitting positions where the back is upright (For details refer to the book Yoga: Asanas – Positions). Some Dharana (concentration) techniques can be done while lying on one's back but Dhyana (meditation) techniques must always be practiced while sitting with the back upright. This is because the individual must remain conscious during meditation.

SAMADHI – SUPERMEDITATION TECHNIQUES

The eighth step of the Original Yoga System is named Samadhi. Samadhi is the third stage of mental control. The Sanskrit word Dhi is the root of the word Samadhi. The word Dhi means 'meditation'. The word Samadhi is a combination of two words: Sam and Dhi. The word Sam means 'super' or 'superior', the word Samadhi means 'supermeditation'.

Samadhi is the process of uninterruptedly holding an object in the mind. According to the Yoga system, if meditation lasts for 1,728 seconds (that is 29 minutes), supermeditation is actualized. In the last stage Dhyana (meditation) reaches a climax. Meditation is so deep at this point that the conscious does not break off from the object in focus and in fact the feeling of self disappears. This state is named Samadhi (supermeditation). According to the Original Yoga System, if supermeditation lasts for 48 minutes without diversion or waning of attention, Kaivalya is actualized. The Sanskrit word Kaivalya means 'spiritual freedom'. In the Kaivalya state, the individual surpasses the borders of material energy and experiences the soul beyond matter. He/she is emancipated from material slavery and enjoys spiritual freedom.

A current Hindu sect of our day presents itself as 'kaivalya yoga' to hide its actual identity. By using so-called 'yoga' practices as a ruse, this sect washes people's brains with their harmful beliefs. Controlled inhaling and exhaling brings on calmness and peace. The peaceful mind concentrates and becomes stabilized. The stabilized mind is able to concentrate on the inner spiritual light. Thus the individual begins focusing on material objects and by the end focuses on spiritual objects.

Just as a natural crystal takes on the colors of the objects surrounding it, when the mind attains silence, it takes on the shape of the objects it is concentrating on. For this duration, the one who knows, knowledge, and the object of knowledge become one. This climax of meditation is named Samadhi (supermeditation). Concentrating the mind on a specific object is Dharana, that is concentration. Continual and uninterrupted concentration is Dhyana, that is meditation. When the mind plunges into real self and loses the feeling of the distinction of individual self, Samadhi, that is supermeditation is actualized. When concentration, meditation, and supermeditation are practiced one after another, Samyama is actualized. Focusing the mind on an object and passing the Dharana, Dhyana, and Samadhi steps is named Samyama, these three steps together are known as Samyama.

WAYS YOGA KEEPS YOU FIT

Flex Time

Improved flexibility is one of the first and most obvious benefits of yoga. During your first class, you probably won't be able to touch your toes, never mind do a backbend. But if you stick with it, you'll notice a gradual loosening, and eventually, seemingly impossible poses will become possible. You'll also probably notice that aches and pains start to disappear. That's no coincidence. Tight hips can strain the knee joint due to improper alignment of the thigh and shinbones. Tight hamstrings can lead to a flattening of the lumbar spine, which can cause back pain. And inflexibility in muscles and connective tissue, such as fascia and ligaments, can cause poor posture.

Strength Test

Strong muscles do more than look good. They also protect us from conditions like arthritis and back pain, and help prevent falls in elderly people. And when you build strength through yoga, you balance it with flexibility. If you just went to the gym and lifted weights, you might build strength at the expense of flexibility.

Standing Orders

Your head is like a bowling ball—big, round, and heavy. When it's balanced directly over an erect spine, it takes much less work for your neck and back muscles to support it. Move it several inches forward, however, and you start to strain those muscles. Hold up that forward-leaning bowling ball for eight or 12 hours a day and it's no wonder you're tired. And fatigue might not be your only problem. Poor posture can cause back, neck, and other muscle and joint problems. As you slump, your body may compensate by flattening the normal inward curves in your neck and lower back. This can cause pain and degenerative arthritis of the spine.

Joint Account

Each time you practice yoga, you take your joints through their full range of motion. This can help prevent degenerative arthritis or mitigate disability by "squeezing and soaking" areas of cartilage that normally aren't used. Joint cartilage is like a sponge; it receives fresh nutrients only when its fluid is squeezed out and a new supply can be soaked up. Without proper sustenance, neglected areas of cartilage can eventually wear out, exposing the underlying bone like worn-out brake pads.

Spinal Rap

Spinal disks—the shock absorbers between the vertebrae that can herniate and compress nerves—crave movement. That's the only way they get their nutrients. If you've got a well-balanced asana practice with plenty of backbends, forward bends, and twists, you'll help keep your disks supple.

Bone Zone

It's well documented that weight-bearing exercise strengthens bones and helps ward off osteoporosis. Many postures in yoga require that you lift your own weight. And some, like Downward- and Upward-Facing Dog, help strengthen the arm bones, which are particularly vulnerable to osteoporotic fractures. In an unpublished study conducted at California State University, Los Angeles, yoga practice increased bone density in the vertebrae. Yoga's ability to lower levels of the stress hormone cortisol (see Number 11) may help keep calcium in the bones.

Flow Chart

Yoga gets your blood flowing. More specifically, the relaxation exercises you learn in yoga can help your circulation, especially in your hands and feet. Yoga also gets more oxygen to your cells, which function better as a result. Twisting poses are thought to wring out venous blood from internal organs and allow oxygenated blood to flow in once the twist is released. Inverted poses, such as Headstand, Handstand, and Shoulderstand, encourage venous blood from the legs and pelvis to flow back to the heart, where it can be pumped to the lungs to be freshly oxygenated. This can help if you have swelling in your legs from heart or kidney problems. Yoga also boosts levels of hemoglobin and red blood cells, which carry oxygen to the tissues. And it thins the blood by making platelets less sticky and by cutting the level of clot-promoting proteins in the blood. This can lead to a decrease in heart attacks and strokes since blood clots are often the cause of these killers.

Lymph Lesson

When you contract and stretch muscles, move organs around, and come in and out of yoga postures, you increase the drainage of lymph (a viscous fluid rich in immune cells). This helps the lymphatic system fight infection, destroy cancerous cells, and dispose of the toxic waste products of cellular functioning.

Heart Start

When you regularly get your heart rate into the aerobic range, you lower your risk of heart attack and can relieve depression. While not all yoga is aerobic, if you do it vigorously or take flow or Ashtanga classes, it can boost your heart rate into the aerobic range. But even yoga exercises that don't get your heart rate up that high can improve cardiovascular conditioning. Studies have found that yoga practice lowers the resting heart rate, increases endurance, and can improve your maximum uptake of oxygen during exercise—all reflections of improved aerobic conditioning. One study found that subjects who were taught only pranayama could do more exercise with less oxygen.

Pressure Drop

If you've got high blood pressure, you might benefit from yoga. Two studies of people with hypertension, published in the British medical journal The Lancet, compared the effects of Savasana (Corpse Pose) with simply lying on a couch. After three months, Savasana was associated with a 26-point drop in systolic blood pressure (the top number) and a 15-point drop in diastolic blood pressure (the bottom number—and the higher the initial blood pressure, the bigger the drop.

Worry Thwarts

Yoga lowers cortisol levels. If that doesn't sound like much, consider this. Normally, the adrenal glands secrete cortisol in response to an acute crisis, which temporarily boosts immune function. If your cortisol levels stay high even after the crisis, they can compromise the immune system. Temporary boosts of cortisol help with long-term memory, but chronically high levels undermine memory and may lead to permanent changes in the brain. Additionally, excessive cortisol has been linked with major depression, osteoporosis (it extracts calcium and other minerals from bones and interferes with the laying down of new bone), high blood pressure, and insulin resistance. In rats, high cortisol levels lead to what researchers call "food-seeking behavior" (the kind that drives you to eat when you're upset, angry, or stressed). The body takes those extra calories and distributes them as fat in the abdomen, contributing to weight gain and the risk of diabetes and heart attack.

Happy Hour

Feeling sad? Sit in Lotus. Better yet, rise up into a backbend or soar royally into King Dancer Pose. While it's not as simple as that, one study found that a consistent yoga practice improved depression and led to a significant increase in serotonin levels and a decrease in the levels of monoamine oxidase (an enzyme that breaks down neurotransmitters) and cortisol. At the University of Wisconsin, Richard Davidson, Ph.D., found that the left prefrontal cortex showed heightened activity in meditators, a finding that has been correlated with greater levels of happiness and better immune function. More dramatic left-sided activation was found in dedicated, long-term practitioners.

Weighty Matters

Msove more, eat less—that's the adage of many a dieter. Yoga can help on both fronts. A regular practice gets you moving and burns calories, and the spiritual and emotional dimensions of your practice may encourage you to address any eating and weight problems on a deeper level. Yoga may also inspire you to become a more conscious eater.

Low Show

Yoga lowers blood sugar and LDL ("bad") cholesterol and boosts HDL ("good") cholesterol. In people with diabetes, yoga has been found to lower blood sugar in several ways: by lowering cortisol and adrenaline levels, encouraging weight loss, and improving sensitivity to the effects of insulin. Get your blood sugar levels down, and you decrease your risk of diabetic complications such as heart attack, kidney failure, and blindness.

Brain Waves

An important component of yoga is focusing on the present. Studies have found that regularyoga practice improves coordination, reaction time, memory, and even IQ scores. People who practice Transcendental Meditation demonstrate the ability to solve problems and acquire and recall information better—probably because they're less distracted by their thoughts, which can play over and over like an endless tape loop.

Nerve Center

Yoga encourages you to relax, slow your breath, and focus on the present, shifting the balance from the sympathetic nervous system (or the fight-or-flight response) to the parasympathetic nervous system. The latter is calming and restorative; it lowers breathing and heart rates, decreases blood pressure, and increases blood flow to the intestines and reproductive organs—comprising what Herbert Benson, M.D., calls the relaxation response.

Space Place

Regularly practicing yoga increases proprioception (the ability to feel what your body is doing and where it is in space) and improves balance. People with bad posture or dysfunctional movement patterns usually have poor proprioception, which has been linked to knee problems and back pain. Better balance could mean fewer falls. For the elderly, this translates into more independence and delayed admission to a nursing home or never entering one at all. For the rest of us, postures like Tree Pose can make us feel less wobbly on and off the mat.

Control Center

Some advanced yogis can control their bodies in extraordinary ways, many of which are mediated by the nervous system. Scientists have monitored yogis who could induce unusual heart rhythms, generate specific brain wave patterns, and, using a meditation technique, raise the temperature of their hands by 15 degrees Fahrenheit. If they can use yoga to do that, perhaps you could learn to improve blood flow to your pelvis if you're trying to get pregnant or induce relaxation when you're having trouble falling asleep.

Loose Limbs

Do you ever notice yourself holding the telephone or a steering wheel with a death grip or scrunching your face when staring at a computer screen? These unconscious habits can lead to chronic tension, muscle fatigue, and soreness in the wrists, arms, shoulders, neck, and face, which can increase stress and worsen your mood. As you practice yoga, you begin to notice where you hold tension: It might be in your tongue, your eyes, or the muscles of your face and neck. If you simply tune in, you may be able to release some tension in the tongue and eyes. With bigger muscles like the quadriceps, trapezius, and buttocks, it may take years of practice to learn how to relax them.

Chill Pill

Stimulation is good, but too much of it taxes the nervous system. Yoga can provide relief from the hustle and bustle of modern life. Restorative asana, yoga nidra (a form of guided relaxation), Savasana, pranayama, and meditation encourage pratyahara, a turning inward of the senses, which provides downtime for the nervous system. Another by-product of a regular yoga practice, studies suggest, is better sleep—which means you'll be less tired and stressed and less likely to have accidents.

Immune Boon

Asana and pranayama probably improve immune function, but, so far, meditation has the strongest scientific support in this area. It appears to have a beneficial effect on the functioning of the immune system, boosting it when needed (for example, raising antibody levels in response to a vaccine) and lowering it when needed (for instance, mitigating an inappropriately aggressive immune function in an autoimmune disease like psoriasis).

Breathing Room

Yogis tend to take fewer breaths of greater volume, which is both calming and more efficient. A 1998 study published in The Lancet taught a yogic technique known as "complete breathing" to people with lung problems due to congestive heart failure. After one month, their average respiratory rate decreased from 13.4 breaths per minute to 7.6. Meanwhile, their exercise capacity increased significantly, as did the oxygen saturation of their blood. In addition, yoga has been shown to improve various measures of lung function, including the maximum volume of the breath and the efficiency of the exhalation.

Yoga also promotes breathing through the nose, which filters the air, warms it (cold, dry air is more likely to trigger an asthma attack in people who are sensitive), and humidifies it, removing pollen and dirt and other things you'd rather not take into your lungs.

Poop Scoop

Ulcers, irritable bowel syndrome, constipation—all of these can be exacerbated by stress. So if you stress less, you'll suffer less. Yoga, like any physical exercise, can ease constipation—and theoretically lower the risk of colon cancer—because moving the body facilitates more rapid transport of food and waste products through the bowels. And, although it has not been studied scientifically, yogis suspect that twisting poses may be beneficial in getting waste to move through the system.

Peace of Mind

Yoga quells the fluctuations of the mind, according to Patanjali's Yoga Sutra. In other words, it slows down the mental loops of frustration, regret, anger, fear, and desire that can cause stress. And since stress is implicated in so many health problems—from migraines and insomnia to lupus, MS, eczema, high blood pressure, and heart attacks—if you learn to quiet your mind, you'll be likely to live longer and healthier.

Divine Sign

Many of us suffer from chronic low self-esteem. If you handle this negatively—take drugs, overeat, work too hard, sleep around—you may pay the price in poorer health physically, mentally, and spiritually. If you take a positive approach and practice yoga, you'll sense, initially in brief glimpses and later in more sustained views, that you're worthwhile or, as yogic philosophy teaches, that you are a manifestation of the Divine. If you practice regularly with an intention of self-examination and betterment—not just as a substitute for an aerobics class—you can access a different side of yourself. You'll experience feelings of gratitude, empathy, and forgiveness, as well as a sense that you're part of something bigger. While better health is not the goal of spirituality, it's often a by-product, as documented by repeated scientific studies.

Pain Drain

Yoga can ease your pain. According to several studies, asana, meditation, or a combination of the two, reduced pain in people with arthritis, back pain, fibromyalgia, carpal tunnel syndrome, and other chronic conditions. When you relieve your pain, your mood improves, you're more inclined to be active, and you don't need as much medication.

Heat Treatment

Yoga can help you make changes in your life. In fact, that might be its greatest strength. Tapas, the Sanskrit word for "heat," is the fire, the discipline that fuels yoga practice and that regular practice builds. The tapas you develop can be extended to the rest of your life to overcome inertia and change dysfunctional habits. You may find that without making a particular effort to change things, you start to eat better, exercise more, or finally quit smoking after years of failed attempts.

Guru Gifts

Good yoga teachers can do wonders for your health. Exceptional ones do more than guide you through the postures. They can adjust your posture, gauge when you should go deeper in poses or back off, deliver hard truths with compassion, help you relax, and enhance and personalize your practice. A respectful relationship with a teacher goes a long way toward promoting your health.

Drug Free

If your medicine cabinet looks like a pharmacy, maybe it's time to try yoga. Studies of people with asthma, high blood pressure, Type II diabetes (formerly called adult-onset diabetes), and obsessive-compulsive disorder have shown that yoga helped them lower their dosage of medications and sometimes get off them entirely. The benefits of taking fewer drugs? You'll spend less money, and you're less likely to suffer side effects and risk dangerous drug interactions.

Hostile Makeover

Yoga and meditation build awareness. And the more aware you are, the easier it is to break free of destructive emotions like anger. Studies suggest that chronic anger and hostility are as strongly linked to heart attacks as are smoking, diabetes, and elevated cholesterol. Yoga appears to reduce anger by increasing feelings of compassion and interconnection and by calming the nervous system and the mind. It also increases your ability to step back from the drama of your own life, to remain steady in the face of bad news or unsettling events. You can still react quickly when you need to—and there's evidence that yoga speeds reaction time—but you can take that split second to choose a more thoughtful approach, reducing suffering for yourself and others.

Good Relations

Love may not conquer all, but it certainly can aid in healing. Cultivating the emotional support of friends, family, and community has been demonstrated repeatedly to improve health and healing. A regular yoga practice helps develop friendliness, compassion, and greater equanimity. Along with yogic philosophy's emphasis on avoiding harm to others, telling the truth, and taking only what you need, this may improve many of your relationships.

Sound System

The basics of yoga—asana, pranayama, and meditation—all work to improve your health, but there's more in the yoga toolbox. Consider chanting. It tends to prolong exhalation, which shifts the balance toward the parasympathetic nervous system. When done in a group, chanting can be a particularly powerful physical and emotional experience. A recent study from

Sweden's Karolinska Institute suggests that humming sounds—like those made while chanting Om—open the sinuses and facilitate drainage.

Vision Quest

If you contemplate an image in your mind's eye, as you do in yoga nidra and other practices, you can effect change in your body. Several studies have found that guided imagery reduced postoperative pain, decreased the frequency of headaches, and improved the quality of life for people with cancer and HIV.

Clean Machine

Kriyas, or cleansing practices, are another element of yoga. They include everything from rapid breathing exercises to elaborate internal cleansings of the intestines. Jala neti, which entails a gentle lavage of the nasal passages with salt water, removes pollen and viruses from the nose, keeps mucus from building up, and helps drains the sinuses.

Karma Concept

Karma yoga (service to others) is integral to yogic philosophy. And while you may not be inclined to serve others, your health might improve if you do. A study at the University of Michigan found that older people who volunteered a little less than an hour per week were three times as likely to be alive seven years later. Serving others can give meaning to your life, and your problems may not seem so daunting when you see what other people are dealing with.

Healing Hope

In much of conventional medicine, most patients are passive recipients of care. In yoga, it's what you do for yourself that matters. Yoga gives you the tools to help you change, and you might start to feel better the first time you try practicing. You may also notice that the more you commit to practice, the more you benefit. This results in three things: You get involved in your own care, you discover that your involvement gives you the power to effect change, and seeing that you can effect change gives you hope. And hope itself can be healing.

Connective Tissue

As you read all the ways yoga improves your health, you probably noticed a lot of overlap. That's because they're intensely interwoven. Change your posture and you change the way you breathe. Change your breathing and you change your nervous system. This is one of the great lessons of yoga: Everything is connected—your hipbone to your anklebone, you to your community, your community to the world. This interconnection is vital to understanding yoga. This holistic system simultaneously taps into many mechanisms that have additive and even multiplicative effects. This synergy may be the most important way of all that yoga heals.

Placebo Power

Just believing you will get better can make you better. Unfortunately, many conventional scientists believe that if something works by eliciting the placebo effect, it doesn't count. But most patients just want to get better, so if chanting a mantra—like you might do at the beginning or end of yoga class or throughout a meditation or in the course of your day—facilitates healing, even if it's just a placebo effect, why not do it?

SOCIAL LIFE AND YOGA

The science and art of Yoga, has for millennia guided man in his search for truth. Even in his personal and social life, Yoga has given him the tools and techniques with which he can find happiness, spiritual realization and social harmony.

ROLE OF YOGIC CONCEPTS

Various yogic concepts have guided man towards shaping his life and the interpersonal relationships in his social life.

- Vasudeva Kudumbakam - The whole world is one family. This is an excellent concept which helps one to understand that division on the basis of class, creed, religion and geographical distribution are all 'man made' obstructions towards oneness. One can then look upon all as his own and can bond with everyone irrespective of any barrier.
- Pancha Kosha - The concept of our five sheaths or bodies helps us to understand how all our actions, emotions and even thoughts can influence our surroundings and that "No man is an island". The concept of "nara" or psychic disassociation help us to be aware of why things happen to us and others in our daily life.
- Chaturvidha Purusharthas - The four legitimate goals of life tell us how we can set legitimate goals in this life and work towards attaining them in the right way, following our dharma to attain artha (material prosperity), kama (emotional prosperity) and finally the attainment to the real goal of our life, moksha (spiritual prosperity).
- Chatur Ashramas - This concept of the four different stages in life, helps us to know how,what and when to perform the various activities in our life.

Brahmacharya is the period from birth till 27 years and is the period for study, conserving the creative impulse and channeling it towards elevating spiritual pursuits. Grahasta is the period of responsibility, spanning the period from 27 - 54 years in which we learn to care about others in the family and the social network, fulfilling our dharma towards both the young and the old.

Vanaprasta or retirement is the period after 54 years when one's life can be played over again and again in the mind with a sense of fulfillment and satisfaction having not to worry about anything at all.

Sanyasa is the period of life when after performing our duties to the best of our ability for 81 years and after having attained perfection in life we renounce everything for the divine.

- Pancha Klesha: Avidya (ignorance), Asmita (ego), Raaga (attraction), Dwesha (repulsion) and Abinivesha (urge to live at any cost) are the five Kleshas or mental afflictions with which we are born into this human life. Through Yoga we can understand how these control our life and see their effects on our behaviour. These 'kleshas' hinder our personal and social life and must be destroyed through the practice of Patanjali's Kriya Yoga which is tapas, swadyaya and iswar pranidhana (atman prasadhanam).
- Nishkama Karma: Selfless action and the performance of our duty without any motive, are qualities extolled by the Bhagavad Gita which is one of the main yogic texts. Performing one's duty for the sake of the duty itself and not with any other motive helps us to develop detachment (vairagya) which is a quality vital for a good life.
- Karmasu Koushalam: 'Skill in action' is Yoga says Yogeshwar Krishna in the Bhagavad Gita. 'To do our best and leave the rest' is how Pujya Swamiji Gitananda Giri Guru Maharaj used to describe the best way of life. Even if we don't practice the other aspects of yoga, we can be 'living' yoga, by performing all our duties skill fully and to the best of our ability. A great artist, doctor, worker, singer or sportsman can be a Yogi by performing doing their duty to perfection and without care for the rewards of the action,even if they do not practice any asana, pranayama etc..
- Samatvam: 'Yoga is equanimity ' says the Bhagavad Gita. Development of a complete personality who is neither affected by praise nor blame

through development of vairagya (detachment) leads to the state of "stitha prajna" or "sama bhava". This is a state of mind which is equally predisposed to all that happens, be it good or bad. Such a human is a boon to society and a pleasure to live and work with.

ROLE OF THE PANCHA YAMA AND PANCHA NIYAMA

The pancha yama and pancha niyama provide a strong moral and ethical foundation for our personal and social life. They guide our attitudes with regard to the right and wrong in our life and in relation to our self, our family unit and the entire social system.

- Pancha Yama:
  Ahimsa - Non - violence
  Aatya - truthfulness
  Asteya - non-stealing
  Bramhacharya - proper channeling of the creative impulse
  Aparigraha - non - coveted-ness

These are the "do not's" in a yoga sadhak's life. Do not kill, do not be untruthful, do not steal, do not waste your god given creativity and do not covet that which does not belong to you.

These guide us to say a big "NO" to our lower self and the lower impulses of violence etc. When we apply these to our life we can definitely have better personal and social relationships as social beings.

- Ancha Niyama
  Soucha - cleanliness
  Santhosha - contentment
  Tapas - discipline
  Swadyaya - study of one's-self
  Ishwar pranidhana - gratitude to the divine self.
  (atman prasadhanam)

The pancha niyamas guide us with "DO'S" - do be clean, do be contented, do be disciplined, do self - study (introspection) and do be thankful to the divine for all of his blessings.

They help us to say a big "YES" to our higher self and the higher impulses. Definitely a person with such qualities is a God-send to humanity.

Even when we are unable to live the yama and niyama completely, even the attempt by us to do so will bear fruit and make each one of us a better person and help us to be of value to those around us and a valuable person to live with in our family and society. These are values which need to be introduced to the youth in order to make them aware and conscious of these wonderful concepts of daily living which are qualities to be imbibed with joy and not learnt with fear or compulsion.

The parents can by example show their children the importance of these qualities and when the children see the good examples of their parents living there principles they will surely follow suit sooner than later.

ROLE OF THE OTHER ASPECTS OF YOGA

Living a happy and healthy life on all planes is possible through the unified practice of hatha yoga asanas & pranayamas, dharana, dhyana and bakthi yoga especially when performed consciously and with awareness. Asanas help to develop strength, flexibility, will power, good health, and stability and thus when practiced as a whole give a person a 'stable and unified strong personality'.

Pranayama helps us to control our emotions which are linked to breathing and the pranamaya kosha (the vital energy sheath or body). Slow, deep and rhythmic breathing helps to control stress and overcome emotional hang-ups. Dharana and Dhyana help us to focus our mid and dwell in it and thus help us to channel our creative energy in a wholistic manner towards the right type of evolutionary activities. They help us to understand our self better and in the process become better humans in this social world.

Bhakti Yoga, enables us to realise the greatness of the Divine and understand our puniness as compared to the power of the Divine or nature. We realize that we are but 'puppets on a string' following his commands on the stage of the world and then perform our activities with the intention of them being an offering to the divine and gratefully receive HIS blessings.

YOGA FOR PEOPLE IN PRISON

Cessnock Correctional Centre has a weekly yoga class for participants of the Phoenix program. Phoenix is an alcohol and other drug (AOD) program for male inmates in the minimum-security section of Cessnock jail. There are a number of education programs including anger-management, sobriety maintenance, parenting, meditation and yoga. A Buddhist monk runs the meditation class each week and I teach the yoga class.

THE PRISON ENVIRONMENT

Prisoners in minimum security have work duties they perform from about 10am until 2pm Monday to Friday. At 4pm there is 'muster' where they receive their individual meals that they eat in their cells. Cells are locked from 5pm until 9am. There is quite a large area where prisoners are able to wander. There are some recreational facilities like tennis courts and gym equipment Most of the walking area is concrete. There is razor wire all around the compound. Prison officers monitor the movement of prisoners through 'A block' where Phoenix is located and where the inmates have their cells. Much of the daily routine of a prisoner is highly regulated. The routine may change at any time without notice or reason. Prisoners are regularly moved on short-notice to other prisons.

THE PRISON POPULATION

People in the minimum-security section have greater freedom than in the other higher security sections. They are often awaiting parole hearings and so are committed to staying out of trouble, being seen as a model prisoner and generally looking like they are ready for and deserving of parole.

A study by Carcach and Grant (2000) found that the rate of imprisonment for Australians born in Vietnam, Oceania, New Zealand, Lebanon and Turkey exceeded the rate of those born in Australia. This is reflected somewhat in the attendees in the yoga class. Carcach and Grant also found that the prison population is an aging population. A disproportionate number of prisoners are Indigenous Australians (Human Rights and Equal Opportunity Commission, 2003, p.18). The literacy and numeracy level of prisoners is significantly lower than that of the general population (See Appendix).

THE NEEDS OF STUDENTS IN A YOGA CLASS

The nature of the prison environment has a profound influence on the people within it. The lack of control in many aspects of their lives creates mental tension. And although this paper is about the needs of prisoners, the job of the prison officer appears to be one associated with many risks and stresses for reasons not dissimilar to the reasons prisoners experience stress and tension. Mental tension is played out in the body as physical tension that is further compounded by the focus on weight training and most walking surfaces being concrete.

The health related issues most commonly raised by prisoners who attend yoga class are difficulty sleeping, agitation/anxiety, pain and physical tension. The clear structure of the Satyananda yoga class allows students to relax into a routine they know well. There are no surprises about what is coming next. Yoga nidra is an essential element to the class as is short relaxation. Students appreciate the benefits they feel with the asanas but yoga nidra gives them the opportunity to let go. Many who complain of not being able to sleep are able to rest completely in yoga nidra.

Sankalpa is a powerful tool for people especially those in prison. It is important to explain this concept carefully so as not to compound existing aspects of the person's character that led to imprisonment in the first place. Many people in prison have difficulty learning and English may not be their first language so a thorough explanation of Sankalpa is very important. Visualisations in Yoga nidra are kept simple and are often scenes from nature. The reason for this is that it connects prisoners to the natural environment as opposed to the very artificial one in which they live, it is reasonably safe for the psyche of the average student and finally, because there is a high turnover of students these visualisations are OK for a newcomer as well as the more experienced student.

Because the class usually has new students mixed with longer-term students the asana aspect of the class plan needs to be pitched at the 'general' level but also needs to be flexible to meet the needs of the students at the time. Many students have injuries. Pranayama practices give students invaluable tools to manage stress. Abdominal breathing, full yogic breath, ujjayi and nadi shodana feature in most classes.

Another aspect of the yoga class within prison is the use of language. Particular attention is paid to descriptions of movements, effects of practices or descriptions of the self or the body that are positive or sacred. For example, in using language like the symbolism of a golden thread along the spine, the lightness of a standing posture or the courage and fearlessness of a warrior, the student is given an opportunity to think differently about himself and perhaps begin to develop other aspects of his character.

The Needs of Students after Release from Prison

Corrective Services have developed the practice of 'Through care'. This is similar to 'discharge planning' within the health system. Prisoners are involved in programs within the prison that they can then continue with once they are released. This provides continuity with the aim of reducing the rate of recidivism by linking the person with the outside community in a way that is positive and supportive.

Satyananda Yoga as 'Through care'

Satyananda Yoga has a lot to offer prisoners within prison but also post-release. There is a clear structure to the class. Students can expect the same structure in whatever class they attend whether in prison or in the community. The systematic progression of students supports students to work at their own pace and to honour their body and their capabilities whatever they are. The student in prison is encouraged to take responsibility for this aspect of their lives and this continues in to the community post-release. The network of Satyananda teachers is such that the newly released prisoner is able to readily access classes. The Satyananda network also means that the yoga teacher in prison can provide the student with information about the nearest available class prior to release from prison.

For the prisoner for whom AOD is an issue yoga helps them to develop skills to manage stress. This is relevant within prison but is particularly relevant outside of prison where ex-prisoners often find the community hostile and unsupportive. This lack of support in turn leads people towards other options for survival that have worked in the past like drug taking and crime. Yoga practices like yoga nidra and the pranayama practices provide skills that compliment the cognitive/psychological focus of sobriety maintenance programs.

Teaching Challenges

Creating a yogic environment within the prison is particularly challenging. The space provided at Cessnock prison is carpeted and air-conditioned. It has ample natural light and good artificial light if required. It will accommodate a maximum of 8 people. It is located on the 2nd floor directly above the weight training area. The weight training area is an open area and training is usually accompanied to music at great volume. Outside the room is a main thoroughfare and the loudspeaker can be intrusive as the students are always listening to hear if they are being called. Observances like shoes off in the 'yoga room' and 'no chatting' helps to create a yogic atmosphere as does a candle and incense. After 18 months I have just introduced 'Hari Om Tat Sat" in classes where the majority of students are experienced.

Many students are poorly educated and may not have English as their first language. Words like 'inhalation', 'exhalation', 'symmetry' and even 'navel' may require substitution or explanation. Because the class operates essentially as a casual class it can be difficult to progress the longer-term students. This is most noticeable in pranayama and less so in asana practices where a range of options can be given.

YOGA ENCOURAGES OVERALL HEALTH AND WELLNESS

Yoga is not just about working out, it's about a healthy lifestyle. The practice of yoga allows students to be still in a world consumed with chaos. Peace and tranquility achieved through focused training appeals to everyone. Yoga's deep breathing and meditation practices help foster an inner shift from to-do lists, kids and spouse's needs, financial concerns and relational struggles to something a little bit bigger than the issues you face. Yoga helps relieve stress and unclutter the mind, and helps you get more focused.

YOGA HAS MANY FACES

One of the benefis of yoga is that you can choose a yoga style that is tailored to your lifestyle, such as hot yoga, power yoga, relaxation yoga, prenatal yoga, etc. Whether you prefer you're at home, in a private session, watching a DVD or at a studio or gym, there are a huge variety of options available to suit your goals and needs.

If you are a yoga beginner, Hatha yoga, which focuses on basic postures at a comfortable pace, would be great for you. If you want to increase strength through using more of your own body's resistance, power yoga may be right for you. There is a great online yoga program at Gaiam Yoga Studio that focuses on Hatha yoga. If you are ready for a deeper practice, Advanced Yoga, or Bikram, also called "hot yoga," may be just what you are looking for. In Bikram yoga, the room temperature is set to around 100 degrees Fahrenheit, resulting in greaterelimination of toxins from the body through the increased production of sweat. No matter your fitness level, fat percentage, or health history, yoga has a place for you.

Strength training and flexibility

Yoga's focus on strength training and flexibility is an incredible benefit to your body. The postures are meant to strengthen your body from the inside-out, so you don't just look good, you feel good too. Each of the yoga poses is built to reinforce the muscles around the spine, the very center of your body, which is the core from which everything else operates. When the core is working properly, posture is improved, thus alleviating back, shoulder and neck pain.

The digestive system gets back on track when the stretching in yoga is coupled with a healthy, organic diet, which can relieve constipation, irritable bowl syndrome (IBS) and acid reflux. Another one of the benefits of yoga is that stretching and holding of postures also causes muscles to lengthen, which gives the body a longer, leaner look.

How Does Power yoga Build Muscle?

A more advanced form of yoga can amplify these effects. Adapted from the basic Ashtanga yoga, power yoga requires increased amounts of energy, focus and strength. Although power yoga is an evolvement of the basics, it certainly is not a basic course. But how does it help build muscle? Deeper, more focused participation is required, because most poses are held for five full breaths versus the usual one to three breaths. Muscles are challenged as the mind and body have to work together simultaneously to hold a position or continue a succession without giving up. Breathing, posing, moving and increasing flexibility happen all together at one time, which solicits a new level of discipline in your mind and body.

Power yoga and the core

Isometric exercises are one of the best ways to build core strength. Isometric, stemming from the words "same" and "length," simply translates to holding one position without moving. Power yoga uses isometric exercises along with other postures that are designed to make the core and back stronger. Flexibility and balance stem from your core, so it is very important to train this area of the body. In turn, you can increase the strangth and health of your entire body. Generally a higher-temperature room is used in this practice to help keep the muscles warm and release additional toxins from the body.

Power Yoga's Effect on the Total Body

Here's a list of some of the most beneficial aspects of power yoga:

- It increases endurance, strength and flexibility.
- Mental endurance and physical stamina are tested through holding postures for extended breaths.
- Arm and shoulder strength is multiplied as you use your own body weight for resistance.
- Lats and other back muscles begin to support the spine better than before.
- Abdominals and obliques are refined and sharpened through building core muscles.

- Poor and average posture begins to correct itself over time.
- Hip flexors are stretched and rebuilt.
- Glutes, quads, hamstrings, and calves are tightened and lengthened where they need to be.

No matter what ails your aching body, or if you just want to take your fitness to a higher level, power yoga's ability to build muscle has an undeniably effect on the total body.

PHYSIOLOGICAL BENEFITS OF YOGA

Physicians and scientists are discovering brand new health benefits of yoga everyday. Studies show it can relieve the symptoms of several common and potentially life-threatening illnesses such as arthritis, arteriosclerosis, chronic fatigue, diabetes, AIDS, asthma and obesity.

Asthma

Studies conducted at yoga institutions in India have reported impressive success in improving asthma. It has also been proved that asthma attacks can usually be prevented by yoga methods without resorting to drugs. Physicians have found that the addition of improved concentration abilities and yogic meditation together with the practice of simple postures and pranayama makes treatment more effective. Yoga practice also results in greater reduction in anxiety scores than drug therapy. Doctors believe that yoga practice helps patients by enabling them to gain access to their own internal experience and increased self-awareness.

Respiration Problems

Patients who practice yoga have a better chance of gaining the ability to control their breathing problems. With the help of yogic breathing exercises, it is possible to control an attack of severe shortness of breath without having to seek medical help. Various studies have confirmed the beneficial effects of yoga for patients with respiratory problems.

High Blood Pressure

The relaxation and exercise components of yoga have a major role to play in the treatment and prevention of high blood pressure (hypertension). A combination of biofeedback and yogic breathing and relaxation techniques has been found to lower blood pressure and reduce the need for high blood pressure medication in people suffering from it.

Pain Management

Yoga is believed to reduce pain by helping the brain's pain center regulate the gate-controlling mechanism located in the spinal cord and the secretion of natural painkillers in the body. Breathing exercises used in yoga can also reduce pain. Because muscles tend to relax when you exhale, lengthening the time of exhalation can help produce relaxation and reduce tension. Awareness of breathing helps to achieve calmer, slower respiration and aid in relaxation and pain management. Yoga's inclusion of relaxation techniques and meditation can also help reduce pain. Part of the effectiveness of yoga in reducing pain is due to its focus on self-awareness. This self-awareness can have a protective effect and allow for early preventive action.

Back Pain

Back pain is the most common reason to seek medical attention. Yoga has consistently been used to cure and prevent back pain by enhancing strength and flexibility. Both acute and long-term stress can lead to muscle tension and exacerbate back problems.

Arthritis

Yoga's gentle exercises designed to provide relief to needed joints had been Yoga's slow-motion movements and gentle pressures reach deep into troubled joints. In addition, the easy stretches in conjunction with deep breathing exercises relieve the tension that binds up the muscles and further tightens the joints. Yoga is exercise and relaxation rolled into one - the perfect anti-arthritis formula.

Weight Reduction

Regular yoga practice can help in weight management. Firstly, some of the asanas stimulate sluggish glands to increase their hormonal secretions. The thyroid gland, especially, has a big effect on our weight because it affects body metabolism. There are several asanas, such as the shoulder stand and the fish posture, which are specific for the thyroid gland. Fat metabolism is also increased, so fat is converted to muscle and energy. This means that, as well as losing fat, you will have better muscle tone and a higher vitality level.

Yogic practices that reduce anxiety tend to reduce anxious eating. In addition, yoga deep breathing increases the oxygen intake to the body cells, including the fat cells. This causes increased oxidation or burning up of fat cells. Yogic exercises induce more continuous and deeper breathing which gradually burns, sometimes forcefully, many of the calories already ingested.

Psychological Benefits

Regular yoga practice creates mental clarity and calmness, increases body awareness, relieves chronic stress patterns, relaxes the mind, centers attention and sharpens concentration.

Self-Awareness

Yoga strives to increase self-awareness on both a physical and psychological level. Patients who study yoga learn to induce relaxation and then to use the technique whenever pain appears. Practicing yoga can provide chronic pain sufferers with useful tools to actively cope with their pain and help counter feelings of helplessness and depression.

Mental Performance

A common technique used in yoga is breathing through one nostril at a time. Electroencephalogram (EEG) studies of the electrical impulses of the brain have shown that breathing through one nostril results in increased activity on the opposite side of the brain.

Some experts suggest that the regular practice of breathing through one nostril may help improve communication between the right and left side of the brain. Studies have also shown that this increased brain activity is associated with better performance and doctors even suggest that yoga can enhance cognitive performance.

Mood Change And Vitality

Mental health and physical energy are difficult to quantify, but virtually everyone who participates in yoga over a period of time reports a positive effect on outlook and energy level. Yogic stretching and breathing exercises have been seen to result in an invigorating effect on both mental and physical energy and improved mood.

Spiritual Benefits

When you achieve the yogic spirit, you can begin knowing yourself at peace. The value of discovering one's self and of enjoying one's self as is, begins a journey into being rather than doing. Life can then be lived practicing "yoga off the mat".

Pride

Pride, and especially anxiety about pride, is something which Hatha Yoga seeks to diminish or eliminate. To one who has been dejected because he cannot do his work properly when he becomes tired, irritable, or haggard, any degree of refreshment may be accompanied by additional degrees of self-respect. Furthermore, one who has benefited from yoga may be moved to help his friends who are obviously in need, he may instruct others and be rewarded with appreciation due a to teacher. But if one succeeds in achieving skill which provides health and self-confidence, one may justly raise his self-esteem simply by observing himself living the improved results as an achieved fact.

KNOWLEDGE

Yogic theory and practice lead to increased self-knowledge. This knowledge is not merely that of the practical kind relating to techniques, but especially of a spiritual sort pertaining to grasping something about the nature of the self at rest. Knowing the self at rest, at peace, as a being rather than merely as an agent or doer, is a genuine kind of knowledge which usually gets lost in the rush of activities and push of desires. The value of discovering one's self and of enjoying one's self as it is, rather than as it is going to be, is indeed a value as well as a kind of knowledge.

3

Yoga and Health Based Exercise Programme

YOGA BASED EXERCISE PROGRAMME

Stroke is the leading cause of adult disability in the United States, with more than 4.7 million people who have had a stroke alive in the United States today.1 The majority of people who have had strokes have mild to moderate neurologic deficits.2 Many are physically deconditioned and have a high prevalence of cardiovascular risk factors that are potentially modifiable with exercise.3 Even the fittest people who have had a stroke tend to have an impaired health status compared with age-matched control subjects.4 Many people who have had strokes experience adverse health events that can be attributed to a reduced level of activity.3 Stroke is a condition associated with increased risk for falls.5 Forster and Young5 reported that 73 per cent of elderly people who have had strokes fell within 6 months after discharge from the hospital. With the rising number of people surviving strokes today, there is a vital need for exercise programs designed to improve and maintain the physical fitness and quality of life of this population.

The majority of people who have had a stroke plateau in neurological and functional recovery and are not expected to make improvements more than 5 months after the stroke.6 Several investigators, however, have found that improvements in muscle force, balance, aerobic capacity, and timed mobility in subjects with chronic poststroke hemiparesis can be achieved with exercise training. In subjects whose stroke occurred more than 1 year prior, Weiss et al7demonstrated improvements in muscle force, balance, and timed mobility after performing 12 weeks of a lower-extremity progressive resisted exercise training program at 70 per cent of one repetition maximum. Potempa et al8 and Macko et al9reported improved aerobic capacity in people greater than 6 months poststroke, following exercise with a bicycle ergometer8 or after treadmill training.9 Teixeira-Salmela et al10 noted increases in muscle force and mobility in subjects greater than 9 months poststroke with a combination of lower-extremity progressive resistive exercises and aerobic endurance training utilizing a treadmill, stepping machine, or stationary cycle.10 Dean et al11 noted improved walking speed and lower-extremity force production in subjects greater than 3 months poststroke with a task-related circuit training regimen. The training regimen included 10 workstation tasks designed to improve muscle performance in the affected lower extremity and to provide practice of various locomotor skills.11 Several investigators have demonstrated improved upper extremity motor ability in people who were more than 6 months or 1 year poststroke with the application of contraint-induced movement therapy. Contraint-induced movement therapy involves constraining movements of the less-affected upper extremity with a sling or glove for 90 per cent of the waking hours for 2 weeks, while undergoing intensive training of the more affected limb 5 to 6 hours per day in a clinical setting and home-based activities.17

Yoga is one of India's oldest and most extensive psychospiritual traditions. It has evolved over 5,000 years to encompass a vast body of moral and ethical precepts, mental attitudes, and physical practices.18 The word "yoga" is derived from the Sanskrit verb "yuj" meaning to yoke or unite. Commonly, yoga is translated to imply the union of body, mind, and spirit.19 There are 8 main forms of yoga.Hatha yoga is the most recognized and practiced form of yoga in the Western world.19 Many forms of yoga encompass 8 elements, known as the "eight-fold path" of yoga, which include yamas (moral disciplines), niyamas (self-restraint),pranayama (breath control), asanas (physical poses), pratyahara (sensory inhibition), dharana (concentration), dhyana (meditation), and samadhi (blissful state). All forms seek to achieve the goal of enlightenment, or the realization of one's true self.20

Yoga therapeutics is defined by International Association of Yoga Therapists as the application of yoga for health benefits.21 Practitioners of yoga therapy integrate yoga concepts with Western medical and psychological knowledge,21for example, by using body awareness and breathing activities, physical postures, and meditation with an understanding of pathological conditions such as back pain or depression in the management of people with these conditions. Whereas traditional yoga practice is primarily concerned with personal enlightenment of people without pathology, yoga therapy focuses on a holistic treatment for people with various somatic or psychological dysfunctions. According to Feuerstein,18the goals of yoga therapy are to promote health benefits and to promote self-awareness for the purpose of enlightenment. Yoga therapy offers an alternative approach to conventional exercise training, and it also can be adapted to meet the needs of people with physical limitations.19 Although there have been no studies that have investigated the effects of yoga on people who have had a stroke or hemiparesis, Bell and Seyfer22 have described adaptations of yoga postures that can be applied to people with neurologic conditions such as multiple sclerosis and stroke.

Yoga therapy has been used for relief of stress and anxiety and to manage epilepsy. The one randomized controlled study conducted to compare the effects of yoga, sham yoga, and no yoga therapy on the management of people with epilepsy yielded inconclusive results.23 Yoga's role in the management of depression has been investigated, and it has been reported to be beneficial for college students who exhibit a high level of depressive symptoms.24 Yogic breathing exercises also have been found to lead to improvements in people with melancholic depression that are comparable to the use of imipramine.25

Proponents of yoga believe it offers a holistic approach to rehabilitation, which includes eliciting relaxation through meditation.26 With the exception of a case report describing an application of yoga therapeutics to a patient with Parkinson disease,27 there have been no studies investigating the effects of a yoga-based program on people with neurologic disorders. Eliciting relaxation, however, may promote positive effects on carotid atherosclerosis, hypertension, diabetes, and coronary artery disease, which are identified as risk factors associated with stroke occurrence or reoccurrence. Effects such as these may add substantial benefits to people following a stroke beyond the use of yoga as an alternate method of physical activity.

A regular practice of yoga has been shown to improve flexibility and muscle force in adults without known pathology,37 vital capacity in college students without pathology,38 aerobic capacity in men without pathology,39 and motor speed (frequency of successive finger taps in 30 seconds) in adults without pathology.40 Tran and co-workers37 reported improvements in upper- and lower-extremity torques measured with an isokinetic device at a speeds of 30°/s and 60°/s; ability to hold a lower-extremity isometric muscle contraction; shoulder, ankle, and spinal flexibility; and aerobic capacity in 10 adult subjects without known pathology after a practice of hatha yoga activities 2 times per week for 8 weeks.

Birkel and Edgren38 found improvements in the vital capacity of college students after practicing hatha yoga activities 2 times per week for 15 weeks. Ray et al39conducted a randomized controlled comparison of men without known pathology participating in either a hatha yoga regimen or an exercise training program for 1 hour daily for 6 months. Although both groups demonstrated improvement in several pulmonary function tests, only the yoga group improved in maximum oxygen uptake and decreased perceived exertion after maximal exercise testing with a bicycle ergometer. Dash and Telles40 found improved motor speed in a 30-second finger-tapping test in adults without pathology who participated in yoga activities 8 hours per day for 30 days compared with a group of adults without pathology who received no intervention. Although Dash and Telles40 reported improved motor speed in repetitive finger motion, it is unclear whether these changes can be generalized to repetitive motor activities of the lower extremities. Balance and mobility require the ability to generate forces to control the body segments and position in space. Musculoskeletal components that influence stability and control include joint range of motion, spinal flexibility, and muscle properties such as force production and endurance. Musculoskeletal problems may greatly influence postural stability and control.41 Decreased range of motion and muscle weakness have been observed in people following a stroke.42 Studies of outcomes have revealed that voluntary muscle force is closely correlated to gait performance in people following a stroke,43 and it may contribute to the balance and mobility problems of these people.44,45 We were interested in knowing whether yoga therapy might be useful for people who have had a stroke. The purpose of this study, therefore, was to investigate the effects of a yoga-based exercise program on balance, mobility, and quality of life for people with chronic poststroke hemiparesis.

METHOD

Subjects

A single-subject study design was used with each of the 4 subjects who participated in this study. Nonconcurrent multiple baselines were used. The subjects were recruited from the community surrounding Keene, NH. Newspaper advertisements and postings at public bulletin boards and senior centers were used to recruit the subjects. People were considered for participation in the study if: (1) more than 9 months had elapsed since their stroke; (2) they were moderately impaired in lower-extremity motor function (a lower-extremity motor score between 15/34 and 27/34 on the Fugl-Meyer Sensorimotor Assessment46); (3) they were able to ambulate independently or with supervision, with or without an assistive device or orthosis; and (4) they had completed all rehabilitation. Subjects were excluded if they had: (1) a medical condition that interfered with participation in exercise programs, (2) a score of less than 15/30 on the Folstein Mini-Mental Status Examination,47 or (3) receptive aphasia that interfered with the ability to follow 2-step commands.

Preliminary screening of subjects was done by use of telephone interview. The purpose and procedures of our study were explained, and verbal consent to participate was obtained. An interview and examination were then arranged in each subject's home. The subjects were again informed of our study's purpose and procedures, and they signed a written consent form. Five people were screened for possible inclusion in this study; 1 person was excluded because the Fugl-Meyer Sensorimotor Assessment lower-extremity score was 32/34.

Subject 1.

Subject 1 was 71-year-old man who had a right cerebrovascular accident (CVA) 8 years before the start of our study, which caused left hemiparesis

(Tab. 1). He had a history of hypertension, hypercholesterolemia, restless leg syndrome, sleep apnea, degenerative joint disease of both knees and shoulders, and chronic low back pain. Immediately following his stroke, he spent several weeks in acute care and inpatient rehabilitation facilities. He was discharged to his home and completed his rehabilitation in an outpatient setting. He had 2 seizures in the year following his stroke. He underwent a right total knee replacement (TKR) 2 years after his stroke and a left TKR 4 years after his stroke. After the left TKR, he received short-term inpatient and outpatient rehabilitation. He retired, approximately 6 years prior to his stroke, after working for 32 years as a computer hardware repair technician. He lived alone in a suburban single-story home and had 3 sons who lived out of the immediate area. He was active in several community and church programs. He could ambulate independently without the use of assistive or orthotic devices within the home; however, he used a railing when going up and down stairs and a straight cane when ambulating outside of his home. He reported that he occasionally stumbled and lost his balance.

He had fallen 3 times in the year before our study was initiated without sustaining a serious injury. He was independent in all self-care activities and did light household tasks. He drove, did his own grocery shopping, and managed the household finances. Before the initiation of this study, subject 1 had not received physical therapy or occupational therapy since completing rehabilitation following his TKR 4 years previously. He stated he did not routinely exercise but occasionally took a leisurely walk for approximately 1 block. He avoided walking long distances or walking quickly because he said this activity increased his low back pain.

Subject 2.

Subject 2 was a 49-year-old woman who had a right CVA with subsequent left hemiparesis 1.5 years before our study began. She had a history of hypertension that began during a pregnancy 12 years before her stroke, but she had not been treated for hypertension since that time. After her stroke, she spent 3 weeks in an acute care hospital, followed by 5 weeks in an inpatient rehabilitation setting. She was discharged to her home and received several weeks of outpatient rehabilitation. She reported no other medical conditions. She resided in a rural environment in a single-story home with her husband, 1 young adult daughter, and 1 teenaged daughter. She had returned to driving and to working as a bookkeeper 20 to 30 hours per week approximately 6 months following her stroke.

She reported feeling off balance and occasionally stumbled while walking on uneven terrain. She had not fallen since being discharged from rehabilitation. She could perform all basic self-care activities independently. She had returned to performing most household duties but reported substantial fatigue at times and the need for frequent rests. She reported that grocery shopping was especially fatiguing. Her Fugl-Meyer Sensorimotor Assessment scores. She had not received physical therapy or occupational therapy more than 1 year before the start of our study. She performed a home exercise program that included standing balance and left lower-extremity weight-bearing activities or walked approximately 0.8 kg (0.5 mile) every day.

Subject 3.

Subject 3 was a 59-year-old woman who had a left CVA resulting in right hemiparesis 4.25 years before the start of our study. She had been diagnosed with cerebrovasculitis 5 years ago, after sustaining a right CVA that led to mild left hemiparesis. Her medical history included having fibromyalgia, type 2 diabetes, pulmonary fibrosis, hypertension, congenital absence of the left internal carotid artery, depression, and anxiety. Following the left CVA, she spent several weeks in an acute care facility and then had inpatient rehabilitation. She was discharged to her home where she resided with her husband. She received home health services, including those from a nurse, a home health aide, a physical therapist, and an occupational therapist. She had 2 episodes of care consisting of outpatient physical therapy and occupational therapy after receiving median, ulnar, and tibial nerve blocks and botulinum toxin injections in the gastrocnemius, soleus, posterior tibialis, and flexor digitorum longus muscles to correct an equinovarus deformity and to improve her mobility and activities of daily living (ADL). These therapeutic interventions occurred approximately 1 to 2 years before the initiation of our study.

At the time of our study, subject 3 was divorced and lived in an assisted living facility. She had 2 adult children from a previous marriage. Before her stroke, she had worked as a clerk and a cake decorator. She had also played the organ for church services and as a hobby before the stroke. Most recently, she played the organ one-handed, created computer greeting cards, and attended support groups, activities, and outings organized at her assisted-living facility. She was discharged from outpatient physical therapy approximately 1 month before the start of our study. She required minimal assistance for climbing up to 14 steps and used one railing. She was independent in bed mobility and transfers using bed rails. Her primary mode of indoor locomotion was a manual wheelchair that she propelled with her left extremities. She used a power scooter for long distances outside the facility. She required assistance for lower-extremity dressing and for showering, but she was independent in all other basic self-care activities. She reported difficulty with problem solving and concentration and stated that she had blurred vision. She said she had a fear of falling, but had not fallen since her most recent stroke. Her Fugl-Meyer Sensorimotor Assessment scores. She exhibited moderate to severe resistance to passive movement in all joints of the right extremities. Before our study was initiated, she did daily passive and active-assistive range-of-motion activities with a certified nursing assistant and weekly active-assistive range-of-motion activities in a therapeutic pool with a certified nursing assistant. She also walked 22.5 to 30 m (75–100 ft) each day independently.

Subject 4.

Subject 4 was a 61-year-old woman who had a left CVA 9 months before the start of our study, which resulted in right hemiparesis, nonfluent expressive aphasia, mild receptive aphasia, and mild apraxia. She had 2 left CVAs at 12 months and 13 months prior to this latest CVA that left her with a mild right hemiparesis. Following her most recent stroke, she spent several weeks in acute care and inpatient rehabilitation before being discharged to her home. She was independent in self-care activities and mobility. Before her initial strokes, she had been employed as an assembly-line worker and enjoyed outdoor recreation, including biking. After her first 2 strokes, she had returned to driving and biking, but she was unable to return to work. She was an active volunteer at the local hospital. Since the most recent stroke, she had returned to driving, but had been unable to return to biking or volunteer work.

She was an active member of Al-Anon and attended therapeutic recreational activities every other week. She had been divorced for several years and lived in a suburban single-story home with her adult son who was developmentally disabled. She was independent in all basic self-care activities; however, she reported that all self-care and household tasks took a very long time to complete and were very fatiguing. She said she felt unsteady while walking on uneven terrain and walked slowly. She had fallen once in the year before our study without sustaining a serious injury. Before the initiation of our study, she had not received physical therapy or occupational therapy for 5 months. She said she did not have a routine exercise program, but she did take leisurely walks 3 times per week for approximately 0.8 to 1.6 km (0.5–1 mile).

Procedure

An interview and examination were conducted with each subject. Demographic and descriptive information was obtained. Subjects were asked questions regarding their medical and social history and level of physical activity. To determine each subject's level of physical and cognitive impairment, testing consisting of the Fugl-Meyer Sensorimotor Assessment46 and the Folstein Mini-Mental State Examination47 was performed. The interviews and initial physical and cognitive examinations were conducted by a physical therapist with 17 years of clinical experience (JVB).

A physical therapist assistant (HM) and a physical therapist (SC) collected data on the primary outcome variables throughout the study. They conducted baseline testing on each subject after the subjects were accepted into our study and before their participation in the yoga exercise program, and they conducted testing each week during the intervention phase and at the completion of the intervention phase. Multiple baseline tests were conducted once a week for each subject at home. Primary outcome data were collected during the baseline phase for 5 weeks for subject 1, for 4 weeks for subject 2, for 7 weeks for subject 3, and for 6 weeks for subject 4. Because subjects became available at different times and had some limitations on how long they were able to be involved in the study, we determined the length of these baseline periods before our study began. Subjects were assigned baseline periods from the shortest to the longest in the order they began the study. At the completion of the baseline phase, each subject participated in an 8-week intervention phase during which the primary outcome data were collected weekly.

Tests and Measures

The primary outcome variables were balance (Berg Balance Scale [BBS]48) and timed mobility (Timed Movement Battery [TMB]49). A secondary outcome variable was perceived quality of life (Stroke Impact Scale [SIS] Version 2.050). These variables were selected to reflect areas of known difficulty in this population. Balance has been found to be the most important factor associated with the ability to perform basic mobility in people with hemiparesis secondary to a stroke.51 Only a small percentage of people who have had a stroke achieve the efficiency and skill needed for community ambulation.52 In addition, many people who survive a stroke report that they have an impaired health status4 and that they have difficulty engaging in recreational activities or social interactions.53Overall, our goal in selecting outcome measures was to include relevant tests that could be reliably and accurately administered and that were likely to detect possible changes in performance over time. We chose more than one outcome variable because we wanted to assess replication of the effects of the yoga intervention across both subjects and behaviors.54

The BBS48 consists of 14 items that require a person to maintain or assume positions of varying difficulty. The ability to perform each task is graded from 0 to 4, with a total possible score of 56.48 Intrarater and interrater reliability of BBS scores were found to be what we would consider excellent (intraclass correlation coefficient [ICC]=.97 and.98) in a combined group of 113 elderly subjects (mean age=83.5 years, SD=5.3) and 70 subjects (mean age=71.6 years, SD=10.1) who had had a stroke.55 Strong correlations have been reported between BBS scores and both Barthel Index of Activities of Daily Living scores (r=.87–.93) and Fugl-Meyer Sensorimotor Assessment scores (r=.70–.82) over a 12-week period in 60 subjects with stroke, substantiating the construct validity of data obtained with this instrument in people who have had a stroke.56 Stevenson57 has reported that a change of ±6 points on the BBS is necessary to be 90 per cent confident that a clinically meaningful change has occurred in people who have had a stroke. The TMB49 is designed to measure mobility and consists of 11 movement tasks performed at 2 speeds, self-selected (SS) and maximum movement (MM). The time for each of the movement tasks has been reported to have what we would again consider excellent intrarater reliability (ICC=.998–.999) and interrater reliability (ICC=.87–.999) in a group of 20 frail elderly subjects (mean age=81.2 years, SD=6.44, range=69–94), which included people who had had a stroke.58The TMB scores demonstrated moderate to high correlations in 30 community-dwelling subjects (mean age=77.5 years, SD=7.0, range=65–92) with scores on an 18-item ADL/instrumental activities of daily living (IADL) scale (rs=.84 [SS],.84 [MM]), BBS scores (rs=-.83 [SS], -.80 [MM]), Barthel Index of Activities of Daily Living scores (rs=-.73 [SS], -.67 [MM]), and Timed Up & Go Test values (r=.89 [SS],.79 [MM]), supporting the construct and concurrent validity in community-dwelling elderly people with and without difficulty in ADL.49 The validity of data obtained with the TMB has not been reported for people who have had strokes. It is not known how much change in the TMB scores reflect a genuine and meaningful change in performance.

Seven movement tasks were timed with subject 3, 8 movement tasks were timed with subject 1, and all 11 movement tasks were timed with subjects 2 and 4. All 11 movement tasks were not used with subjects 1 and 3 because of physical or environmental constraints. Subjects 1 and 3 were unable to perform the floor-stand task without assistance. Subject 1 did not have more than 2 steps in his home to perform up-and-down-steps tasks. Subject 3 also was unable to step over a 15-cm (6-in) obstacle or perform up-and-down-steps tasks without assistance. Each movement task was timed at both SS and MM speeds. The difference between the SS and MM scores indicates the reserve speed (RS), which is considered a capacity measure and is defined as the ability to safely perform activities at speeds faster than usual. Reserve speed may be an important measure of how people can adapt to the various temporal demands in the environment necessary for efficient community mobility49 and was therefore included as a measure in our study.

For all subjects, perceived quality of life was measured using the SIS Version 2.050 3 times: at baseline testing, just before the intervention period, and after the intervention period. The SIS was administered to all subjects by the primary author (JVB). The SIS is a stroke-specific quality-of-life instrument administered by direct interview, and it includes 64 items within 8 domains. There are 4 physical domains (strength, hand function, mobility, and ADL/IADL) as well as emotion, communication, memory, and participation domains. The subject also rates perceived percentage of recovery on a visual analog scale. Intraclass correlation coefficients for test-retest reliability of the scores for all domains have been shown to be high (ICC=.70–.92), except for the emotion domain (ICC=.57) in 25 subjects with mild to moderate stroke.50

Validity of the SIS scores was examined by comparing the SIS scores with scores obtained with existing stroke outcome measures (Fugl-Meyer Sensorimotor Assessment, Functional Independence Measure, Barthel Index of Activities of Daily Living, Medical Outcomes Study 36-Item Short-Form Health Survey [SF-36], Geriatric Depression Scale, Instrumental Activities of Daily Living Scale, Duke Mobility Scale, National Institutes of Health Stroke Scale, and Folstein Mini-Mental State Examination). The correlations were what we consider moderate to strong (ICC=.44–.84) in people who had had a mild to moderate stroke and who were in the acute phase of recovery (1–6 months after a stroke).50 Scores for the SIS domains appear responsive to change during recovery 1 to 6 months after a stroke.50 According to Duncan and co-workers,50 a change of SIS domain scores of at least 10 points represents a clinically meaningful change in perceived quality of life.

RELIABILITY TESTING OF TESTS AND MEASURES

Before the study was initiated, reliability testing of the primary outcome measures as we used them in our study was done between the primary author and the 2 data collectors. Three subjects who had had a stroke were simultaneously rated by 3 raters on the BBS and TMB tasks. Reliability was determined by calculating the percentage of exact agreements for the scores on the BBS items and by agreement within 0.2 second on the TMB scores. Agreement across the individual BBS scores averaged 89 per cent, and agreement for the TMB SS and MM scores averaged 64 per cent and 61 per cent, respectively, across these 3 subjects. Additional protocol clarification and education of the raters regarding specific timing endpoints for the TMB walking tasks and timed tasks of the BBS improved the level of agreement with an additional subject to 93 per cent for the BBS items and 100 per cent agreement (±0.2 second) for both the TMB SS and MM individual task scores.

Data Analysis

Data were visually analyzed to determine stability and trends in the baseline and intervention phases. We used Ottenbacher's suggestion that the baseline should be considered stable if 80 per cent to 90 per cent of the data points in the baseline phase fall within 15 per cent of the mean.54 Because some authors62 have argued that visual analysis alone may not be a reliable and accurate method for supporting clinical decisions, we used the 2-standard-deviation–band method to determine if changes occurred in balance and timed mobility between the baseline and intervention phases for each subject. We chose the 2-standard-deviation band–method over the split-middle method because the variability of some of the baseline data and because some subjects did not show an obvious baseline trend. According to Ottenbacher,54 the 2 advantages of the 2-standard-deviation-band method are that it can be used with a small (less than 10) number of data points in the baseline, and it can be applied to baseline data that are fluctuating. With the 2-standard-deviation-band method, fluctuations in baseline data lead to a larger standard-deviation band that is used for comparison to performance during the intervention phase; an overall larger change in performance then is required to conclude that a genuine change in performance has occurred.54

Two consecutive data points beyond the 2-standard-deviation band were used to determine whether there was a change for the BBS and TMB data.62 We considered a clinically meaningful change in performance of the BBS to be present if the BBS changed by at least 6 points.

RESULTS

Berg Balance Scale

Visual analysis of the BBS data revealed some variability in baseline scores for all subjects. Only subjects 1 and 3, however, demonstrated unstable baselines according to Ottenbacher's criteria.40 The results of the data analysis for the primary outcome variables using the 2-standard-deviation–band method are summarized. Individual data trends for the BBS scores for all subjects. For 3 of the 4 subjects (subjects 2, 3, and 4), there was an improvement in BBS scores in the intervention phase with at least 2 consecutive data points above the 2-standard–deviation band. Only subjects 3 and 4, however, demonstrated what we consider clinically meaningful changes in balance performance.

Timed Movement Battery

Visual analysis of the TMB data revealed some variability in baseline scores for all subjects. Unstable baselines occurred in subject 1's TMB SS scores, in subject 3's TMB SS and MM scores, and in subject 4's TMB MM scores. The results of the data analysis for all subjects using the 2-standard-deviation–band method are summarized. Individual trends in TMB data for each subject. Using the 2-standard-deviation-band method, 3 of 4 subjects improved on total TMB SS scores, whereas only 1 subject improved on the total TMB MM scores. There was no difference in TMB RS scores between the 2 phases for any subject. Subjects demonstrated variability in the individual TMB tasks that improved during the intervention phase, with subjects 1 and 2 demonstrating improvements in the greatest number of movements at SS speed and subject 2 demonstrating the greatest number of improvements in MM speed tasks. Subject 3 demonstrated no difference in performance of any TMB SS or MM speed task.

Stroke Impact Scale, Version 2.0

The SIS scores for all subjects. Subject 1 demonstrated what we considered meaningful improvement in the physical, emotion, and participation domains between preintervention and postintervention scores. Subject 2 demonstrated what we define as meaningful improvement in scores for all domains between prebaseline and preintervention scores and further improvement between the preintervention and postintervention scores in the physical and memory domains. Subject 3 demonstrated meaningful improvement between prebaseline and preintervention scores and between preintervention and postintervention scores in the communication, emotional, and social participation domains, but not in the physical or memory domains. Subject 4 demonstrated meaningful improvement between the preintervention and postintervention scores in the memory, emotion, and participation domains.

DISCUSSION

The single-case experimental design can provide researchers with valuable information about people's response to an intervention and the characteristics of subjects that show beneficial results versus the characteristics of those who do not demonstrate such results. Traditional experimental designs (ie, one-group or control group pretest-posttest designs) deal with generalizations and often overlook an individual's characteristics. Although generalizations are necessary to understand outcomes within a specific population, we believe that this information is most helpful to the clinician when it can be used to understand or predict individual performance.62

All subjects in our study demonstrated some positive effect in the primary and secondary outcome variables. Not all of the subjects had similar responses to the yoga intervention, and there were several differences among the subjects that may have contributed to the variance in the results. Subject 1 had improvement in total TMB SS scores but not in the BBS or total TMB MM scores. Using the criteria suggested by Ottenbacher,54 however, the TMB SS baseline phase was not stable. Our confidence about whether there was really an improvement in TMB SS scores after the intervention phase would have been strengthened if a longer baseline period would have led to greater stability in baseline scores.

Subject 1 reported that he did not adhere to the daily independent yoga activities. Low adherence to home-based exercise protocols in older adults has been reported previously.63,64 Jette and co-workers65 reported an 89 per cent rate of adherence to a home-based exercise program among elderly people with the use of behavioral incentives to encourage adherence. The use of behavioral incentives may have improved adherence to the independent yoga activities.

Subject 2 demonstrated the greatest number of changes compared with the other subjects. The baseline BBS scores were considered to be stable; however, the scores were becoming greater at each test session. Improvements in BBS scores after the introduction of the yoga intervention met the criteria for change using the 2 standard-deviation-band method; however, in our opinion, the 2-point gain in BBS scores does not represent a clinically meaningful change. The results of the total TMB scores indicate there was an improvement in the speed of performing the mobility tasks at both SS and MM speeds.

Subject 2 reported consistent adherence to the daily independent yoga activities throughout our study. She demonstrated a commitment to self-improvement by committing to a daily exercise routine on her own after rehabilitation ended and before the initiation of our study. We believe this may explain the trend of improvements during the baseline phase. The total TMB RS score initially declined in the baseline phase, indicating less capacity to move faster than her usual speed. This appears to have happened primarily because the SS scores improved during the baseline phase, with little change in the MM scores during the baseline phase. During the intervention phase, the RS scores increased steadily back to the initial baseline level. There was approximately a 14-second improvement in both total SS and MM scores from the beginning of baseline testing to the end of the intervention. Subject 2 demonstrated a return to the initial RS score; however, she was performing the tasks at faster speeds.

Collectively, our data may suggest that subject 2 gained the capacity to move at faster than usual speeds. The SIS scores for subject 2 demonstrated improvement in all domains after the baseline phase, and the scores were unchanged or continued to improve after the intervention phase. These results appear to indicate that there was a perceived improvement across all domains before the introduction of the intervention. We cannot determine whether the attention given to her by the investigators, her desire for self-improvement, the yoga intervention, or some combination of these factors contributed to this perceived improvement.

Subject 3 did not show improvement in any movement task of the TMB. Among all subjects, she had the greatest number of impairments, comorbid conditions, and prescription medications. She also had the most limitations in mobility. Over the course of the intervention phase, she participated less in the asanas portion of the program because of increasing complaints of pain. She stated she feared getting into some of the more challenging yoga postures because of concerns that they might have increased her pain severity. She continued with all other less physically demanding aspects of the program, including performing portions of the daily independent yoga activities. During the expression/sharing segments of the program, she expressed emotional and spiritual issues of frustration, feelings of isolation, fear and uncertainty about her future, and questions concerning the meaning and purpose of her life. Emotional dysfunction has been strongly associated with health-related quality of life66 and limitations in physical functioning, work, and leisure pursuits in people after a stroke.4 Yoga therapy practitioners believe that acknowledgment and empathetic support given while a person expresses emotional and spiritual feelings may greatly facilitate healing of the person's body, mind, and spirit.20 Despite her limited participation in the asanas portion of the intervention, subject 3 demonstrated what we believe is a clinically meaningful improvement in BBS scores after the intervention. Perhaps daily participation in some of the yoga activities enhanced her attention and concentration and decreased her physical impairments enough to affect her postural stability and control while performing the BBS tasks. It would have been interesting to determine whether changes in her perception of overall physical functioning and measures of mobility would have improved with a longer duration of the yoga intervention.

Subject 4 reported that she did not adhere to the independent yoga exercise program. Because of her aphasia, it was difficult to determine if she understood the instructions for the independent yoga activities even though demonstration was used and illustrations were provided. She indicated that she understood what to do, but she did not do the activities routinely because of time constraints and fatigue from performing daily household chores and going on frequent social outings. Her aphasia did not appear to hinder her participation in the physical segment of the yoga intervention. Her ability to verbally participate in the sharing segments, however, was limited. We found it difficult to ascertain whether she understood or received benefit from the educational segments or body awareness activities, because she was unable to express her experiences or discuss how she incorporated the yoga concepts into her daily life.

Despite the limitations imposed by her communication deficits, subject 4 showed what we consider to be a clinically meaningful improvement in balance. She was able to participate fully in the asanas portions of the program in the presence and guidance of the yoga-therapy teacher. These results appear consistent with the results of other investigations into the effects of various exercise training programs on people with long-standing poststroke hemiparesis.7,11 The results of the SIS appear to indicate meaningful improvement in subject 4's perception of memory, emotion, and social participation after the yoga intervention. The scores for the physical domain showed very little change after both the baseline and intervention phases. We question the interpretation of the SIS results with this subject, because the SIS has not been tested with people with communication difficulties.50

Overall, our results suggest that yoga may be beneficial for people with chronic poststroke hemiparesis, but further investigation is warranted. Our data suggest that the BBS may not be sensitive to detect changes that may occur in some people with high-level balance deficits, a finding previously reported by other authors.67 For example, subject 2's mean BBS baseline score was 4 points from the maximum possible score before the intervention began. In future studies, we recommend that measures sensitive to changes in postural stability, such as the Dynamic Gait Index41 or measures of postural sway, be used. In contrast, we believe the TMB appears to be an appropriate measure of timed mobility for this patient population, but this does not provide information about the factors that may be influencing speed of movement. In addition, no information is available to determine what are clinically meaningful changes in TMB scores. Our recommendation for future investigations is to include additional impairment measures to clarify the relationship between changes in impairments and changes in speed of performing movement tasks to be able to determine the effects of yoga on flexibility, muscle force, endurance, and motor function in people with chronic poststroke hemipáresis.

YOGA AND MINDFULNESS FOR A HEALTHY HEART?

Many studies report the benefits of using relaxation techniques, such as yoga, to work away anxiety, stress, and even depression and pain. However, few researchers also have looked for improvements in overall well-being or for changes in physiological markers for a specific disease. Until now. Cleveland Clinic's Joan Fox, PhD, and Thomas Morledge, MD, recently joined forces to do just that. Together, they have delved further into the subject of mind over matter to better understand whether and how yoga and a practice called mindfulness positively affect cardiovascular health.

"Studies show that 70 to 80 percent of all chronic disease, such as cardiovascular disease, is caused by lifestyle. Thus, the potential for improving health and decreasing health-care costs is enormous," says Dr. Fox, who is with the Department of Molecular Cardiology, the Robert and Suzanne Tomsich Department of Cardiovascular Medicine, and Center for Integrative Medicine. Her co-investigator, Dr. Morledge, is with the Wellness Institute's Center for Integrative Medicine.

The duo set out to study the effectiveness of regularly practicing yoga or mindfulness in decreasing negative emotions and increasing positive emotions — unique to their research — and in modulating some of the physiological pathways that may lead to the development of cardiovascular disease. Sixty-two individuals with moderate cardiovascular risk were enrolled in the study. They were randomly assigned to one of three groups: One that practiced yoga postures, meditation and breathing exercises; a second that used mindfulness — a central teaching of Buddhist meditation described as a calm awareness of one's body functions, feelings, consciousness, etc. — including discussion of concepts of the practice, various mindfulness meditations, relaxation practices and some yoga; and a control group, whose sessions were based on those of a typical conventional stress-reduction program, such as muscle relaxation exercises, lectures on health and wellness, and stretching exercises as recommended by the American Heart Association. All groups were asked to practice at home daily for 24 weeks, as well as meeting weekly for the first 12 weeks. About 75 percent completed the 12 weeks and 60 percent the 24 weeks. Negative emotions such as anxiety, depression and psychological stress were assessed using validated questionnaires. Questionnaires also were used to assess changes in emotional and spiritual well-being. Sympathetic nervous system activity was assessed by blood pressure, heart rate and heart rate variability recordings.

Another unique feature of the study involved collecting blood and urine samples to measure the concentration of inflammatory markers, or molecules produced by immune cells that are thought to contribute to the damage to the vessel wall that ends up in atherosclerotic lesions.

> "Our preliminary analyses suggests that all three groups received benefits in terms of decreased scores on questionnaires that assess negative emotions such as stress, anxiety and depression and also increased scores on well-being questionnaires," Dr. Fox says. "Although the control group showed improvements in these scores, the improvements in the yoga and mindfulness groups were significantly greater than those for the control group."

Most of the physiological outcome data has yet to be analyzed, although preliminary data for one of the inflammatory markers shows a significantly greater decrease in the mindfulness group compared to the control group.

YOGA AND PSYCHOTHERAPY

Yoga is compatible with other approaches and can be combined with them, as described e.g. by Lohman (1999). The principles of modern psychotherapy and traditional Indian medicine (Ayurveda) overlap. In fact Satvavajaya or psychotherapy is one of three principal categories of treatment approaches as described in Ayurvedic classics (Nespor and Singh 1986). The classical Satvavajaya is based on three principles:

1. Replacement of emotions (an undesirable emotion can be replaced or neutralized by other incompatible emotion),
2. Assurances,
3. Psychological shock.

The author had an opportunity to observe an experienced professor of ayurveda performing an exemplary psychotherapeutic sessions in English with his patients. He used empathy and unconditional positive regard, as many Western psychotherapists would. The replacement of emotions took place by gently switching emotions e.g. from the mother-in-law (anger) to children (love). He also used reframing (a negative event was presented in a more positive way), and employed various stories and metaphors that directly or indirectly related to patients' problems and possible solutions. Such an approach was used e.g. by M. H. Erickson in the West.

ADVANTAGES OF YOGA

There are many relevant reasons why addicted people should practice yoga.

- Stress, anxiety and depression relieving effects of yoga (e. g. Michalsen et al. 2005, Pilkingtona et al. 2005).
- Safer social network. According to the author's experience yoga-minded people are less prone to addictive behaviour.
- Yoga enables safe management of some psychosomatic problems such as insomnia, headaches, and some painful problems. It may be possible in this way to avoid addictive analgesic or sedative drugs (Goyeche 1979).
- In the author's experience, yoga and relaxation, as the part of a complex treatment programme, can counterbalance less pleasant aspects of treatment, strengthen therapeutic relationship, and decrease the number of patients leaving the programme prematurely (Nespor and Frouzova 1985).
- Yoga and meditation develop and emphasize self-awareness, which is important in many ways. It is a common experience that sufficient self-awareness is required e.g. for early identification of internal or external clues triggering craving for alcohol or drugs.
- Yoga compensates for long sitting during psychotherapy. In-patients are frequently obliged to sit during psychotherapeutic activities for up to 4.5 hours. This can prove tiring and uncomfortable. Yogic practices, especially those with the spine in the horizontal posture such as "cat" or marjariasana variations are useful to counterbalance this.
- The author presumes that yoga also enhances spirituality. The term spirituality, however esoteric it may look, has become the serious topic of medical research. In September 2006 the Database of American National Library of Medicine contained 2496 references to the search word "spirituality". Lower occurrence of daily smoking in spiritually minded people has been identified in the Czech population (17.6 per cent in those believing in God and 28.6 per cent in those not believing) (Sovinova et al. 2006). Among substance-dependent individuals, higher levels of religious faith and spirituality is associated with a more optimistic life orientation, greater perceived social support, higher resilience to stress, and lower levels of anxiety (Pardini et al.. 2003).

Some Problems with Yoga

When the author was 26 years old he visited a noted Czech professor to whom he suggested that all his addicted patients could be cured by means of yoga. Having been offered the opportunity to test the claims the author found that it was not quite so easy; and that there were some problems, such as:

- Long-term compliance of patients (the enthusiasm for yoga of most patients was much less than the author expected).

- Systemic (domestic) interactions (e.g. lack of understanding of yoga by family members).
- Practical problems (for some patients it was difficult to find time and place to practice).
- The trainees were competitive and not patient enough.
- The need of a qualified teacher to modify the practice according to the needs of an individual. As somebody said: "An individual should not adapt to yoga, not yoga should adapt to him." It is especially important in physically or mentally challenged people.

Despite these problems, the author still believes that yoga is useful for this patient population. The aim of this paper is to investigate the above mentioned problems in more detail.

Formal sessions of yoga

The yoga protocol has been described in a previous paper (Nespor 2000). The structure of two typical 30 to 45 minute sessions is outlined below. Regardless of the duration, the lesson is usually divided into three roughly equal thirds. This scheme is not rigid and can be modified according to the situation.

- 1st third: Physical exercises of Yoga
- 2nd third: Full yoga breath and/or some simple pranayama and some short story symbolically related to common patients' problems.
- 3rd third: Relaxation with sankalpa (resolve)

Most of the following practices are described according to Satyananda (1996).

An example of a yoga session (30 minutes)

Marjariasana (Cat stretch pose): Instructions: Place the hands flat on the floor beneath the shoulders with the fingers facing forward. Inhale while raising the head and lowering the spine and create a hollow between your shoulder blades. Exhale while lowering the head and stretching the spine upward. The trainees may be instructed to emphasize the movement of the thoracic spine while inhaling, and the lumbar spine while exhaling.

Vyaghrasana (Tiger's stretch): This usually commences from the marjariasana (cat's pose) which is for trainees easy enough. Instructions: While inhaling straighten the right leg, stretching it up and back. Bend the right knee and point the toes toward the head. Look up and try to touch the toes to the back of the head. Hold the breath for a few seconds in this position. While exhaling, straighten the right leg, bend the knee and swing the leg under the hips. At the same time arch the back up and bend the head down. The right foot should not touch the floor. Press the knee against the chest and, if possible, touch the nose to the knee. Fix the eyes on the knee for few seconds while holding the breath out. With the next inhalation start to repeat these movements 5 times or so. Then repeat it with the left leg. Shashankasana (Hare pose): This is also started from marjariasana. Instructions: While exhaling move downward and back so that the head and the arms rest on the floor in front of the knees. If you want to relax, just observe your natural nasal breath As you breathe deeply be aware of your abdomen. After a while return back to marjariasana.

Sphinx asana and its variations: Instructions: Lie on the stomach. Bend the arms and place the forearms on the floor with the palms facing downward. The upper arms are vertical. Raise the head but relax all the muscles which are not necessary to maintain correct pose. The possible variations include hitting one's buttocks with the heels, gentle rotations of the head and spine. Backward bending should be increased during inhalation and relaxed during exhalation.

Jyestikasana: Instructions: Lie down on your belly with the legs straight and the forehead resting on the fingers, with both hands interlocked, palms facing up. Be aware of your body and let it relax. Then observe your breath. Supta udarakarshanasana (sleeping abdominal stretch pose or supine rotation with the knee bend): Lie on your back, bend the knees and place soles flat on the ground in front of the buttocks. Keep the knees and feet together. Interlock the fingers of both hands and place the palms under the back of the head. While breathing out slowly lower the legs to the right. The knees move down to the floor. At the same time move the head in the opposite direction. Hold the breath in final position for few seconds. While breathing in move the legs back to the upright position. Repeat to the opposite direction. Repeat 5 times.

Spontaneous abdominal breathing: I usually let the trainees to be aware of their spontaneous abdominal breathing on the back with the legs bent. Only after that we practice deep abdominal breathing, as something based on spontaneous abdominal breathing. Eventually we also add thoracic and clavicular breathing.

Full Yoga Breath

Stories symbolically related to common patients' problems. An example of a story: Swami Satyananda often received visitors who sought his advice in spiritual or personal matters. Some visitors were satisfied with his advice but some were not. They objected "Yes, but it can be done so and so."

> "It is also good," replied usually Swami Satyananda. A disciple once asked Swamiji doubtfully: "Is it really also good?"
>
> "Of course," replied Swamiji. "Karma of some people does not allow them to accept good advice. They have to commit mistakes, to suffer and to learn through their painful experiences. That is why it is also good."

This story is liberating. It shows that even our mistakes can be instrumental to our ultimate awakening. In the same time it shows that it is better to avoid these mistakes and related suffering. Brief yoga nidra or yogic relaxation. During yoga nidra, I tend to offer to the trainees three sets of images they can choose from. Images for vata types (air and ether prevail; these people need grounding, stability, the feeling of safety): You are looking at the quiet surface of a lake. Its firm reliable banks are full of flowers whose fragrance is sweet. Somebody at the bank is singing a calming, sweet song. Images for pitta types (fire and water prevails; they need calmness and detachment): You are in rocky maintains at night. You see a pine, rooted firmly in the stony soil. There is plenty of free space around. Far away above your head Moon and stars spill their silver light all around. You feel pleasant breeze bringing to you cool fragrance of jasmine from some distant valley. Somebody is playing there a flute and its melody is detached and calm. Images for kapha types (earth and water prevails; these people need stimulation): You are looking at Sun high at sky.

It shines brightly and colours the clouds by its orange and yellow light. The clouds move to the horizon. You smell sharp fragrance of eucalypt. Somebody is playing fast and skilfully a drum far away. Alternative symbolic imagery for everybody: You see a quiet surface of a lake reflecting nature around it. Similarly your mind, calm and sober, perceives things as they are. Now see a river, mighty and moving on and on. Similarly you are able to overcome every obstacle if pursuing good and appropriate goals. Finally you see a strong, healthy pine tree with strong roots in the soil and its branches open to the sky. This tree is resistant against storms and winds. Similarly you are grounded in reality and in the same time open to positive spiritual influences. You are able to cope with all challenges in this way.

Namaste: Beforehand I usually explain that this mean „I bow to the highest in you which is the same as the highest in me." I found this simple practice very useful. Our patients need very much to learn to respect themselves and others. They like this practice.

An example of a yoga session (45 minutes)

Marjariasana (Cat) on forearms. This variant diverts blood from pelvic area which is useful after long sitting.

Vyaghrasana (Tiger's stretch)

Shashankasana (Hare pose):

Sarpasana (snake): Lie on the stomach, interlock the fingers and place them on top of the buttocks. Raise the head, neck and chest from the floor. Push the hands back and up. Squeeze the shoulder blades together and look forward. Hold for as long as comfortable. Then return to the starting position and relax the whole body. Tiryaka Bhunjangasana (twisting cobra).

Ardha shalabhasana (a variant of half locust pose): Lie on the stomach, legs are together and the forehead touches the floor. Stretch the arms above the head and place them and the chin on the floor. Simultaneously raise the stretched left leg, the head and right arm. Hold for as long as comfortable. Then lower the leg, head and arm. Repeat the same movement with the right leg and left arm. Jyestikasana: Lie down on your stomach with the legs straight and the forehead resting on the fingers of both hands interlocked and palms facing up. Be aware of your body and let it relax. Then observe your breath for a while.

Supta udarakarshanasana.

Spontaneous abdominal breathing and full yoga breath.

Seetkari. Cooling pranayamas seetkari and sheetali, according to Satyananda (1996) cool the body and the mind as well and decrease thirst. They are recommended in ayurveda especially for pitta (fire) personalities. Maybe they can also help to cope with craving for alcohol. The advantage of Seetkari compared with sheetali is, that seetkari can be performed in its mild form, inconspicuously, even during daily activities. Seetkari is practiced as follows: Hold the teeth lightly together and separate the lips. The tongue is passive in khechari mudra. Breathe slowly and deeply through the teeth. At the end of inhalation close the lips and keep the tongue where it is and breathe out slowly through the nose. Inconspicuous variant: Lips are separated very little and breathing is not as deep as during the normal practice of seetkari.

A story, yoga nidra and namaste.

Yoga Outside Formal Sessions

Beside formal practice of yoga, I frequently use the elements of yoga during other activities. E.g. we may practice a little at the end of psychotherapy workshops. It is especially useful after long sitting or when we have dealt with some difficult and heavy psychological material. This "miniyoga" is also helpful to deal with tiredness and boredom. It works not only in addicts. Once I gave a lecture to business people. When I arrived, I found them tired and bored. We exercised a little bit and their mood instantly changed. When these people gave their feedback to the organizers of the workshop, my lecture was considered the best. I suspect that it was because of what we did, and not because of what I said.

Some examples of "miniyoga"

Heavenly stretch or dynamic Tadasana

For our purposes I call it "Delights of abstinent life". Begin in standing position with the feet slightly apart. The weight of the body is equally distributed on both feet. Raise the arms over the head. Interlock the fingers and turn the palm upwards. Place the hands on the top of the head. Fix your eyes at the point on the wall slightly above the level of your head. Inhale and stretch the arms, shoulders and chest upward. Raise the heels coming up onto the toes. Stretch the body from the bottom. Hold the breath and the position for a few seconds. Lower the heels while breathing out and bring the hands to the top of the head. Practise 5 to 10 times.

Chopping the wood or Kashtha Takshanasana

For our purposes I call it "Hammering the pillars of abstinence". The only difference from the practice as it is described in Satyananda (1996) is that I do not practise in squatting position but in standing posture and bend the knees slightly while moving the hands down and exhaling. The full posture would be too difficult for most of my patients.

Wings

Begin in standing position with the feet slightly apart. Lift the arms sideways to the level of shoulders. While inhaling move the hands stretched backwards, and let the chest expand. While exhaling the stretched hands move to the front of the body so that the palms and fingers touch each and the head bow with the chin touching the chest at the end of exhalation. Practise 5 times or so. I usually add to this practice that the patients leave behind them all the problems which alcohol or drug abuse caused in the past, and move on to the better future.

Bow and Arrow (Akarna dhanurasana)

We practice as described in Satyananda (1996). Usually I ask the patients to target a positive aim in the external world when the right hand is pulling the bow-string, and an aim in the internal world when the left hand is pulling.

I am

Begin in standing position with the feet apart on distance of the width of the shoulders. During inhalation move stretched arms sideways. At the end of exhalation the palms are on the level of the head. During exhalation beat your chest gently with the fists and pronounce long "I". Repeat this once more and during next exhalation repeat in the same way "am". A variation: Instead of "I am", we laugh at all drug dealers and alcohol or gambling industry because they will get nothing from us in the future.

Hero

Step with the right foot askew forward a slight bend the right knee. Arch the back, expand the chest and push it forward. Clasp the hands and stay for a while breathing naturally. Repeat this with the other side. Those who try to overcome addiction are heroes. The first bravery is to acknowledge one's addiction; the second one is to cope with it and the third one to persist.

Tadasana (static)

Sometimes I use it instead of relaxation, if it is - not possible to lie down. At the end I often suggest: "You are standing in a firm, steady and relaxed manner now and you can stand so in your life as well."

Adding Colour to Aura

It is not a yogic practice. With the legs widely apart we pick up balls of colour energy from the well on the floor and improve with them our auras (yellow is intellect, green health, blue calmness and detachment, violet spirituality and abstinence, pink youthfulness, orange independence and rainbow gives beauty and strengthens immunity.

THE PROBLEM OF COMPLIANCE

As mentioned earlier, the main challenge when using yoga in substance dependent patients is the long-term regular practice outside the hospital. The aim of this paper is to identify possible barriers which hinder regular unsupervised practice and to consider the ways how these problems can be overcome.

MATERIAL AND METHODS

A questionnaire

We prepared an original questionnaire which was administered to in-patients and former in-patients. They were asked to answer a set of simple questions such as:

- How do your feel after yoga session?
- Do you intend to practice yoga outside the hospital?
- Are there any possible hindrances in regular yoga practice at home?
- If so, how these hindrances can be overcome?

Subjects

The subjects were:

- The group 53 current male in-patients treated for addictive diseases and 50 current female in-patients treated for the same problems. Their age was on the average 38.2 years (SD=11.8).
- The group of 44 former male in-patients treated for addictive diseases and 9 female former in-patients treated for the same problem. Their age was on the average 43.1 years (SD=12.7).

Results

Most patients felt after yoga session better or much better. That is why it is surprising that most of them do no intend to practice yoga regularly.

Former and current in-patients: Feelings after the yoga session during in-patient treatment (n=156, missing answers: 5)

- Much better: 47 (31.1 per cent of relevant answers)
- Better: 59 (39.1 per cent. of relevant answers)
- The same: 37 (24.5 per cent of relevant answers)

- Worse: 3 (2.0 per cent of relevant answers)
- Much worse: 2 (1.3 per cent of relevant answers)

How often in-patients intend to practice yoga at home (n=103, missing answers: 3)

- Not at all: 23 (23 per cent)
- Less than once a week: 19 (19 per cent)
- Once a week: 24 (24 per cent)
- 2 – 4 - times a week: 19 (9 per cent)
- 5- 6 - times a week: 5 (5 per cent)
- Daily: 7 (7 per cent)

How often former in-patients practice yoga at home (n=53, missing answers: 0)

- Not at all: 32 (64 per cent)
- Less than once a week: 5 (9.4 per cent)
- Once a week: 11 (20.1 per cent)
- 2 - 4x times a week: 3 (5.7 per cent)
- 5- 6x times a week: 0 (0 per cent)
- Daily: 2 (3.7 per cent)

The obstacles

The main obstacles included laziness (29), other interests and sports (14), lack of time (12), problems with privacy and housing (11), health limitations and age (9), problems related to family members and friends (8), lack of information (6), lack of interest (3) and that it is difficult to practice alone (3).

DISCUSSION

The feeling after a yoga session predictably improved in most patients. It is in accordance with our previous paper written many years ago (Nespor and Frouzova 1985). It is surprising that many patients, even if they feel better, do not intend to practice every day and they do not practice. I believe that the above mentioned obstacles are not specific to the people with addictive diseases. Many of these obstacles are relevant also to the general population of yoga trainees.

Regularity: Most patients like yoga and did not mention any obstacles to regular practice. Despite this, they do not intend to practice regularly in the future. Maybe it should be repeated more often that regular practice is one of the crucial factors of successful use of yoga in health management. Laziness and indolence: This most common obstacle it not easy to overcome. It may be useful if trainees are able to motivate themselves, e.g. to remind themselves that after investing some effort and inconvenience (such as getting up early) in yoga they will be rewarded by pleasant feelings afterwards.

Other interests, sports: Our aim is not to replace healthy and useful interests by yoga. But most of our patients have unhelpful hobbies which should be substituted. It may help to contemplate ways how their healthy interests can be accommodated with yoga or sometimes even integrated with yoga (e.g. mantra repetition during walking).

Lack of time: Time can be organized better. For example, yoga can be practiced instead of unnecessarily long sleep or even better instead of watching TV. A 2004 report estimates that young Americans aged 13-24 years watch nearly 14 hours of television a week (Brier 2004). 73.4 per cent of Czech population watched TV daily in 2005. The problem of lack of time has more specific context. Some addicted people want to pay their debts (both financial and moral) as soon as possible. Because of that they become exhausted. Their self-control deteriorates. Such life-style increases the risk of relapse. It is absolutely necessary for them to maintain balance between duties and rest. Yoga fits well into this. It is also possible to emphasize, that regular practice of yoga can increase productivity.

Family members, friends: It may be difficult to explain to relatives why one practices yoga, and a trainee may feel ashamed. This obstacle is mentioned frequently and may be also serious. The relatives, if possible, should be informed about yoga by a therapist. The aims of yoga in addicted people should be explained. Alternatively trainees should be encouraged to explain the reasons why they practice to their relatives themselves.

Privacy, housing: This may be a serious problem. It was much more often mentioned by current in-patients than the former in-patients. This can be explained by the excessive anxieties of in-patients regarding their future. Such apprehension decreased with continuing abstinence outside the hospital; beside this, the social situation of the people who abstain from alcohol usually radically improves. Possible solutions to the problems of privacy may be to practice silently early in the morning when other people sleep, information about yoga, its meaning and usefulness to family members may also help. There are also many practices which can be used inconspicuously (e.g. mantra) or outside home in parks, etc. It is also possible to include yoga practices into normal daily activities (relaxation during waiting, mantra or full yoga breath during walking etc.) sometimes.

Health problems, pain: Assurances can be given that carefully selected yoga practices are safe and helpful. Even very old or physically challenged people can benefit form suitable yogic practices. Lack of information: To assure that basic principles and practices are simple. To give the trainee addresses of yoga classes outside hospital. Trainees should be recommended practical books about yoga. It is difficult alone: Patients should be supplied with contact details of yoga classes or clubs that are willing to accept them. They may also attend our yoga class after their dismissal, but it may be rather complicated for them because these classes do not take place in the evenings.

Religion: It is possible to argue that yoga is compatible with any religion and that yoga is practiced by people of different confessions both in India and all over the world. This problem seemed to be negligible for most patients. Yoga may deepen the individual's religious and spiritual life. Unpleasant feelings: This objection appeared rarely. Yoga is usually perceived as pleasant. The reasons somebody may feel pain includes overstretching and competitiveness, lack of experience or lack of mental and physical flexibility.

It is not interesting: This objection was rare. I try to include interesting elements and colourful stories in the lessons. Commuting: This obstacle was mentioned only once. Perhaps emphasizing that the practice in private is most important and to enhance it by retreats etc. from time to time.

HEALTH AND EXERCISE SCIENCE PROGRAM

PROGRAM DESCRIPTION

The Health and Exercise Science Program at the Jefferson College of Health Sciences is a four-year, Bachelor of Science degree program. The blend of classroom, laboratory, and clinical components is designed to prepare students for careers in Health and Exercise Science and/or post-baccalaureate education.

A Bachelor of Science degree in Health and Exercise Science from Jefferson College of Health Sciences prepares graduates for careers in college, clinical, corporate, and commercial settings, including personal fitness consulting/ training, cardiopulmonary rehabilitation, hospital and/or corporate wellness, community health and obesity prevention, and industrial rehabilitation/ worksite fitness. Students enrolled in the program will have the flexibility to develop knowledge, skills, and abilities to pursue post-baccalaureate education in medicine, occupational or physical therapy, exercise science, public health or other graduate and/or professional allied health programs. Health and Exercise Science program graduates will be eligible to pursue certifications with the American College of Sports Medicine, National Strength and Conditioning Association and other organizations requiring a Bachelor's degree and clinical experience.

Program Philosophy

The educational philosophy of the HES program is based on the concepts of learner-centered teaching, experiential learning and academic excellence. The HES program features a complementary relationship between general education and professional studies, between academic and personal development, between service and individual growth, and between the JCHS campus and the larger community.

The overarching vision of HES is to help people establish and maintain physically active, healthy lifestyles. This includes helping people develop the essential beliefs, attitudes, knowledge, and skills associated with maintaining lifelong physical activity habits that promote individual responsibility toward optimal health and fitness. Additionally, and equally important, is helping people to develop collective efficacy, communities of learned citizens that value active living, are confidence in their ability to live actively, and are committed to our transformation to a physically active society. Physically active citizens behave in ways that recognize and support societal changes and policies aimed at building healthy, supportive environments that are conducive to the practice of safe, effective, and inclusive physical activity and health behaviors that are available to all people.

Program Mission

The mission of the Health and Exercise Science program is to provide an academic environment that will enable students to develop knowledge, skills, and abilities in the areas of health and exercise science. Through a focused curriculum, faculty-student interactions, clinical opportunities, and service learning, graduates of the Health and Exercise Science program will cultivate the competencies and proficiencies required for entry-level professional practice or continuation to graduate-level education.

Program Goals and Objectives

By the conclusion of the program of study, successful graduates will:

- Apply biophysical and behavioral theory and research from health and exercise science to critically analyze health, exercise, and fitness processes, behaviors, and outcomes.
- Demonstrate integration of health and exercise science scholarship into clinical practice through:
  - Assessment, design, and implementation of individual and group exercise programs and fitness activities for persons of all ages who are apparently healthy and those with controlled disease.
  - Application of skills in evaluating health behaviors and risk factors, conducting fitness assessments, writing appropriate exercise prescriptions, and motivating individuals to modify negative health habits and maintain positive lifestyle behaviors for health promotion.
- Demonstrate competence, professionalism, cultural sensitivity, and a commitment to life-long learning as a leader of health and fitness programs in college, clinical, corporate and/or commercial settings in which clients participate in health promoting and fitness-related activities.
- Develop knowledge, skills, and abilities requisite for post-baccalaureate education in health and exercise science, other medical/allied health fields, and/or professional certification/career placement.

- Complete minimally 500 hours of practical experience in supervised clinical exercise program settings.

Community Service Requirement

The Health and Exercise Science program believes in promoting the mission and vision of Jefferson College of Health Sciences both in the classroom as well as in the community. Part of that mission includes "holistic development of the individual" and "participation in the local and global community". Combining these two aspects of the College mission statement, the HES program requires that all full-time students enrolled in the HES program as of Fall 2012 complete a total of 10 hours of community service per semester of full-time enrollment.

Students will be expected to record, document, and verify their community service work before the designated semester deadlines. Failure to complete the required amount of community service work by this deadline will result in an administrative "hold" on the student's academic account until all community service work is satisfactorily completed and associated paperwork is submitted. Community service work is required to enhance academic learning and professional practice by applying knowledge gained in the classroom to a practical environment and/or providing an opportunity for students to learn new skills outside the classroom that supplement their overall experience as a student of Jefferson College of Health Sciences.

Technical Standards

The HES Program has adopted technical standards that HES graduates are expected to hold that align with those put forth by the American College of Sports Medicine (ACSM). These standards reflect reasonable expectations of the HES student's knowledge, skills, and abilities (KSAs) in eight content areas and what may be required of an ACSM Health/Fitness Instructor® or Exercise Specialist®. They are not all inclusive nor do they reflect what may be required for employment or post-baccalaureate education.

Technical Performance Standards

Successful graduates of the HES Program are expected to demonstrate the following KSAs in eight content areas:

EXERCISE & HUMAN BIOPHYSICAL SCIENCES

Functional Anatomy and Biomechanics

- Describe the basic structures of bone, skeletal muscle, and connective tissues.
- Describe the basic anatomy of the heart, cardiovasacular system, and respiratory system.

- Identify the major bones and muscles and their actions. Major muscles include, but not limited to: trapezius, pectoralis major, latissimus dorsi, biceps, triceps, abdominal, erector spinae, gluteus maximus, quadriceps, hamstrings and gastrocnemius.
- Define the following terms: supination, pronation, flexion, extension, adduction, abduction, hyperextension, rotation and circumduction.
- List and describe the types of joints in the body.
- Knowledge to describe the plane in which each muscle action occurs.
- Identify the interrelationships among centre of gravity, base of support, balance and stability.
- Describe the following abnormal curvatures of the spine: lordosis, scoliosis, kyphosis.
- Describe and demonstrate exercises designed to enhance muscular strength and/or endurance of specific major muscle groups.
- Describe and demonstrate exercises for enhancing musculoskeletal flexibility.
- Knowledge to describe the myostatic stretch reflex.
- Knowledge to identify the primary action and joint range of motion for each major muscle group.
- Describe the structure and nature of movement in the major joints of the body.
- Ability to locate the anatomic landmarks for palpation of peripheral pulses; locate the brachial artery and correctly place the cuff and stethoscope in position of blood pressure measurement.
- Ability to locate the common sites for measurement of skinfold thickness, skeletal diameters, girth measurements for estimation of body composition.
- Describe the biomechanical principles that underlie the performance of the following activities: walking, jogging, running, swimming, cycling, weight lifting, and carrying or moving objects.

Exercise Physiology

- Define aerobic and anaerobic metabolism.
- Identify the role of aerobic, anaerobic and ATP-PC systems in the performance of various physical activities.
- Define the following terms: ischemia, angina pectoris, tachycardia, bradychardia, myocardial infarction, cardiac output, stroke volume, lactic acid, oxygen consumption, hyperventilation, systolic blood pressure, diastolic blood pressure.
- Describe the roles of carbohydrates, fats, proteins as fuels for aerobic and anaerobic metabolism.
- Demonstrate an understanding of the components of fitness: cardiorespiratory fitness, muscular strength, muscular endurance, flexibility, body composition.

- Describe the normal cardiorespiratory responses to static and dynamic exercise in terms of heart rate, blood pressure and oxygen consumption.
- Describe how heart rate, blood pressure and oxygen responses change with adaptation to chronic exercise training and how men and women may differ in response.
- Knowledge of the physiological adaptations associated with strength training.
- Ability to identify and apply to both groups and individuals methods used to monitor exercise intensity, including heart rate and rating of perceived exertion.
- Identify the physiological principles related to warm up and cool down.
- Describe the common theories of muscle fatigue and delayed onset muscle soreness (DOMS).
- Knowledge of the physiological adaptations that occur at rest and during submaximal and maximal exercise following chronic aerobic and anaerobic training.
- Knowledge of the differences in cardiorespiratory response to acute graded exercise between conditioned and deconditioned individuals.
- Define the major components of motor fitness: agility, speed, balance, coordination, power.
- Knowledge of the structure of the skeletal muscle fiber and basic mechanism of contraction.
- Knowledge of the characteristics of fast and slow twitch muscle fibers.
- Knowledge of contraction of muscle in terms of the sliding filament theory
- Explain twitch, summation, and tetanus in terms of muscle contraction.
- Discuss the physiological principles involved in promoting gains in muscular strength and endurance.
- Knowledge to define muscle fatigue as it relates to task, intensity, duration and the accumulative effects of exercise.
- Demonstrate an understanding of the relationship between number of repetitions, intensity, number of sets, and rest with regard to strength training.
- Knowledge of the basic properties of cardiac muscle and the normal pathways of conduction in the heart.
- Describe the response of the following variables to steady state submaximal exercise and maximal exercise: heart rate, stroke volume, cardiac output, pulmonary ventilation, tidal volume, respiratory rate, arteriovenous difference.

- Knowledge of the differences in the cardiorespiratory responses to static exercise compared with dynamic exercise, including possible hazards and contraindications.
- Describe the blood pressure responses associated with exercise and changes in body position.
- Define and describe the implications of anaerobic threshold as it relates to physical conditioning programs and cardiovascular assessment.
- Knowledge of and ability to describe the physiological adaptations of the respiratory system that occur at rest and during submaximal and maximal exercise following chronic aerobic and anaerobic training.
- Describe how much each of the following differ from the normal condition: dyspnea, hypoxia, hypoventilation.
- Discuss the physiological basis of the major components of physical fitness: flexibility, cardiovascular fitness, muscular strength, muscular endurance, and body composition.
- Explain how the principle of specificity relates to the components of fitness.
- Explain the concept of detraining or reversibility of conditioning and its implications in fitness programs.
- Identify the physical and physiological signs of over overtraining and how to provide recommendations for these problems.
- Describe the physiologic and metabolic responses to exercise associated with chronic disease (e.g., heart disease, hypertension, diabetes mellitus, and pulmonary disease.

CLINICAL AND MEDICAL CONSIDERATIONS

Pathophysiology/Risk Factors

- Identify risk factors for coronary artery disease (CAD) and designate those that may be favorably modified by regular and appropriate physical activity habits.
- Define the following terms: total cholesterol, high density lipoprotein cholesterol (HDL-C), low density lipoprotein cholesterol (LDL-C), total cholesterol/high density lipoprotein cholesterol ratio, anemia and hypertension.
- Be familiar with the plasma cholesterol levels for various ages as recommended by the National Cholesterol Education Program.
- Knowledge of the risk factor concept of CAD and the influence of heredity and lifestyle on the development of CAD.
- Demonstrate an understanding of the pathophysiology of atherosclerosis and how this process is potentially influenced by physical activity.

- Ability to discuss in detail how lifestyle factors, including nutrition, physical activity and heredity influence lipid and lipoprotein profiles.
- Identify the following cardiovascular risk factors or conditions which may require consultation with medical personnel prior to participation in testing or training, including inappropriate changes in resting or exercise heart rate and blood pressure, new onset discomfort in chest, neck, shoulder or arm, changes in the pattern of discomfort during rest or exercise, fainting or dizzy spells and claudication.
- Identify the following respiratory risk factors which may require consultation with medical professionals prior to participation in testing or training, including, asthma, exercise induced asthma, extreme breathlessness at rest, mild exertion or during sleep, bronchitis, emphysema.
- Identify the following metabolic risk factors which may require consultation with medical professionals prior to participation in testing or training including bodyweight more than 20 per cent above optimal, BMI > 30, thyroid disease, diabetes or glucose intolerance, hypoglycemia.
- Identify the following musculoskeletal risk factors or conditions which may require consultation with medical professionals prior to participation in testing or training including: osteoarthritis, osteoporosis, tendonitis, rheumatoid arthritis, acute or chronic back pain.

Screening, Health Appraisal and Fitness Testing

- Knowledge of the importance of a heath/medical history.
- Knowledge of the value of a medical clearance prior to exercise participation.
- Skill to measure pulse rate accurately both at rest and during exercise.
- Ability to obtain a health history and risk appraisal that includes past and present medical history, family history or CAD, orthopedic limitations, prescribed medications, activity patterns, nutritional habits, stress and anxiety levels, smoking and use of alcohol.
- Describe the categories of participants who should receive medical clearance prior to administration of an exercise test or participation in an exercise program.
- Identify relative and absolute contraindications to exercise testing or participation.
- Discuss the limitations of informed consent and medical clearances prior to exercise testing.

- Ability to obtain informed consent.
- Explain the purpose and procedures for monitoring clients prior to, during, and after cardiorespiratory fitness testing.
- Demonstrate the ability to instruct participants in the use of equipment and test procedures.
- Ability to describe the purpose or testing, select and appropriate submaximal or maximal protocol and conduct an assessment of cardiovascular fitness on the cycle or the treadmill.
- Demonstrate the ability to measure heart rate, blood pressure and RPE accurately at rest and during exercise according to established guidelines.
- Ability to locate and measure skinfold sites and girth measurements used for estimating body composition.
- Ability to describe the purpose of testing, select appropriate protocols and conduct assessments of muscular strength, muscular endurance, and flexibility assessment.
- Skill in various techniques of assessing body composition.
- Demonstrate various techniques of assessing body composition and discuss the advantages/disadvantages and limitations of the various techniques.
- Ability to interpret information obtained from the cardiorespiratory fitness test and the muscular strength and endurance, flexibility and body composition assessments for apparently healthy individuals and those with stable disease.
- Identify appropriate criteria for terminating a fitness evaluation and demonstrate proper procedures to be followed after discontinuing such a test.
- Discuss modification of protocols and procedures for cardiorespiratory fitness tests in children, adolescents, and older adults.
- Knowledge of common drugs from each of the following classes of medications and describe the principle action and the effects on exercise testing and prescription: Antianginals, Antihypertensives, Antiarrhytmics, Bronchodolators, Hypoglycemics, Psychotropics, Vasodilators.
- Ability to identify the effects of the following substances on exercise response: antihistamines, tranquilizers, alcohol, diet pills, cold tablets, caffeine, and nicotine.
- Skill in techniques for calibration of a cycle ergometer and a motor-driven treadmill.

HUMAN DEVELOPMENT AND AGING

- List the benefits and risks associated with exercise training in pre- and post pubescent youth.

- Identify benefits and precautions associated with resistance and endurance training in the older adult.
- Describe the changes that occur in maturation from childhood to older adulthood for the following areas: skeletal muscle, bone structure, reaction and movement time, coordination, tolerance to hot and cold environments, maximal oxygen consumption, strength, flexibility, body composition, resting and maximal heart rate, resting and maximal blood pressure.
- Ability to modify cardiovascular and resistance exercises based on age and physical condition.
- Demonstrate and understand the effect of the aging process on the muscular skeletal and cardiovascular structure and function at rest, during exercise and during recovery.
- Characterize the differences in the development of an exercise prescription for children, adolescents and older participants.
- Describe the unique adaptations to exercise training in children, adolescents and older participants with regard to strength, functional capacity, and motor skills.
- Describe common orthopedic and cardiovascular considerations of older participants and what modifications in exercise prescription are indicated.
- Describe specific leadership techniques that might be used for participants of all ages.

PSYCHOLOGY, HUMAN BEHAVIOR AND COUNSELING

- Ability to identify and define at least five behavioral strategies to enhance exercise and health behavior change (i.e. reinforcement, goal setting, social support).
- Ability to list and define five important elements that should be included in each counseling session.
- Knowledge of specific techniques to enhance motivation (e.g., posters, recognition, bulletin boards, games, competitions). Define extrinsic and intrinsic reinforcement and give examples of each.
- Knowledge of the stages of motivational readiness.
- Ability to list and describe three counseling approaches that may assist less motivated clients to increase their physical activity levels.
- Ability to list and describe the specific strategies aimed at encouraging the initiation of exercise, adherence and return to participation in an exercise program.
- Knowledge of symptoms of anxiety and depression that may necessitate referral.
- Describe the potential manifestation of test anxiety (i.e., performance, appraisal threat) during exercise testing and how it may disrupt accurate physiological responses to exercise.

SAFETY, INJURY PREVENTION, AND EMERGENCY PROCEDURES

- Demonstrate skills necessary to obtain basic life support and cardiopulmonary resuscitation certification.
- Describe appropriate emergency procedures (i.e., telephone procedures, written emergency procedures, personnel responsibilities, etc.) in a variety of exercise settings.
- Describe basic first aid procedures for exercise-related injuries such as: bleeding, strains/sprains, fractures, and exercise intolerance (dizziness, syncope and heat injury).
- Knowledge of basic precautions taken in a group exercise setting to ensure participant safety.
- Ability to identify the physiological and physical signs and symptoms of overtraining.
- List the effects of temperature, humidity, altitude and pollution upon the physiological response to exercise.
- Define shin splints, sprains, strains, tennis elbow, bursitis, stress fracture, tendonitis, patella femoral pain syndrome, low back discomfort, plantar fasciitis, and rotator cuff tendonitis
- Knowledge of hypothetical concerns and potential risks that may be associated with the use of exercises such as straight leg sit ups, double leg raises, full squats, hurdlers stretch, yoga plough, forceful back extension and standing bent-over toe touch.
- Demonstrate knowledge of safety plans, emergency procedures, and first aid techniques needed during fitness evaluations, exercise testing, and exercise training.
- Identify the components that create and maintain a safe environment.
- Discuss and instructors responsibilities, limitations, and the legal implications of carrying out emergency procedures.
- Ability to describe potential musculoskeletal injuries (eg. contusions, sprains, strains, fractures), cardiovascular/pulmonary complications (e.g. tachycardia, bradycardia, hypotension/hypertension, tachypnea) and metabolic abnormalities (e.g. fainting/syncope, hypogylcemia/hyperglycemia, hypothermia/hyperthermia).
- Knowledge of the components of an equipment maintenance / repair program and how it may be used to evaluate the condition of exercise equipment to reduce the potential risk of injury.

EXERCISE PRESCRIPTION AND PROGRAMMING

- State the recommended intensity, duration, frequency, and type of physical activity necessary for development of cardiorespiratory fitness in an apparently healthy population.

- Differentiate between the amount of physical activity required health benefits and the amount of exercise required for fitness development.
- Describe and demonstrate exercises for the improvement and maintenance of muscular endurance and muscular strength of specific muscle groups.
- Describe the principles of overload, specificity and progression and how they relate to exercise programming.
- Demonstrate an understanding for the components incorporated into an exercise session and their proper sequence (i.e., pre-exercise evaluation, warm-up, aerobic stimulus phase, cool-down, muscular strength and/or endurance and flexibility).
- Define overload, specificity of exercise conditioning, use-disuse, progressive resistance, isotonic, isometric, isokinetic, concentric, eccentric, atrophy, hypertrophy, sets, repetitions, plyometrics, Valsalva maneuver.
- Demonstrate various methods for establishing and monitoring levels of exercise intensity such as heart rate. and perceived exertion METs.
- Skills to teach participants how to use RPE and heart rate to adjust the intensity of the exercise session.
- Ability to calculate training heart rates using two methods: percent of age-predicted maximum heart rate and heart reserve (Karvonen).
- Skill to teach and demonstrate appropriate modifications in specific exercises for the following groups: older adults, pregnancy and postnatal women, obese persons and persons with low back pain.
- Ability to recognize proper and improper technique in the use of resistive exercise equipment such as stability balls, weights, bands, resistance bars, and water exercise equipment.
- Ability to recognize proper and improper technique in the use of cardiovascular conditioning exercise equipment (e.g. steps, cycles)
- Ability to evaluate flexibility and prescribe appropriate flexibility exercises for all major muscle groups.
- Ability to design resistive exercise programs to increase or maintain muscular strength and/or endurance.
- Design, implement, and evaluate individualized and group exercise programs based on health history and physical fitness assessments.
- Ability to modify exercises based on age and physical condition.
- Knowledge, skills and abilities to calculate energy cost, VO2, METs and target heart rates and apply information to exercise prescription.
- Ability to convert weights from pounds (lb) to kilograms (kg) and speed from miles per hour (mph) to meters per minute (m/min).
- Ability to convert METs to VO2 expressed as mL/kg/.min, L/min and or ml/kgFFW/min.

- Ability to calculate energy cost in METs and kilocalories for given exercise intensities in stepping exercise, cycle ergometry and during horizontal and graded walking and running.
- Ability to explain and implement exercise prescription guidelines for apparently healthy clients, increased risk clients and clients with controlled disease.
- Ability to adapt mode, duration, frequency, intensity, progression, level of supervision, and monitoring techniques in exercise programs for patients with controlled disease (heart disease, diabetes mellitus, obesity, hypertension), musculoskeletal problems, pregnancy/postpartum, and exercise-induced asthma.
- Knowledge of special precautions and modifications of exercise programming for participation at altitude, different ambient temperatures, humidity, and environmental pollution.
- Knowledge of the importance of recording exercise sessions and performing periodic evaluations to assess changes in fitness status.
- Knowledge of the advantages and disadvantages if implementation of interval, continuous and circuit training programs.
- Ability to design training programs using interval, continuous and circuit training programs.
- Ability to discuss the advantages and disadvantages of various commercial exercise equipment in developing cardiorespiratory fitness, muscular strength, and muscular endurance.
- Knowledge of the types of exercise programs available in the community and how these programs are appropriate for various populations.

NUTRITION AND WEIGHT MANAGEMENT

- Define the following terms: obesity, overweight, percent fat, lean body mass, anorexia nervosa, bulimia, and body fat distribution.
- Knowledge of the relationship between body composition and health.
- Compare the effects of diet plus exercise, diet alone, and exercise alone as methods for modifying body composition.
- Knowledge of the importance of an adequate daily energy intake for healthy weight management.
- Identify the functions of fat and water soluble vitamins.
- Ability to describe the importance of maintaining normal hydration before, during and after exercise.
- Demonstrate familiarity with the USDA Food Pyramid and US Dietary Guidelines.
- Ability to describe the importance of calcium and iron in women's health.

- Ability to describe the myths and consequences associated with inappropriate weight loss methods: saunas, vibrating belts, body wraps, electric simulators, sweat suits and fad diets.
- List the number of kilocalories in one gram of the following: fat, carbohydrate, protein, and alcohol.
- List the number of kilocalories in one pound of fat.
- Describe the health implications of variation in body fat distribution patterns and the significance of waist/hip ratio.
- Knowledge of guidelines for caloric intake for an individual desiring to lose or gain weight.
- Discuss common nutritional ergogenic aids, their purported mechanism of action and any risks and/or benefits (e.g., carbohydrate, protein/amino acids, vitamins, minerals, sodium bicarbonate, bee pollen etc).
- Knowledge of nutritional factors related to the female athlete triad syndrome (i.e., eating disorders, menstrual cycle abnormalities, and osteoporosis).
- Knowledge of the NIH Consensus statement of health risks of obesity, Nutrition for Physical Fitness Position Paper of the American Dietetic Association, and the ACSM Position Stand on proper and improper weight loss programs.
- Knowledge of NECP II guidelines for lipid management.

PROGRAM ADMINISTRATION & MANAGEMENT, QUALITY ASSURANCE, AND OUTCOME ASSESSMENT

- Understand the health fitness instructor's supportive role in administration and program management within a health/fitness facility
- Demonstrate an ability to administer fitness related programs within established budgetary guidelines.
- Demonstrate an ability to develop marketing materials for the purpose of promoting fitness related programs.
- Describe various sales techniques for prospective program clients/participants.
- Describe the documentation required when a client shows signs or symptoms during an exercise session which should be referred to a physician.
- Demonstrate the ability to create and maintain records pertaining to participant exercise adherence, retention and goal setting.
- Demonstrate the ability to develop and administer educational programs (i.e., lectures, workshops etc.) and educational materials (i.e., participant handouts).

- Demonstrate and understanding of management of a fitness department (e.g., working with a budget, training exercise leaders, scheduling, running staff meetings, etc.).
- Discuss the importance of tracking and evaluating membership

Additionally, the successful HES graduate must be able to apply the knowledge, skills, and dispositions necessary to function in a broad variety of health and exercise settings with diverse individuals. Client safety and provision of quality services is paramount. Students in the Health and Exercise Science Program are expected to demonstrate:

Observation Skills:

- Ability to observe a client's response to programming, changes in client's physical condition, body alignment, exercise technique, gait, posture and functional abilities, interpret instrument panels/ displays, assess the environment, and gather information from data sources and professional literature.

Communication Skills:

- Ability to communicate clearly, effectively and efficiently in English, both orally and in writing, with patients and their families, other health care providers, peers, faculty, community or other professional groups.
- Ability to use nonverbal behavior to effectively and appropriately communicate messages.
- Ability to recognize, interpret and respond to the nonverbal behavior of others.
- Ability to read at a competency level necessary to safely and efficiently carry out the essential functions of a task.
- Ability to document clearly, legibly and using appropriate scholarly and professional terminology.

Motor Skills:

- Demonstrate satisfactory movement skills necessary to model and instruct appropriate exercise technique.
- Demonstrate satisfactory physical conditioning and motor ability necessary to assure safety when working with clients.
- Demonstrate motor control necessary to manipulate/operate equipment controls and use assessment tools.

Intellectual Conceptual Skills:

- Ability to collect, interpret and assess data about clients.
- Ability to prioritize multiple tasks, integrate information and make decisions.

- Ability to problem-solve.
- Demonstrate critical thinking skills sufficient for safe and sound clinical judgment and discretion.
- Ability to apply knowledge of health and exercise interventions in a variety of settings and situations.
- Ability to recognize and respond appropriately to emergency and potentially hazardous situations.

Behavior:

- Ability to interact appropriately with individuals of all ages, genders, races, socio-economic, religious, lifestyle and cultural backgrounds.
- Ability to cope effectively with the stresses of academic demands and clinical situations.
- Ability to work collaboratively with HES students, faculty, and clinical staff.
- Demonstrate emotional health and stability required to fully utilize intellectual capabilities, demonstrate good judgment and render services required in diverse health and exercise settings.

4

Scope of Yoga for Refinement of Educational Process

Since time honored the lore of the Yoga was developed and refined by the Indian sages in search of the real-most state of human nature. In course of time that traditionally evolved system of Yoga has been a science of consciousness development and finally in modern time Yoga was seen as the science of possibilities, latent within oneself and helpful in dealing with crucial problems of human life. After the popularization of health promotion potentials of Yoga practices among masses, certain other applied aspects of the Yoga system, concerned with human resource development, have been remained to be substantiated scientifically. That's why modern educationists are taking interest in improving the quality of education with the help of Yoga system. Education system, not only in India but the modern globalizing world also really is in great need of taking help of Yoga system. It is seriously being felt that besides the development of national strength and scientific mentality among the students, the aim of education should be the liberation of mind and soul as well.

THE ROLE OF INDIA IN SPREADING YOGA PRINCIPLES

India, as the cradle of Yoga, is the most qualified country in the world to spread Yoga at the national as well as at the international levels. The Indian Government should therefore have the responsibility to accomplish this by appointing a qualified institution to organize the project at global level.

The first phase of the project should dealmainly with the training of motivated teachers to be integrated m the Indian public schools as well as in the schools of participating foreign countries. Teachers should be trained for different levels of schools. To achieve this goal, the existing qualified Yoga institutions should be strengthened and new ones should be created.

Even using the modern means of audio-visual communication like television and other modern technologies, the universal divulgation of Yoga is a very long process and requires a strong financial and organizational commitment from member countries and organizations participating in the project.

THE PROPOSED UNIVERSITY OF PEACE AND GLOBAL YOGA EDUCATION

As Yoga is considered one of the ways to achieve brotherhood, peace and harmony among people in the world, the University of Peace, to be created in Alandi, in collaboration with United Earth organization, could be entrusted, among other responsibilities, to divulge Yoga in India and world-wide.

Alandi should be the starting point for spreading this new awareness in global education. Hopefully, Alandi Peace University will be the first of many such universities to be created world-wide. In my vision, I see the University of Peace managed by a council of illuminated and motivated people, deeply involved in spreading knowledge and educational principles which should promote the transformation of human behaviour and lead to brotherhood, peace and harmony among people. In this noble process,Yoga has a universal validity. The University of Peace, in accepting to include Yoga, and divulge it as a scientific system of integrated learning, hopefully will help the western universities to introduce this science in their regular curriculum.

CHANGING CONCEPT OF YOGA-DOWN THE AGES

It has been discussed in the earlier lines that the lore of the Yoga system was evolved by the extensive chain of seer and sages in search of the real-most state of human nature and all Yogic techniques were developed to support the emergence of transcendental meditative state (Patanjali, 4th century AD), however, the harmonious way of living with oneself along with the environment has also been the subject of Yoga. The remarkable part of Vaidic literature, Kathopanisad elucidates that Yoga is a system of holistic life where all the facets of human life as well of personality get due consideration as inevitable elements of a whole system". In Bhagavad-Gita, composed by the sage Veda-Vyasa, the practical implication of Yoga in active life situations has been wonderfully elaborated. There yoga is assumed as the state of equanimity at psychic level, which makes life free of stress so that one can perform his best in an effective manner. After having been derived from the Sanskrit root 'Yuj', in the ancient time, meaning 'to unite' or 'to combine', Yoga has been understood afterwards (during 6th to 12th century AD) as a state of union of opposite pairs, forms the human Pranic and/or psychic system.

In the modern period, after having been redefined by Swami Vivekananda (1893) as a traditional Indian system compatible with modern sciences, Yoga is presently being defined as a system of personality-development, transformation of consciousness and integration within the human system leading to the complete well being. It is quite obvious by the definition of

Yoga given by Swami Ranganathananda of the Ramakrishna Mission that "The science of Yoga is thus the science of man in depth, the science of conscious evolution or the science of human possibilities. It is a unique science in that it encompasses, matter, life and consciousness in one sweep and bridges the gap between science (as it is understood today) and Spirituality." The outstanding figure of contemporary Yoga, Sri Aurbindo defined yoga as a methodical effort towards self-perfection. It is a process by which the limitations and imperfections in man are washed away which result into an all round personality development at the physical mental, intellectual emotional and spiritual levels (Sri Satprem, 1975). Swami Rama of Himalayan Institute, America asserted that 'Purpose of yoga is not to introduce an omnipresent god, but to attain the self-awareness. Yoga may also be seen as modification of the interaction between the self and the non-self, it suggests modification of individual's attitude and approach towards the environment (Tripathi and Singh 1984).

ROLE OF YOGA IN EDUCATION

Commonly, the term Yoga education has been referred to as the training and teaching process of Yoga, though it should also be seen as the application of Yoga techniques to bestow better support to the education process. The target of both the disciplines is the same and that is enhancement of socially useful potentials of human personality. To achieve this target, the system of Yoga lays foundation stones whereupon the education system may flourish in all areas. Modern educationists are taking interest in improving the quality of education with the help of the Yoga system. Therefore it is a high time to think seriously on inclusion of Yoga and Yogic values in education system. Here Yogic values refer to the holistic and spiritual approach towards life and the world. Yoga in education should lead to the development of harmonious personality and behavior at all the levels. An atmosphere should be created where the students study yoga with their own enthusiasm. To the whole the higher level of education is the fittest for integration of Yoga. In the current Indian perspective, the role to be played by the education system is facing new challenges. Normally the main aims of education have been the physical, psychological, interpersonal, professional and spiritual refinement of a personality. In modern Indian perspective it is deemed that the system of education should also be helpful in the attainment of the objectives of socialism and democracy mentioned in Indian constitution too. Besides, to attain refinement at the level of thoughts (intellectual development) and feelings (affective aspect), contributing to the development of national character and scientific mentality among the people, at present it is seriously being felt that the aim of education should also include the liberation of mind and soul as well. Normally, in the education process, one is taught and asked to store in mind as much as possible, there is not any format for the appreciation in the education system regarding the values for optimal mental usage and getting rid of the burden of information, to become tranquil for a while. The system of Yoga may offer this kind of training and teaching.

Presently it is being seriously sensed that as the classical Indian tradition established four Noble Aims (Purusarth) in human life i.e. Ethics (Dharma), Earning (Artha), Enjoyment (Kama) and Emancipation (Moksha), which are equally essential and significant for sublime human existence in present time too, the education system should also impart the teaching and training of the moral (Dharma), socioeconomic (Artha), psychological (Kama) and spiritual (Moksha) values to the students. In different words Acharya Vinoba Bhave (1997), the spiritual heir of Mahatma Gandhi suggested the same, that 'education in India is to be based on three principles: Yoga (spiritual training), Udyoga (vocational training) and Sahayoga (social training)'. Expressing the views 'On the integration of Yoga with modern education' Swami Rama asserted (1981) that Yoga should become a part of education in India. According to Swami Rama 'Education process should include 3 steps:

1st step-Education at home.

2nd step-Environmental education.

3rd step -Self-education.

On the whole certain thrust areas positively concerned with educational process have been identified, where the potential of Yogic practices are duly proved i.e. treatment of physical difficulties, improvement of mental health and developing resistance to stress, promotion of emotional balance and control on hyperactivity, however, many other prospective aspects of yoga-practices, may be helpful in giving good support to the education process, are still to be evaluated substantially. These positive aspects of yoga are: promotion of will power and development of perseverance in students, education and training about inner-Self, comprising introduction with corporeal Sheath (physical body) of the Self, development of awareness of vital sheath (psychosomatic system) of the Self, accessing to the psychic sheath (psychological system) of the Self, approaching the Gnostic sheath of the Self escorting finally to the realization of the beatific sheath. The said process of education and training about inner-Self, obviously also takes in the process of pursuit of the transcendental state of psyche leading to the development of wide-ranging awareness, unfoldment of creative consciousness and promotion of uniqueness or talent in the students.

Self- Education (Education of Self-Realization)

Yoga renders self-education. Yoga is nothing but the education of self-awareness. Yoga teaches how to live with wisdom, not with the worldly orientations. Present education system causes orientation towards external world to such an extent that one gradually starts losing the awareness of his being i. e. self-awareness. The present education system conveys no training to develop an acquaintance with the abstract internal world of our Self. There is essentially a need to learn to understand the subtle realities concerned with the inert aspects of self-existence. Yoga system can impart progressive training for the development of self-awareness and educate us about the realities of our being and becoming. How the process of Self-Education in Yoga takes place, has been obviously elucidated in the famous dialogue of Varuna (the teacher) and Bhrigu in Tattiriyopanisad (3/ 1-6). Following the instructions of Varuna, Bhrigu after going through the actualization process of five sheaths or levels of the Self, successively i.e. Corporeal Sheath (Annamaya Kosha), Vital Sheath (Pranamaya Kosha), Mental Sheath (Manomaya Kosha), Gnostic Sheath (Vijnanamaya Kosha) and Beatific Sheath (Anandamaya Kosha), attained Self-realization. On the basis of this dialogue or instruction, the process of self education is quite clear and it comprises five progressive steps or levels as below:

- Introduction With Corporeal Sheath or Level (Physical Boby) of the Self: To be introduced with the aspects of one's physical health through the practices of yogic postures in order to approach internal muscular states by different rhythmic external voluntary muscular activities. This is the most external level.
- Development of Awareness of Vital Sheath or Level (Psychosomatic System) of the Self: To develop an awareness about the functioning of internal vegetative and vital system and to establish an adequate communication with internal system leading to a good control over them by the practices of yogic breathing, postures and meditation.
  The education and training concerned with the above two levels of self-education is covered in the system of Hatha-yoga and are the subject matter of Bahiranga yoga.
- Finding the Mental Sheath (Psychological Processes) of the Self: The practices applied to regulate the mental sheath of the self are Pranayama (Bioenergy-control), Pratyahara (abstraction) and Dharana (concentration). For the modification and management of this level, the practices of Pranayama (Bioenergy-control) specially breathing by abdomen, helps in calming down the mind by getting rid of emotions. In Pratyahara (abstraction) abstracting the senses and mind from the external world the aspirant makes attempts to discipline the mind by contemplation on introspection of mental reflections while keeping them in an orderly manner. By the practices of Dharana (concentration) the fluctuations of mind are controlled. A disciplined mind is only fit for further evolution.
- Approaching the Gnostic sheath of the Self: The method of attainment of Gnostic sheath or level starts with simple, natural, moral and peaceful living. It needs sincere practice of Eightlimbic system of Yoga starting with the practice of abstinence and

observances (Yama and Niyama), further including the yogic exercises of postures and breathing practices and finally leading to meditation. After being absorbed in meditation, one may realize any reasonableness or cognizance of ultimate Self.

Occasionally in a peaceful solitude environment,

- Whenever one's mind is free from violence, lust, temptation, fear and worries,
- And is wholesome, contented and relaxed,
- With the help of any sensefull verse, melodious tune, sylvan scene, blissful feeling
- one's body, bioenergy and mind are in relaxation.

All at once it may make one oblivious of his self. At once at a stage several components of Yoga are spontaneously met together, which lead one's consciousness to the state of Samadhi. Samadhi (transcendental state) further leads to the attainment of wisdom. The trial of making this rare but spontaneous natural creative stage into an attainable one is the subject-matter of Yoga system.

At the level of Gnostic Sheath of the Self, one is able to understand about what is normally unseen. The Gnostic sheath of the Self, attained in somewhat advanced level of Samadhi, is the source of wisdom and creative intelligence. This level of Self is helpful in creating true art of artists, in composing poetry for the poets, inventions to scientists, as well as pious divine bliss to devotees and saints and solution to seekers. We try to become scientists without knowing the rootstock and real meaning of the science. The real science comes out from within through the process of internalization. In Yoga we learn how to internalize. In Yoga one learns to relax his body, senses, vital system and mind leading to the state of Samadhi. Through this only, the gap between science, spirituality and religion may be filled and then we can enter to the next step of evolution of consciousness as well as civilization.

The students should be suggested to find time whenever it is feasible to them, to sit quiet and calm for 5 or 6 minutes while keeping their spine straight, twice or thrice in a day. They should practice to calm down the rate of respiration and try to internalize their mind, as in meditation, After a couple of years, a sincere practitioner may be able to approach his Gnostic level of Self. It will be helpful in making him a good scientist or artist or writer.

Thus the popularly accepted system for education and training concerned with the above-said two sheaths or levels of self in Yoga, is Raja-yoga and the widely prescribed approach is the Eightlimbic system, propounded by Patanjali.

- Realization of Beatific Sheath: The realization of this final-most level of the self is not possible by any education and training process. It can not be included in the usual education system. It is the subject matter of Laya-yoga and might be realized after a prolonged spiritual retreat, which is not be expected from a normal human being. However, since time honored it has been regarded as the culminating point of the education process in India. The path of knowledge (Jnana-yoga) or the path of devotion (Bhakti-yoga) is helpful in realization of the beatific level of the Self.

BALANCING BOTH HEMISPHERES OF THE BRAIN

Science tells us that there are two hemispheres in our brain, the right and the left. These two hemispheres perform different functions. The functions of the left hemisphere are linear, logical and intellectual. Those of the right hemisphere are artistic, creative and intuitive. If we consider these facts, the education system does not allow the child to develop the full potential of the right and left hemispheres of the brain. The trend of education has been through books. You read, memorize, sit for an exam and receive a grade. Either you pass or fail. Again you have to read, memorize, sit for an exam and get your grade.

The subjects which are taught follow a linear, logical system, whether it is maths, history, geography, physics, chemistry or medicine, whether it is advanced education or secondary education. In this process only one side of the brain is stimulated - the linear, logical side.

In order to balance the other aspects, we teach children the arts. We encourage them to practise music, to paint, to perform plays. We encourage them to use their creativity. But if you compare the influence of the different lobes of the brain, you will find that the linear and logical are more pronounced than the artistic and creative. This is one point.

DEVELOPING THE WHOLE MIND

The second point is that the brain is only the medium through which we educate our mind. The mind is a composition of four different faculties, which in yogic terminology are defined as manas, buddhi, chitta and ahamkara. The word manas means to rationalize, to think about something. Buddhi means intellect. Chitta is an area of consciousness where impressions are stored. Ahamkara is the concept of ego.

In the modern education system we are feeding only one aspect of the mind - buddhi. We are not dealing with the manas aspect, which deals with the faculty to know what is right and what is wrong. We are not dealing with chitta, where impressions of knowledge are stored in the form of memory and experience. Nor are we dealing with ahamkara, the ego. Rather we are cramming buddhi with information without boosting up the other aspects of our mind. Therefore, despite all our education, we are not able to apply it constructively and creatively in our lives.

Despite all our understanding of right and wrong, we become confused if we have to decide what we need to do. At the same time, as teachers and as parents, most of the time we ignore the psychological samskaras and the psychological nature of the child.

There is an Urdu couplet which says, "Let me tell you the grand things I have done in my life. I have studied and after receiving an education, I did my service and after completing my service, I received my pension and after receiving my pension, I died. This is life." But is this everything in life? No. It is important for each one of us to provide opportunities for our children to recognize themselves, to use their potential, to develop and awaken their personality, without parents imposing their own personal ideologies on them.

The problem is not only with education. The problem is also with the parents. Parents have not been educated. You might have studied at Oxford or Harvard; you might have received the highest degree available, but you are not educated. A degree is not education. It is only a certificate which allows you to lead a life with, possibly, self-esteem, if that. A degree is only a passport to attain satisfaction, job status and recognition from other people. But a degree is not an indication of your education.

Proper education can only be received when you allow children to use their intuitive abilities along with their intellectual abilities, when you allow them to overcome their fears and inhibitions, to overcome the psychological pressures which are created without you imposing your own conditions on them. This is what we found when we set up SALT in San Francisco. We interviewed many elementary, high school and college students. We found that each one had a psychological block in learning, remembering and memorizing. By nature children are different to their grown-up counterparts. In order to study, grown-ups may need to sit down at a desk with books, but children don't need to.

Yoga in the Classroom

The system of educating children has to be different. It has to be combined with certain practices which can remove their psychological blocks, which can make them aware of the psychological changes that happen in their body and brain, which can make them aware of their own distractions and which can give them the ability to focus on the theme of the subject they are studying.

So what did we do? We started with very simple yoga practices in the classroom environment, taking some hints from the work of RYE (Research on Yoga in Education) with children in Europe. In RYE schools the classes begin and end with the practice of two asanas and one pranayama. So if a child has to sit through six or eight classes during the day, he or she is practising two asanas and one pranayama sixteen times each day at the beginning and at the end of each class.

In Europe, the schools have a psychologist who monitors the performance, behaviour and aptitude of the child and who tries to create a support group for the child in the home environment. When the children who were practising yoga in the classroom were monitored, a marked improvement in their responses, creativity, receptivity, memory, willpower and behaviour was found. The children were more relaxed, focused, one-pointed and tranquil than their counterparts in other classes who were not practising yoga and who were more destructive, restless, violent and distracted.

In America we took pointers and hints from RYE, but we incorporated extra things along with yoga. We incorporated soft background music in the classroom so that children are not under constant psychological pressure to study. Having music around is a subconscious distraction and subconscious relaxation. For our experiment we chose the classical music of Bach.

The teachers started teaching pranayama to the students. The students were told to breathe in and out in unison with the help of a big grandfather clock. When the pendulum swung to one side, everybody was supposed to breathe in and when the pendulum swung to the other side, everybody was supposed to breathe out. After a few moments the breathing pattern had become regular and was coordinated with the swing of the pendulum. The teachers then gave instructions when the students were breathing out and became silent when the students were breathing in.

Now you may wonder what this has to do with education. But it is very important and relevant because psychologists have said that when we breathe in, we create psychological, emotional and rational blocks in our mind. The energy of the body, brain and mind is withdrawn. When we breathe out, relaxation takes place in the body, in the nervous system, in the mind and in the brain. If you provide information when the physical systems are relaxed, it is retained by the brain and not easily forgotten.

Developing Awareness and Rapport

This also helps to bring in the concept of awareness. When I visit schools I often find teachers teaching the subject to the students without awareness. While the training is going on in the class, there is an absence of awareness. Students are taking down notes mechanically, whether they understand the subject or not. That is not the worry of the teachers. The students also know that the teacher is not concerned, so why should they bother? So, there is a gap in the relationship between student and teacher. That gap is a very crucial component which can build up the personality of the student, which is non-existent. However, if you incorporate some methods of concentration, then rapport develops as well as awareness.

Please remember that yoga in the classroom is not confined to the physical practices and breathing techniques that are taught. Rather, the teacher has to be aware when to speak and when to be silent. Speech is the medium of instruction, but at the same time silence is also the medium of instruction because silence allows you to assimilate what you have just heard. So don't only speak. After ten minutes give the children a three minute break or after five minutes have a one minute break. Become silent and ask everybody to be silent.

In the period of silence get the children to play a game of observing their own breath. Ask them to count their breath backwards from fifteen to one. Inhalation and exhalation is taken as one count and as one breath. Fifteen breaths equal about one minute. Then again begin your instructions. This is another important point. Speech and silence have to be combined.

Alertness and dynamic instructions have to be combined with passive visualization. You instruct, you stimulate their intellect, but at the same time you have to give them a chance to visualize passively what they have just heard which has stimulated their intellect. You have to develop a rapport with every student - not that of a teacher but that of a considerate friend to whom they can come and say, "Look, I am having such and such a difficulty with my studies, what can I do?" You should be able to guide them.

There is a well-known story about the Sufi saint Mulla Nasruddin. One day he was sitting near a well trying to fill an earthen pot with water. But the earthen pot had a crack in it. So everything he poured into it would flow out through the crack. People scoffed at him and said, "You must be crazy. How can you expect to fill this pot with water when it is cracked and all the water is leaking out?" He replied, "Who cares? I am only concerned with filling the pot. I do not care whether the pot is cracked or not."

As teachers we are repeating the same things. We are concerned with giving children information. We are not concerned whether they retain it or not. So what is the result? You study history and geography at night and in the morning you have already forgotten it.

THE MEANING OF EDUCATION AND YOGA

There is at present a need to clarify the meaning and aim of Education, just as it is necessary to clarify the meaning and aim of Yoga. Yoga is often identified exclusively with Hatha Yoga and thus its true psychological nature remains quite veiled. Similarly, Education is often identified with vocational training or with some kind of mental culture, but its fundamental nature of integral psychological process remains quite veiled. "Yoga", as Swami Vivekananda has said, "may be regarded as a means of compressing one's evolution into a single life or a few months or even a few hours of bodily existence." And, Education too, when rightly understood, would mean a rapid psychological process towards perfection. Education is a search for knowledge, and it is a search for values. It is also an uncovering of the layers of faculties, cultivation of them and perfection of them. It is a process of the discovery of the self, and it aims at a true self-knowledge, which gives liberation from ego and imperfections. Sa vidya ya vimuktaye. Education is a search for that knowledge which would fulfil oneself individually and as a harmonious member of the universe. But this is also the meaning of Yoga. By Yoga, says

Sri Aurobindo, "We mean...a methodised effort towards self-perfection by the expression of the potentialities latent in the being and a union of the human individual with the universal and transcendent existence we see partially expressed in man and in the cosmos." In the right view of Yoga and of Education, we find, Education and Yoga are one and identical process.

THE NEED FOR RESEARCH IN YOGA FOR PURPOSES OF NEW EDUCATION

In our own times, there is a crisis in the field of knowledge. With the advancement of Science, there has come about an accelerated process of accumulation of knowledge of Facts and also the manipulation of Facts. But it has also come to be realised that Science cannot give the knowledge of Values. And yet, it is increasingly felt that the knowledge of Values is even more important than the knowledge of Facts. How then to attain the knowledge of Values? Moreover, mere knowledge of Values is not sufficient. In Education, we would like to develop those methods by which values would spontaneously grow and manifest among those who are being educated. What are then the best methods by which students can be so trained as to enable them to embody the highest Values?

Yoga is the answer to these questions. Yoga gives the knowledge of Values and the methods of embodying Values. But it should be stressed that Yoga is neither religion, nor morality, nor philosophy. Its attitude and method are entirely scientific. Yoga aims at a direct contact, verifiable experience and union with the Supreme Value.

It is noteworthy that the logic of modern experiments in educational methodology seems to point to the need of a yogic orientation in education. The ideas of individual differentiation, the stress on multiple methods of teaching for different categories of students, recognition of the phenomena of genius, insistence on the development of the latent faculties of the child, emphasis on creativity and on an integral development of personality, and an ardent attempt at implementing the idea of freedom, and that of consulting the child in his own development - these have created a new atmosphere perfectly ready for a plunge in the direction where the truths of Yoga will be found increasingly relevant.

But in the past, -Yoga has largely been and more particularly so in the middle past, life-negating. On the other hand, modern education is science-based; and in science and technology, there is the affirmation of Life and of Life in Matter. Science-based education is thus life-affirming education. If, therefore, Yoga is to be relevant to modern education, it will have to cease to be life-negating. A life-affirming Yoga is a necessity, and a research in this Yoga is centrally relevant to the solution of the modern problems of education. It is also important to note that Education Commission Report have directed that education in India should be science-based and yet in coherence with the spiritual values. Indeed, if this recommendation is to be implemented, the research in Yoga which reconciles Spirit and Matter is indispensable.

Indeed, there has been a good deal of research in Yoga since a number of decades in the wake of the Renaissance in India, and a good deal of experimentation has been attempted to relate this research to the problems of education. It is in the light of this research and experimentation that we can make a few suggestions that would be useful in arriving at a new yogic basis of education and the way in which Yoga can permeate the entire spirit of education and even in the actual processes of education.

New Education in the Light of Recent Research in Yoga

Yoga and yogic research affirm that there are principles and means by which there can be achieved a greater perfection of the body, life and mind than can ordinarily be conceived or imagined. It is also affirmed that there are great hidden faculties and powers which can be awakened by a methodised effort. Finally, there is a supreme affirmation that there are great psychological superconscient states and powers which are central to the creative and integral perfection of personality.

But a mere learning about Yoga is not Yoga, and even the most catholic book on Yoga cannot be a substitute for the direct yogic practice. Nor can Yoga be practised in a casual way or only as a part-time preoccupation. Yoga to be properly practised must be taken up as a sovereign and central occupation and it must govern and permeate every aspect of life and its activity. Yogic research affirms that there is no aspect of life or knowledge which cannot be dealt with by Yoga and that therefore there is no need to make a gulf between Yoga and Life, between yogic knowledge and mundane knowledge. All disciplines of knowledge can in this view be made the vehicles of yogic knowledge. In the words of Sri Aurobindo:

The Yogin's aim in the sciences that make for knowledge should be to discover and understand the workings of the Divine Consciousness- Puissance in man and creatures and things and forces, her creative significances, her execution of mysteries, the symbols in which she arranges the manifestation. The Yogin's aim in the practical sciences, whether mental and physical or occult and psychic, should be to enter into the ways of the Divine and his processes, to know the materials and means for the work given to us so that we may use that knowledge for a conscious and faultless expression of the spirit's mastery, joy and self-fulfilment. The Yogin's aim in the Arts should not be a mere aesthetic, mental or vital gratification, but, seeing the Divine everywhere, worshipping it with a revelation of the meaning of its works, to express that One Divine in gods and men and creatures and objects. The theory that sees an intimate connection between religious aspiration and the truest Art is in essence right; but we must substitute for the mixed and doubtful religious motive a spiritual aspiration, vision, interpreting experience. For the wider and more comprehensive the seeing, the more it contains in itself the sense of the hidden Divine in humanity and in all things and rises beyond a superficial religiosity into the spiritual life, the more luminous, flexible, deep and powerful will the Art be that springs from the high motive.

In the light of life-affirming Yoga, life is meaningful, and life itself could be so organised as to serve as a natural means of education. Also, a complete yogic education is a life-long process, and yet, in so far as it truly gives a meaning to the life-development, it must determine the entire process of the education of the child and the youth. The secret of this life-long education is a constant aspiration for progress and perfection, a thirst for progress, and a zeal, utsaha, for self-perfection should govern the rhythm and law of self-development. To progress constantly is to remain young perpetually, and constant progress comes by perpetual education.

To limit the hours of education during the day and during the year, to organise education on the idea of finishing it one day, to bifurcate education in curricular and extra- curricular courses, to regard studies as work and games as a mere play and pastime, to give exclusive value to reading, writing, reasoning and eloquence and to regard all else as secondary or a mere decoration, -- these tendencies are inimical to the conception of all life as education, and all education as Yoga.

Yoga is essentially a creative process of the flowering of personality, and yogic research gives us the secret of the perfection and integration of personality. In recent times, a stress is being laid on education for an all-round personality. There has come about a recognition that there are in us various personalities, conflicting personalities, and thus conflicting potentialities of our profession. It has been pointed out that this entire domain of the secrets of the growth of personality has remained ignored, and the consequences are that most of us possess smothered personalities, and most often we are engaged in the work that has no correspondence with our real genius, with our inner delight of existence. Most of us live in deep suffering, alienated from ourselves. It is this inner suffering that causes ageing, and even in our youth we feel so often old and worn out. These are indeed excellent ideas and they will have a valuable place in the New Education. But yogic research takes us to a still deeper perception. It fathoms into the secret of the true person behind all personalities and discovers there the real power of healing our conflicts and integrating the fullness of all personalities. This is a deep and precious Wisdom, the true self-knowledge of self-perfection, which reveals that the secret of perpetual youth is not a mere progression, but a deeper part of progression, namely, the constant harmonisation of our outer work and circumstances with the inner needs of the manifestation of the powers of the real Person seated deep within us. It is this secret of eternal youth that will be the inner soul of the New-Education. The deepest yogic research affirms that: There is a Supreme Reality that is constantly at work; it does not impose itself upon us, but manifests more and more effectively as we aspire to know it and to work for its manifestation. It is this aspiration that must be lit in the temple of our hearts; and if it is lit and continues to burn, then, we are assured, we shall arrive. A thousand-rayed sun of solid mass of knowledge illuminating, by an incessant downpour of its sheer lustre, the universal skies and the hidden and distant secrets of Matter, a most potent drive of energy and action, and an irresistible bursting forth of love, joy and marvellous forms of beauty - these are the new ideals which result from the recent yogic research, and which, if accepted, would infuse a new spirit in education.

PURSUIT OF THE TRANSCENDENTAL STATE OF PSYCHE

The paramount aim of Yoga system is the pursuit of the transcendental state of psyche i.e. Nidhidhyasana, assumed as an essential aspect of the ancient Indian system of study and education. Samadhi leads to the Nididhyasana state which further escorts the wisdom. Here one thing should be clear that the path for transcendental state of psyche is a continuum, as mentioned in the Yoga-Sutra (2/27), not an "all or none" phenomena, as it is commonly understood.

The experience of Samadhi is not a very difficult or rare stage. Like other components of Yoga it is also attainable. Nevertheless, experience of Samadhi needs application of holistic approach to other constituents of Yoga. Samadhi is nothing but a stage of realization of any reasonableness or cognizance of ultimate Self, in a state when the grosser level of self-awareness gradually starts disappearing. Samadhi is a state of consciousness, which begets energy, awareness and delight to the experiencing being for his/her creative thoughts and actions. A Samadhi devoid of creativity is worthless. Moreover, the real creativity is impossible to achieve without attaining Samadhi state. A creative Samadhi is again hard to achieve without adopting high moral values in daily life. Inclusion of moral values paves way to easy accesses of subtlety, depth and strength in other constituents of Yoga and finally facilitates an ascent to Samadhi.

Samadhi (transcendental state) further leads to wisdom. Yoga teaches how to attain wisdom. Knowledge through real vision or wisdom, accomplished by profound meditation, directed to the Samadhi, is the real attainment and learning through mind and senses is a shallow class of knowledge, which leads to complexity. In most of the institutions today, we find that majority of the student are growing with a complexity. Complex living patterns lead to tensions. Methods of peaceful living are not being included in present education system.

Development of General Awareness (Attention Vs Awareness)

The objectives of Yoga, besides causing physical, mental and spiritual unfoldment in an individual, are also the inculcation of social and ecological awareness within oneself. Education in the modern age emphasizes on power and manner of attention. Attention is used to be selective and it may be influenced by the internal affective states. In attention one may overlook many other relevant aspects of reality. Many a times the attention is directed by biases. Yoga system emphasizes on awareness of very subtle aspects, hardly attainable subject of single pointed focus. It leads to the awareness of the external environment in its full extent and awareness of internal environment in its full depth as well as awareness of those aspects, which are beyond internal and external attainability. Commonly 'Awareness' should never be choicefull. More is the choicefullness, more is the attention and less will be the general awareness. Thus the attention and the general awareness are two different phenomena. As far as one is choicelessly aware, one is able to grasp the things, which are hardly attainable, otherwise expected to be overlooked. Yoga proposes that the aspects, which are subtlest, hardly attainable and hidden behind the observable ones, are more important and in reality they are the determinants of observable phenomena. In Yoga we try to grasp such aspects. So the awareness in Yoga refers to the holistic vision. Such kind of choiceless awareness or holistic vision has least scope for stress and emotionality. Diminishing loads on vital vegetative system, it may lead to positive health.

Moreover the said general awareness only may cause a deep comprehension of the principles of Yogic abstinence and observance, prescribed in yogic texts as Yama and Niyama. Normally people are so absorbed in self-centered endeavors and materialistic sensual enjoyments around their world that they are unable to see the pros and cons or good and bad effects of their conducts. Normal materialistic oriented activities cause a kind of delusion with momentary Kef and elation. As long as one does not get rid of it, one is not able to appreciate classically prescribed and universally accepted ethical principles. With the awareness of Yogic values, slowly one experiences the joy present in his surrounding and after a time finds himself deeply connected with his external environment and starts appreciating the truths of ecology. Meanwhile one should also be trained to feel his inner visceral and vegetative activities and to dip into more and more profound psychic aspects. So the general awareness leading to the deeper appreciation and realizations, should be the essence of yoga in education.

Promotion of Uniqueness

While discussing the role of Yoga in education, the individual difference and uniqueness of a person should be given due place. When supreme consciousness is reflected through the individual uniqueness of sundry souls, it gives an exclusive pleasure and vividness in the creation. Otherwise the world will be monotonous. Yoga believed in the uniqueness of the individual soul, that's why in Yoga, many a paths and practices were prescribed for aspirants for their spiritual development. Yoga system is enriched with a wide variety of yoga practices. Though each Yoga-practice modifies some or the other specific component of human personality, seeing the individual difference, it may well be that initially every yoga practice may not suit to each and every individual, even if one may be fit for exercising many kinds of practices later on. However, these practices may be prescribed one by one, observing the changes in nature and temperament of the aspirant, only then at last we can expect promising results of yoga practices.

Unfoldment of Creative Consciousness

Eventually the practice of Yoga may make one self-centered and introverted. This is not always a good direction. There is a difference between yoga and spirituality. In spirituality we are centered on internal aspect of our existence but really in yoga, to attain the internal bliss, peripheral aspects of life are not neglected. In yoga we start with discipline of the peripheral aspect and then with the help of peripheral aspects we proceed for getting internal development. Creativity is the fragrance of internal development. As one's inner-self effloresces, one starts emitting some goodness in his surrounding, in the things present around him. Giving a good order to the external things, which is also useful for the society, is the right manifestation of internal development. All the established Yogis were living in society, contributed something significant for the public and they never overlooked their external world in spite of having no deep attachment for anything, except the internal bliss. Real spiritual development generates vital energy and if one is really energetic he should do something positive and significant, otherwise his energy will be deviated. While producing or making anything, a subtle communication is established between the internal psyche and external material existence. This silent communication with a tongueless environment, either with internal physiology or with external ecology, causes a new dimension for expansion of consciousness. Thus such a way of wordless communication further causes a tendency of creativity and finally leads to the vitality.

For the promotion of uniqueness and creativity, it may be suggested that there should be provision of recess periods in the school-schedule. Present author is able to recollect that during his school-days, there was provision of two recess periods, one of shorter duration and other-one of duration of about equal to one full period. Author feels that there may be three or four free or recess times. Besides the recess periods, the student should be allowed to join the school half an hour before as well as to stay 45 minute after the usual school-timing. The Principal or Vice-Principal and the class-teacher should be present during the said free-times to observe the potential and interests of the students. These recess-period or free-times may be occupied by a student in either of the items out of the following:

- He/she may play with friends.
- He/she may make fun or gossip with friends.
- He/she may do curricular interaction with teachers.
- He/she may offer his/her help or assistance to the teachers
- He/she may attend library.
- He/she may spend his/her time in observation, contemplation or meditation.
- He/she may spend his/her time enjoying with nature in school-garden.
- He/she may offer his/her manual labour, wherever it is needed.
- He/she may complete his/her pending or incomplete work.
- He/she may practice dance, drama, music and other fine-arts activities.

During free times, while interacting with external environment, producing or making anything, a subtle communication is established between the internal psyche and external material existence. This silent communication with the environment, either with internal physiology or with external ecology, causes a new dimension for expansion of consciousness. Thus such a way of wordless communication further causes a tendency of creativity and finally leads to the vitality.

Promotion of Will Power and Perseverance

The path of Yoga is a life-long pursuit in the development of psyche. It needs sincere practice of Eightlimbic system of Yoga starting with the practice of abstinence and observance (Yama and Niyama), including the yogic exercises of postures and breathing practices and finally leading to the meditation. Without inclusion of ethical values and virtue, the agile tendencies may create tension and cause hindrances in the perfection of Dharana that requires a determination for compliance of ethical and spiritual values.

Otherwise in course of Yoga-retreat, an aspirant may face some blockades or obstructions. If the aspirant ably qualifies these bars efficiently, by enhancing his/her will power he/she gets further progress in Yoga otherwise one may be perturbed or truant. In the stage of Dhyana, at times when conscious, subconscious, and unconscious thoughts, feelings and images concerned with the past and present life creep in and if they are unsatisfactory, awful and of a stimulating nature, the individual may deviate from Dhyana. Because the state of Dhyana and delighted state are closely related. The moment affliction sets in, individual loses the state of Dhyana. Without having a consistency and capacity for profound meditation or Dhyana, attainment of Samadhi is just not possible.

Thus the path of Yoga is a test as well as the training of will power. Will power is a quality that plays its major role in every creative performance and success. Firstly, when an aspirant gets due development through the exercise of external yoga techniques, one should start directing himself to the internal yoga techniques. After having performed internal yoga techniques adequately, if one starts feeling monotony and no more pleasure, one should divert oneself to the direction of physical creativity and social service. Thereafter again a stage of confusion comes out, that can only be overcome by observing the path of devotion, as depicted in Bhagavatgita.

Management of Mental Health

The ancient form of Yoga system was not aimed at management of disorders, nevertheless the aspects of health were covered in the foundation texts of Yoga (Shvetashwatara Upanisada/2/12; Bhagavatgita /6/17,23; Yoga-Sutra/1/31,32&2/2). It seems that in the Eight-limbic system of Yoga, Patanjali recommended the observance of Yama and Niyama, for the management of conscious emotional conflicts, whereas, as far as the subconscious emotional conflicts are concerned he recommended Asana and Pranayama. Yama, Niyama are also prerequisites for Asana and Pranayama, because these physical exercises do not cause any emotional training or give rise to any intervening effect in the state of emotional agitation, as it is being expressed as underneath.

Conscious emotional conflicts------can be managed by ---Yama & Niyama

Subconscious emotional conflicts----can be managed by----Pranayama & Pratyahara

Unconscious emotional conflicts-----can be managed by----Dhyana & Samadhi

Stability of body, brought about by the practice of Asana may lead to the emotional stability and psychological well being. Asanas release tensions which are subconscious in nature. It makes the body function harmonious and restores the natural reciprocity of visceral functions. Asanas contributing to the alignment of body and changing the postural reflexes, naturally, produces indirect psychological changes. The psycho-physiological modeling, caused by the practice of Asanas, moderating the functions of autonomic nervous system, induces a balance in the psycho-pranic system.

There is a relationship observed between respiration and emotions as well.

Psychological factors Agitation of Respiration

Rhythmic Respiration (Pranayama) Poised State of mind

Due to the over-oxidation because of the agitated state of vegetative system causes unfavorable metabolic changes in the organism. On the other hand, slow breathing, causing mental relaxation induces good amount of alpha brain waves. It is also found that psychological factors have significant effect on breathing pattern. Its vice versa may also be possible. and it is being observed that voluntary positive control on breathing i.e. Pranayama may change the state of mind.

As far as the applications of yoga-practices for management of mental problems are concerned, the yogic techniques are mostly being used as adjunct to the other psychotherapeutic systems and as a part of psychosomatic rehabilitation and relaxation training. Many psychologists on the basis of their experimental results and clinical experiences found that Yoga is an effective instrument of modification of human behavior. Yoga more closely resembles the methods of psychotherapy rather than a religion or a philosophy (Fritjof Capra, The Turning point, 1981).

Yoga practices were found to be effective in the management of personality disorders (Singh 1986; Tripathi, 1987), mental retardation, hyperkinetic behavior (Subramanyama & Porkodi,1981; and Singh, 1986; Nagendra & Nagarathna, 1984; Maria Bullard 1985); and neurotic reactions (Meares, 1976; Puryear, 1976; Nagarathna, Horia and Nagendra, 1984). Meti (1997) reported electrical activity of the brain like mild electroconvulsive seizure effect as a result of Pranayama, irrespective of types. The research report of Johnson deduced significant difference with higher scores for self-esteem, identity, self- satisfaction, personal worth, behavior and the emotional adjustment seemed to be more positive, less feeling of general maladjustment, less personality disorder and less neurosis. By the regular and prolonged practice of meditation, a remarkable decrease in the use of alcohol, barbiturates, amphetamines, marijuana, LSD and Heroin was noted. Dr. Mears and Franz from Australia published their result that deep meditation has a positive role in emotional stability. Yoga maintains good positive health of the body and mind. Selected routine of yogic exercises can certainly lead to a happy and successful healthy life.

Treatment of Physical Difficulties

From the period of later Upanishads and Yoga-Samhitas, it was duly emphasized that the practice of yogic postures and yogic breathing, in addition to mental and ethical disorders are also able to alleviate physical pains and problems (Yoga Churdamani Upn./109; Hath Pr/1/19 & 2/16-18; Yoga Vasistha/6/1/81/12-42). During 20th century, after the earlier fifties, a large number of medical research reports showing the efficacy of yogic practices in the management of a variety of psychophysiological and functional problems were published in different journals.

Efficacy of Yogic Therapy in Treatment of Various Physical Difficulties

- Effect on Musculo-skeletal System: - All the Asanas bring about good muscular equilibrium. It permits the movement with an economy of energy. The stability of the body-parts leads to the emotional stability and psychological well being. Regular practice of Asanas improves movement in joints, cures different kinds of arthritis problems and corrects the postural defects. Backache muscle spasm, prolapsed intervertebral disc may get relief by yogic practices. (Udupa, et at, 1975)

- Effect on Respiratory System:- Yogic practices e.g. Kapalabhati and Bhastrika strengthen diaphragm muscles. These are very useful in delaying exhaustion in asthma attacks and respiratory insufficiency. By this process the sticky phelegm of Asthma draw out from bronchi. (Udupa, et at 1975)
- Effect on Cardiovascular System:- The gravitation effect during inverted positions like Viparitakarani, Sarvangasana (Shoulder stand) influence functioning of lungs, brain, heart, intestines and movement of body fluids (blood, lymph, cerebrospinal fluid) and so on. So it is a method of treatment for migraine, premenstrual tension. Pranayama extends the walls of blood vessels resulting in increased blood flow to the areas of heart and lungs. The mild retention of Co2 and slow breathing during Pranayama help to dilate blood vessels of the brain, skin and of the coronary system. It is a treatment for angina pectoris. It reduces the workload of heart. Reduction of hypertension through muscular relaxation can be possible by the practice of Shavasana and muscular relaxation (Chandra Patel Datey), Benson, (Udupa, et al, 1975).
- Effect on Neuro-Endocrine System:- Yogic practices have power to change hormones and neurotransmitters. The increased dopamine-beta – hydrooxilase in hypertension is reduced from blood by relaxation with lowering of the pressure.

MANAGEMENT OF STRESS DISORDERS

Stress can be controlled by recommended Yogic technique (Udupa, 1978). The Yoga along-with recommended Yogic diet, reduces tension. The practice of Pratyahara controlling the activities of senses, at both internal and external levels, manages the stresses of personal life and brings composure. The meditation on respiration, as in Vipasana of Bauddha system, was found to modify the state of mind. Moreover, transcendental meditation, which is a meditation on Mantra, was found to have the power of physical changes (Wallace, 1970) like reduction in muscle tone and blood lactate of stress, slowing down of respiration, decrease in metabolism and positive changes on electroencephalogram. One can attain a complete isolation from interior and exterior stimuli. Yoga, taking in above-said techniques, appears as a system of self-healing. Meditation stabilizing the functioning of autonomic nervous system causes remarkable reduction in anxiety and hypertension. The Yogic refinement in psychological attitude (Yama and Niyama of yoga) can reduce tension, improve health and resolve psychological conflicts. Both the internal and external environments can be balanced by such Yogic practice (Tripathi & Singh, 1984).

DIPLOMA OF YOGA TEACHING & LIFE SKILLS

The Diploma of Yoga Teaching is core Shanti yoga™ teaching practicum. It provides you with the knowledge, training and authorisation to teach, and the sheer joy of sharing, the path of classical yoga with others. It allows an intense personal development that prepares you for your role as a teacher by including actual experiential practice, homework, reading/preparation assignments prior to each practicum, assignments and an examination during, and in internship, which includes required components such as teaching, assisting and service if one aspires to become a certified Shanti Yoga Instructor.

Teaching rides on your learning, openness, passion and genuine communication. Your specific level of authorisation as a Shanti Yoga teacher will be based upon you meeting the prerequisites for that authorisation: i.e. your performance during training. You are invited to

- Explore the classical yoga approaches to health and wellness
- Practice
- Study
- Learn to teach a series of 55 minute core Shanti Yoga classes

with your peers and give and receive feedback towards blending the ancient principles of classical yoga with the modern precision of safety and strength for dynamic and inspiring classes that strengthen and streamline the body, enhance posture and body awareness, reduce tension and stress and support the abdominal and lower back care in better overall health and wellbeing.

The uniqueness of this course is the wonderful blend of the healing, physical aspects from mat work and on the meditation cushion, with the sublime, deeper teachings and practices handed down through some of the most esteemed teachers of classical and traditional yoga. This allows for a smooth cultural blend of the West with the East. Additionally, the pioneering techniques of Shantiji through asana (postures) woven together in a rich tapestry with pranayama (yoga breathing), mudras (seals and gestures), bandhas (locks), vinyasa (yoga flow) and yoga nidra (deep relaxation or yogic sleep) add a whole new dimension to your learning and teaching experience.

The aim of the Shanti Yoga™ teacher training education is for you to be an accomplished and qualified yoga practitioner (600 hours, Cert IV in Yoga and Life Education) and teacher (a further 600 hours, Diploma in Yoga Teaching and Life Skills) with a program and style compatible with your environment. Thus yoga teacher training is a great self-directed leaning experience through which you will gain the tremendous benefits of yoga, which include the ability to relax and calm yourself at will. You will then be able to translate this into an effective teaching methodology for your students as you move towards becoming an accomplished teacher.

In this course you will

- Learn how to structure and effectively teach a class
- Cultivate the skill and sensitivity required to fulfil the varying needs of your students
- Learn the art and science of yoga and its related disciplines
- Cultivate the communication, facilitation, learning and teaching skills to effectively share the yoga world view
- Practice teaching under tuition, supervision and guidance
- Enhance your own personal growth as a human being and a yoga teacher

THE PRACTICE OF TEACHING YOGA

As yoga students we're committed to the process and concept of practicing. Even though we may slip here and there, we remember that we aren't competing with anyone—including ourselves—when we're on our mat. We remember that our practice is not the preparation for a scored event and we're not on a timeline to develop postures or gain particular insights.

And, yet, we're committed to the spirit of practice and this means that we're not simply resting on our laurels or going through motions. As practitioners, we're honing our focus, deepening our self-awareness and developing our experience of embodiment. We're repeating postures, sequences and elements of the spiritual practice in order to refine our skills. We're also exploring our edge so that we discover what's beyond our comfort zone.

As yoga teachers it's essential that we see ourselves in the same light: as teachers practicing the art of teaching. Too often, we're overly critical of ability to convey information and inspire students. We ask our students not to be competitive or judgmental in our practice, but our inner-monologue about our own "performance" is often extremely harsh. As educators, we have to remember that we will always be honing our craft—which means we're not always perfect and expecting as much creates unnecessary tension that causes more harm than good. We'll continue to refine our awareness in key areas like anatomy, sequencing, manual adjustments, verbal cueing, and so on. We'll continue to practice witnessing our students clearly and unconditionally. And, we'll continue to develop our voice and clarify our sense of purpose—and, we'll allow both to naturally change over time.

As teachers, we should hold ourselves to an extremely high standard, while, at the same time, remembering that just like our students are practicing down-dog, we're practicing the many, many layers of teaching during our classes. Even more, we need to make inner-room and allowances for the countless mistakes that we'll inevitably make as we teach our classes—after all, we need to make mistakes and have confusion in order to grow. In my trainings, I encourage trainees to be proactive about the practice of teaching by listing several skills that they are currently developing. I hear teachers talk about what postures they're working on—or see pictures and video clips—but I rarely hear what aspects of teaching and knowledge development teachers are currently working on. In order to be transparent and encourage everyone to do the same, I'll end with my list of skills that I'm currently focused on deepening in my practice of teaching yoga. I'd love to hear what you're working on.

- Seeing my students' shoulders with more clarity and accuracy.
- Experimenting with sequencing structures that are unconventional for me.
- Trusting that I can give less instruction from time to time and allow greater quietness.
- Continuing to give simple, clear, accessible instructions without diluting the content.
- Maintaining a steady tempo for longer durations in class.
- Using my students names and giving personalized instruction in the middle of large classes.
- Learning the names of new students more quickly.

5

The Teaching of Yoga and Meditation

INTRODUCTION

Prisons in the US are becoming big business, especially as the government allows private enterprise to run prisons. Current laws concerning drug-related convictions and "Three Strikes" mandates are putting more and more people behind bars. Many more people are becoming "educated" in prisons instead of schools and universities. A few statistics about the U.S. prison system:

- The U.S. incarceration rate is five times greater than most industrialized nations.
- "In 1970 there were fewer than 200,000 prisoners in the U.S.A."
- In 2000 there are nearly 2,000,000 prisoners in the U.S.A.
- The states "spend between $20,000 and $50,000 per year, per inmate."
- "Prisoners currently sleep on floors, in tents, in converted broom closets and gymnasiums, or in double or triple bunks in cells that were designed for one inmate."
- "Approximately 240,000 brutal rapes occur in our prison system each year."
- "Nearly 70 per cent of all U.S. prisoners are serving time for nonviolent offenses."
- "Around sixty percent of federal prison inmates are doing time for drug offenses, up from 18 per cent in 1980."
- "Only about 10 per cent of the prison population sets the brutal tone for most institutions, and they are able to do that because the administration gives no support to the vast majority of inmates who just want to do their time, improve themselves in some way, and get out alive."

(Lozoff, Can We Do Better Than Our Present Prison System?)

The facts paint a grim picture, one that most people do not see or care to hear about, or if they do, they accept as a normal part of society. Inmates are offered few to "no opportunities to learn compassion or take responsibility for what they have done, nor make restitution or offer atonement to their victims in any practical ways." (Lozoff, Can We Do Better...?) When people emerge from doing time, they are little prepared to manage life on the outside. Many through repeated mistakes find their way back into the system.

Fortunately, the picture includes many bright spots. Dedicated individuals from a wide variety of backgrounds and traditions bring programs into the prisons that engage prisoners in a holistic way. What the inmates learn in these programs gives them the opportunity to explore their humanity and learn positive ways of dealing with their problems and circumstances on the inside and outside.

The focus of this exploratory study is yoga and meditation programs in U.S. prisons. The first part of the study was designed to provide an overview of:

- Who conducts yoga and meditation programs?
- What kinds of programs exist?
- When have these programs existed?
- Where do programs exist?
- How are they run?
- What are the outcomes?

The second part of the study was designed to test the feasibility of starting a yoga and meditation program in Cleveland area prisons.

In addition to conducting this study to complete the requirements for the Yogic Studies 2b course at the Satyananda Yoga Academy at Mangrove Mountain in Australia as part of an accreditation process, the results of this study will be used to lay the foundation for developing a sustainable yoga and meditation program for Cleveland area prisons. The experience and benefits of successful programs elsewhere in the U.S. can be presented to prison officials who might be skeptical of allowing such a program.

TEACHING GROUNDED MEDITATION

The mind can be our greatest friend or our greatest enemy, the source of many of our problems or the solution to our problems. Helping students form positive, conscious relationships with their minds is a great gift. This positive relationship with the mind is the basis of true health and happiness.

If we neglect the mind, we are disconnected from our creative potential and can easily fall prey to anxiety and depression. This is because the mind is a powerful force that requires training and maturity if we are to handle it well. Unfortunately, many people shy away from meditation. asana practice gives a wonderfully immediate sense of physical well-being, leaving us feeling refreshed and energized. This is one of the reasons that asanas are so popular. Meditation, on the other hand, is a more daunting discipline, because it asks us to face and train our minds. There are many different forms of meditation, but all lead to the same goal: greater self-awareness. A positive side effect is a state of both physical and psychological health. Meditation also helps us study the mysteries of life and existence, helping us access deeper fulfilment. Ultimately, meditation leads to a grounded, centered, focused state that many describe as enlightened.

STAGES OF MEDITATION

Meditation encompasses three distinct stages. The first is self-regulation, in which we teach our students to consciously alter their body-mind functioning and feelings. For example, teach your students breath awareness with the stated aim of inducing relaxation. Having taught self-regulation, the second stage involves methods of self-exploration, which consist mainly of concentration combined with self-awareness. This allows us to become aware of parts of ourselves that were previously unconscious. Self-exploration techniques develop inner strength and stability. Ultimately, self-exploration techniques open the door to the pursuit of self-liberation and spiritual growth, the linking of our awareness to higher consciousness. This third stage is called self-mastery, which leads to self-realization.

Facing the Mind

Most people do not want to do the work required to develop meditative awareness, because it is challenging to face the mind. It has areas that we like and are comfortable with and areas that we dislike and want to get rid of. It is quite natural to want to avoid facing difficulties, and most people come to meditation because they want to be free from problems, anxiety, and pain. They hope that meditation will allow them to get rid of their problems.

However, meditation teaches us that we cannot get rid of our problems, that life is inherently problematic and challenging. Meditation teaches us instead how to handle problems with greater strength, poise, and courage, and how to use problems as stepping-stones to higher consciousness.

It is essential to remember that the aim of meditation is self-awareness, not a state of bliss that is free from problems and obstacles. If we simply seek ecstasy, and hope to avoid sorrow and suffering, then we are actually seeking the loss of ourselves. The ultimate aim of meditation is to remain grounded in self-awareness under all conditions of joy and sorrow, pleasure and pain, gain and loss.

As teachers, therefore, we need to continuously remind our students to stay grounded in self-awareness under all conditions and not get lost in the experience, no matter what state arises.

Challenges to Meditation

There are several fundamental challenges facing everyone who meditates. The first is the nature of the undisciplined mind itself. An undisciplined mind tends to oscillate between two primary states in meditation: the dull, sleepy state and the restless, dissipated state. It is important for teachers to reassure their students that this oscillation is normal.

Other challenges include old mental patterns and undigested emotions and experiences that come up as we attempt to quiet the mind. As we begin to relax, suppressed experiences resurface, and we need to face, handle, and digest them. We do this by teaching practices that allow the detached witness state that lets us observe the mind without reacting.

It is also important, as teachers, to extol a yogic lifestyle and diet, a simple sattvic life that facilitates meditative experience. If we are exhausted by a stressful existence, then during the quiet times of meditation we will sleep. If we eat excessively, we will feel heavy. We will experience in meditation whatever we bring into it.

Changes in lifestyle are often difficult even when we know they will make us healthier and happier.

Meeting the Challenge

In order to achieve higher states of meditative awareness, we have to undergo a process of training and self-transformation. This is difficult to achieve alone, and it usually requires a teacher. As teachers, there are a number of things we can do to support more grounded meditation practice:

- Inspire your students, giving instructions that invoke courage, sincerity, commitment, and determination. Paint a picture of possibility so that students know what they are aiming for and how much benefit they will achieve once they are on this inner journey of self-discovery.
- Tell your students to contemplate what they want to achieve in life, and resolve to achieve it. They should use meditation as part of this achievement.
- Practice asana prior to meditation to prepare the body-mind, making it easier to sit without sore knees and backs while we focus on the subtler elements of our being.
- Use pPranayama, a wonderful premeditative process that fills us with energy and gives us the strength and stamina to do the work we need to do with our minds. One of the best premeditative pranayama exercises is alternate-nostril breathing.
- Engage in a mixture of meditative practices. Start with a concentration-based style of practice—meditating using the breath and a mantra. Then go into mindfulness practice by observing what is arising. One of the best breaths to use to stay grounded in meditation is Ujjayi, throat breathing, performed very softly and gently.
- During guided meditation, ask your students to observe whether they are feeling grounded or dull and dissipated. If they are dull

or dissipated, they are tomeditate on that state to inquire why this might be happening. Encourage them to gain insight into what changes they need to make in their lives.

- Use self-regulation techniques so that during the practice they can do what they need to do to feel more grounded—for example, use breathing techniques such as Ujjayi or a mantra.
- A symbol of higher consciousness, such as a candle flame, or some image that attracts our minds to higher inspiration, is often a useful tool to spur us on during practice. Tell your students to hold this image in your heart and mind as they practice.
- Above all, remind your students that whatever arises in their minds is just part of a mental process. They must try to keep their awareness on themselves as observers of the process, rather than becoming caught up in the mental states themselves.

LITERATURE REVIEW

A wealth of information does exist on yoga and meditation in the prisons all over the world, much of which can be found on the Internet or in yoga or spiritually based magazines. The majority of the books, articles and videos are from Buddhist organizations and their dharma service. The focus of the research for this study was limited primarily to current programs in yoga and yoga-related meditation in the United States prison system. Most of the articles describe either the author's personal experience teaching, observations of a teacher in the prisons, or an interview of a teacher who teaches in the prisons. Some articles and books are from inmates' perspectives.

The most helpful resources were two annotated listings of resources. Yoga in Prison compiled by Trisha Lamb Feuerstein at the Yoga Research and Education Center in Santa Rosa, California is a forty-seven page document that has three sections: 1) Books/ Articles/Videos, 2) Related Books and Articles, and 3) Yoga Teachers and Organizations Working with Prisoners. Resource Directory for Prisoners compiled by the Naljor Prison dharma Service contains spiritual resources for prisoners broken down by spiritual tradition, plus other resources that are useful for prisoners – pen pals, re-entry services, jobs and continuing education, health and nutrition, and more. Many of the articles, organizations and individuals listed in the reference section were found through these two sources, though many were found by searching on the Internet.

While some studies have been conducted on the efficacy of yoga and meditation in prisons, many of them are now somewhat out of date, and were not consulted for this study. This is an area ripe for more work. In fact, Elizabeth Shaver wrote, "I am currently conducting research and writing my Ph.D. dissertation on the development of spiritual intelligence in inmates who have had significant spiritual experiences while incarcerated." Additionally a conference entitled Indic Wisdom on the Inside: Prison Yoga & Meditation and Spiritual Prison Reform Conference was convened in December of 2001 by the California Institute of Integral Studies and the Association for Transpersonal Psychology. Perhaps more current studies will evolve out of future gatherings such as this one.

While yoga and meditation have been used in the prison environment as long as yoga has existed, this is a relatively new area of work and research in the United States with some of the oldest studies dating to the late 1970s. Two organizations have been involved with this work since the early 1970s. The Human Kindness Foundation in Durham, North Carolina founded by Bo Lozoff continues to work with prisoners through the Prison-Ashram Project. Jon Kabat-Zinn, Ph.D., current Executive Director of the Center for Mindfulness in Medicine, Health Care, and Society at the University of Massachusetts Medical Center (UMMC), founded and directed the UMMC Stress Reduction Clinic and its prison project.

For the purpose of this study, the Internet search was sufficient for finding organizations and individuals working with prisoners in the U.S. prison system.

METHODOLOGY

Once organizations and individuals had been identified, an email questionnaire was sent (see Appendix A) and followed up with a personal telephone call or email. In many cases the original email or telephone number that was listed in Yoga in Prison (Lamb) was outdated and incorrect. Twenty-five individuals and organizations were originally contacted. From the original group, I was referred to five additional teachers. Since the timeframe for the written part of the project was limited, not everyone was able to respond in the time given. Since this project does not end with this research paper, contacts will continue to be made in the coming weeks and months. In total, I received eight email responses to the questionnaire and spoke with five others by telephone.

FINDINGS

Many programs offer yoga in the prisons and many individuals teach yoga on their own in prisons all over the country at the federal, state and county level. Andrew Getz, Executive Director of Youth Horizons, points out that there is "a distinction between yoga programs and programs that incorporate yoga in their curriculum." (Getz, personal communication) Programs that incorporate yoga as a modality tend to mean asana (the physical postures/body awareness) only. These programs include meditation, often rooted in Buddhist teachings, as a separate modality, along with some form of discussion. Programs and teachers who focus on yoga have an inclusive meaning of yoga that incorporates a range of practices including, but not limited to asana, pranayama (breathing practices) and meditation. Yoga instructors teaching "just" yoga also at times guide discussions if that is what seems to be needed on a given day.

Some programs work inside the prisons conducting classes, while others provide services to prisoners through free books, videos, cassettes, CDs and correspondence courses that introduce yoga, meditation and other introspective practices. The Human Kindness Foundation (HKF) is one of the oldest organizations working in the prisons. Bo Lozoff, founder and director of HKF, has taught in over 500 prisons around the country. Today HKF sends thousands of books to inmates. The Tri Yoga Prison Project sends a Prana Vidya booklet that gives information and instruction about the practices o breathing, concentration and meditation.

Yoga and meditation are being taught to a wide variety of prisoners, from girls and boys aged 11-20 in juvenile halls, detention centers and camps to women and men aged 20 to 80 in city jails, minimum-, medium- and maximum-security prisons. All educational levels and ethnicity's are represented, some in greater proportion than others depending on the location in the country. One respondent noted that "prison populations are disproportionally black and Hispanic, but yoga programs tend to attract more whites than people of color." No one mentioned specific physical ailments beyond what exists in the population at large such as back pain, hypertension, and depression to name a few. There was general recognition that prison life is stressful and that yoga provided some relief for participants.

Classes range in style, length, frequency and attendance. Integral Yoga, Kripalu Yoga, Kundalini Yoga and Syda Yoga are among the systems of yoga being taught in the U.S. All include hatha yoga, pranayama, deep relaxation and meditation. Some include chanting. Class length varies between one hour to one-and-a-half hours and even two hours. Some programs occasionally run daylong programs. Classes tend to be held on a weekly basis, though some are only once a month or a few times a year depending on teacher availability and facility location.

Attendance is the biggest wild card. Attendance at some facilities is mandatory, for example at a juvenile facility, while at others it is voluntary. One yoga teacher who taught at the Federal Correctional Institution in Raybrook, New York wrote, "Attendance was very regular because if a participant missed the class, he jeopardized being able to stay in it due to the popularity of the class and the waiting list to get into it." (O'Neill, personal communication) At medium security prison in New Hampshire, missed sessions meant dismissal from the program, but there was no waiting list. By the end of the program so few inmates were involved that the local administration declined to have any further programs. (Gosselin, personal communication) Where attendance is voluntary often a core group comes regularly while others come and go. Another yoga teacher reported that once the women who had been coming regularly to her class were released, another core group did not develop and the class was discontinued due to lack of interest. (Horne, personal communication) Each situation had different factors contributing to attendance levels some of which can be attributed to the relative stability or change in the prison population.

As mentioned previously, a typical range of yoga practices are taught depending on the need of the participants at the session. Since the question was general, the responses were also general – asanas, pranayama, deep relaxation, meditation, discussion. The most beneficial general practices mentioned were pranayama, deep relaxation and meditation. No specific practices were named.

The focus of the classes are all similar, but expressed in many different ways:

- "The emphasis is on embodying one's experience in a genuine way in order to learn how to respond to life...effectively [and] consciously" (Getz, personal communication)
- "To develop love and respect for themselves and others." (Madhu, personal communication)
- "To share with them how they can experience inner peace even in the midst of chaos, noise, disruptions, etc. so prevailing in the prison environment, anywhere, at anytime." (Pozzi, personal communication)
- "Inner wisdom, body wisdom vs. ego mind." (Reynolds, personal communication)
- "Giving inmates the tools to develop their own daily practices." (Stringer, personal communication)
- "To bring a sense of respect into the deepest humanity in each one of us through the practice of yoga." (Hutchins, Interview with Sarahjoy Marsh)

Yoga is simply a tool, a language, for learning to engage the heart and mind in totally new ways that can have an enormously transformative effect no matter where one is.

All the programs whether coordinated by an organization or an individual, began as a result of a yoga teacher offering to teach in the facility. The classes got off the ground after much red tape, delays, background checks, orientations and other bureaucratic delays. Prison officials have even come to a teacher's class before making a final decision. Most of the programs are offered on a volunteer basis as karma yoga, as seva, though a few are funded through the prisons. Whether or not a yoga program is initiated or continues often depends on both the level of support by the prison administration and the availability of the teacher. Organizations that have a core of volunteer teachers are more able to keep a program going.

DISCUSSION

The Findings of this study are limited, yet they do indicate that yoga and meditation are being taught successfully in U.S. prisons under widely varying conditions. It should come as no surprise that yoga teachers are adaptable and where there is will and determination for a program to exist, it does. In some places the programs sound like they are thriving. All these programs and teachers are amazing resources. From my own experience and from reading about other teachers' experiences, teaching in prison is a profound experience for all involved – the teacher and the participants. It is very honest and very human.

6

Alternative Medicine for Health and Yoga

In the past decade we have seen an increased awareness of complementary and alternative medicine (CAM) in both public and governmental sectors. What today is called alternative medicine covers a wide range of disciplines, most of which are guided by the "healing model" of holistic medicine, which emphasizes the complex interplay between multiple factors: biochemical, environmental, psychological, and spiritual, as opposed to the biomedical model which reduces disease to a disturbance in biochemical process and relies heavily on the "curative model" of care.

Healthcare providers today are faced with challenging issues of health-promotion, disease prevention and management of chronic illnesses for which conventional medicine has offered only limited success. An increasingly knowledgeable patient population is now fueling the CAM movement by seeking alternatives to traditional treatments. The use of CAM modalities by Americans between 1990 and 1997 increased from 34 per cent to 42 per cent of the general population. In addition, the total number of visits to CAM providers increased from 427 million to 629 million within this same time period. This number exceeds the total visits to all primary care physicians combined (386 million) in 1997.

Just a decade ago, alternative therapies were readily dismissed by physicians as fringe medicine, however today CAM is now beginning to earn attention and academic stature. The growing number of CAM clinics affiliated with hospitals, the expansion of CAM courses within academic medical education, and the increase in CAM benefits offered by insurers offer clear evidence of this trend.

The costs of CAM approaches and their potential risks and benefits provide a public health rationale for subjecting them to critical appraisal. In pursuit of this vision, the US Congress authorized in 1998 the establishment of a new component of the National Institutes of Health—the National Center for Complementary and Alternative Medicine ("NCCAM")—with a mandate to conduct CAM research, train CAM investigators, and disseminate authoritative information to practitioners and the public. That same year, the Journal of the American Medical Assoc. (JAMA) published a series of scientific studies in a special issue dedicated to alternative medicine. This was the first such effort by a mainstream US medical journal and was an attempt to meet doctors' needs for high-quality scientific information on treatments that more and more patients are trying.

COMPLEMENTARY AND ALTERNATIVE MEDICINE THERAPIES BY CATEGORY

According to NCCAM, CAM is defined as a group of diverse medical and health care systems, practices, and products that are not presently considered to be part of conventional medicine. The many diverse CAM therapies are frequently grouped into five overlapping categories: biologically based therapies, manipulative and body-based interventions, mind-body interventions, "energy" therapies, and alternative medical systems. Below is an overview of some of the common CAM therapies in each category and some basic information on training and licensure. For more information on Licensing, Certifying and Training Standards for CAM therapies than what is provided below, the American Medical Student Association has some good reference information.

BIOLOGICALLY BASED THERAPIES

Naturopathic Medicine

Naturopathic medicine is a distinct system of primary health care - an art, science, philosophy and practice of diagnosis, treatment and prevention of illness. Naturopathic physicians are primary health care practitioners, whose diverse techniques include modern and traditional, scientific and empirical methods. The priciples of Naturopathic medicine are based upon the objective observation of the nature of health and disease, and are continually reexamined in the light of scientific advances. Methods used are consistent with these principles and are chosen upon the basis of patient individuality.

The training program for a naturopathic physician (ND) resembles in part that of a medical physician (MD), and takes place through a 4-year post-graduate training program. The general standard for licensure is graduation from an accredited 4-year ND program, and successful completion of the state licensing board exam. NDs are licensed in every New England State with the exception of Massachusetts and Rhode Island. Legislation to license NDs in Massachusetts, An Act for the Registration of Naturopathic Doctors (SB661/ HB 2603), has recently been under consideration by the Massachusetts legislature, over the strenuous objections of the Massachusetts Medical Society. Currently, there are over 15 naturopathic physicians based in the Bay State.

Herbal Medicine

Herbal medicine is one of the oldest holistic systems of medicine. It uses plants, plant parts, their water or solvent extracts, essential oils, gums, resins, exudates or other form of advanced products made from plant parts used therapeutically to provide proactive support of various physiological systems; or, in a more conventional medical sense, to treat, cure, or prevent a disease in animals or humans. Its therapies are based on the body's capacity to heal itself. It is incorporated in a diverse number of systems of medicine. Many current medications are derived from plants, for example digoxin, tamoxifen, aspirin, morphine, and others.

The practice of herbal medicine is a diverse field with practitioners from many several medicinal traditions using herbal medicine in many different ways. Each tradition has its own standards and as a result there is no formal standard for training. Some healing modalities, including Chinese Herbology and Naturopathic Medicine, have their own certification and licensing processes.

Nutritional Supplements

Because CAM practitioners commonly stress that each individual is unique on a biochemical level, many consider individualized nutritional supplementation to be an effective mode of prevention and treatment. Popularized in the 1970's by Dr. Linus Pauling, this modality is used widely by the general public. The practice of nutritional supplementation is broad and it includes everything from megavitamin therapies and other preparations containing a range of ingredients that can be natural or synthetic.

Nutrition

Nutrition started to become more important as a healing practice in the beginning of the 20th century. Nutritional practices are directed at those who are trying to maintain health and decrease symptoms of illnesses through balanced diets. Alternative practitioners embrace a number of diets that are being evaluated as adjunct therapies for chronic conditions such as cancer, inflammatory disease, cardiovascular disorders, allergies, etc. Examples are macrobiotic diet, raw foods diet, detoxification diet, Gerson therapy, vegetarianism, veganism, the Hay diet and the Pritkin diet.

While no global standard exists for the education requirements for dietitians/nutritionists, there are general standards required by individual licensing, certifying and registering bodies. There are currently 46 states that regulate dietitians or nutritionists through licensure, certification or registration. Both nutritionists and dieticians require licensure in Massachusetts.

MANIPULATIVE AND BODY BASED THERAPIES

Alexander Technique

In the late 19th century, an Australian actor, Frederick Matthias Alexander, observed a correlation between correct posture of the body and the ability to perform certain tasks. In the therapy he developed that is his namesake, stresses are reduced by teaching patients how to hold their bodies and how to move in healthful alignment. Patients' awareness of the way they move and position their bodies helps their body systems to function more efficiently. Many municipalities in Massachusetts have licensed fully-trained practitioners of Alexander Technique and other forms of movement education such as the Feldenkrais® Method (see below) in conjunction with massage therapy. About 40 members of the American Society for the Alexander Technique, one of the profession's certifying bodies, are based in Massachusetts.

Chiropractic

Founded in 1895 by D.D. Palmer of Iowa, chiropractic is a system of healing, based on the belief that restoring normal nerve function can cure disease. Chiropractors practice manipulation, especially of the spinal column, along with massage, physical therapy techniques, nutrition counseling, heat therapy and traction. This is one of the most accepted forms of CAM in the United States. Their practice is conservative, non-invasive and does not involve pharmaceutical products or surgery. Doctors of chiropractic attend accredited chiropractic colleges and can currently be licensed in all 50 states, and their services are reimbursed by many medical insurance plans. Each state has its own state licensing board to monitor the practice of chiropractic, including Massachusetts, whose Board of Chiropractors oversees approximately 1,930 licensees in the Commonwealth.

The Feldenkrais® Method

A system of movement education developed in the 1940s by a Russian born atomic physicist, Dr. Moshe Feldenkrais®, this method teaches patients to avoid certain postures and positions that could lead to the development of disorders of the nervous system. Exercises which emphasize posture and breathing are central to this system. According to research, cerebral palsy and multiple sclerosis patients have found Feldenkrais® therapeutic. Initially taught in Israel and the United States, it has been adopted throughout the world. Many municipalities in Massachusetts have licensed fully-trained practitioners of the Feldenkrais® Method and other forms of movement education such as the Feldenkrais® Method (see below) in conjunction with massage therapy. About 35 practitioners in the Feldenkrais® Guild of North America are based in Massachusetts.

Massage

Massage is an ancient form of healing and maintaining good health. It has been used in many different cultures. Massage has been shown to promote circulation, enhance the immune system's ability to fight illness, relieve muscle pain, and promote digestion. In addition to the physiological benefits of this modality, massage has definite psychological benefits-- it can be used to increase self esteem and to decrease symptoms of depression and is often integrated into various complementary therapies.

There are numerous schools that teach a variety of styles and approaches. While standards differ, training typically includes: anatomy, physiology, pathology, massage theory and technique, and supervised practice. The Commission on Massage Therapy Accreditation currently accredits about 70 schools in the United States. 500 hours is of training is considered to be the average requirement for state or local licensing, although licensing criteria for massage therapy differ greatly by state. Currently 32 states license massage therapy across the country. Last year, with the support of a range of Massachusetts professional bodywork organizations, Massachusetts Rep. Antonio Cabral (D-New Bedford) introduced House Bill 3155, which would establish statewide licensing, and may be up for vote this year.

Osteopathy

Andrew Taylor Still founded the discipline of osteopathy in the 19th century in reaction to hospital conditions and the medicine he saw practiced during the American Civil War. Osteopaths emphasize the relationship between the musculoskeletal system and organ function and use physical manipulation to correct malfunctions. The first osteopathic medical school was established in 1892 in Kirksville, Missouri. Osteopathic doctors are licensed to practice medicine in all states in the United States and have the same professional rights and responsibilities as medical doctors. Their techniques range from gentle massage to high velocity mobilization of the joints and therefore, these practices are particularly useful in treating back and joint pain. Osteopathy emphasizes treating the whole person.

Training of osteopathic physicians parallels that of allopathic physicians. There are 19 four-year osteopathic medical schools in the United States and coursework is similar to that of allopathic medical school, with an additional 300-500 hours of musculo-skeletal coursework. Osteopathic physicians are licensed to practice in all 50 states. DOs are licensed by the states in which they practice. The Massachusetts Board of Registration in Medicine licenses osteopathic physicians in the Bay State, as it does medical doctors and acupuncturists.

Reflexology

Reflexology is a therapy based on the ancient tradition of foot massage. Early twentieth century physicians discovered that there are organs in the body that can be affected by pressure applied to certain zones in the feet or hands. Stimulation of natural healing powers of the entire body occurs when the feet and hands are massaged. This therapy is commonly used in combination with aromatherapy or naturopathy. Reflexology is not licensed in Massachusetts, and the field does not have a unifying certifying body, making it difficult to gauge its prevalence in the Commonwealth.

Rolfing

Dr. Ida Rolf originally developed Rolfing in the 1950s. Rolfing contains elements of massage and is based on realignment and remolding of fascia by using elbows, fingers and knuckles. The main uses of this modality are improvement of posture, therapy for sports injury, and alleviation of persistent muscle pain and respiratory problems. In addition, Rolfing has been used to prevent postural or stress related problems. Athletes, dancers and singers often find Rolfing beneficial. Many municipalities in Massachusetts consider Rolfing to be a form of massage or bodywork and license it as such. There are about 20 Rolfers practicing in Massachusetts who are certified by the Rolf Institute, Rolfing's preeminent professional organization in the US.

MIND-BODY INTERVENTIONS

Western medicine traditionally viewed the mind and body as separate entities. However, in the late 20th century, an appreciation began to develop for the interrelationship between the two.

Biofeedback

The word "biofeedback" was coined in 1969 to describe laboratory procedures that trained research subjects to alter their brain activity, blood pressure, muscle tension, heart rate and other bodily functions that are not normally controlled voluntarily. Biofeedback training is a type of behavior therapy that attempts to change learned responses to stress. It can be very successful in alleviating symptoms (e.g., pain and muscle tension) of a disorder, and its effects can be especially lasting if used in combination with psychotherapy when a patient learns to understand his reactions to stress. Migraine headaches, gastrointestinal cramping (e.g., colitis), high blood pressure, tics, and the frequency and severity of epileptic seizures are some of the ailments treated by biofeedback.

Hypnotherapy (Hypnosis)

Hypnosis is a special psychological state with certain physiological attributes, resembling sleep only superficially and marked by a functioning of the individual at a level of awareness other than the ordinary conscious state. This state is characterized by a degree of increased receptiveness and responsiveness in which inner experiential perceptions are given as much significance as is generally given to external reality. Hypnotherapy is psychotherapy that facilitates suggestion, reeducation, or analysis by hypnosis. It has been officially endorsed as a therapeutic method by medical, psychiatric, dental, and psychological associations throughout the world. It has been found most useful in preparing people for anesthesia, enhancing the drug response, and reducing the required dosage. In childbirth it is particularly helpful, because it is effective in alleviating the mother's discomfort while avoiding drug-induced impairment of the child's physiological function. Hypnosis is highly regarded in the management of otherwise intractable pain, including that of terminal cancer. It is valuable in reducing the widespread fear of dental procedures; the very people whom dentists find most difficult to treat frequently respond best to hypnotic suggestion.

Meditation/Mindfulness

Meditation is private devotion or mental exercise consisting in any of innumerable techniques of concentration, contemplation, and abstraction, regarded as conducive to heightened spiritual awareness or somatic calm. The practice of meditation has occurred worldwide since ancient times in a variety of contexts. In recent medical and psychological studies, skilled meditation practitioners have proved effective in controlling pulse and respiratory rates and to varying degrees, in the symptomatic control of migraine headache, hypertension, and hemophilia, among other conditions. There is currently no formal licensure or certification process for meditation instructors due to the large body of meditation traditions as well as differing opinions in training requirements.

Yoga

In a very basic sense, yoga is a system of exercises for attaining bodily or mental control and well-being. The Sanskrit word "Yoga" comes from the root yug (to join), or yoke (to bind together or to concentrate). Essentially, yoga describes a means of uniting or a method of discipline: to join the body to the mind and together join to the self (soul), or the union between the individual self and the transcendental self. In his classical work The Yoga Sutras, a 2000-year-old treatise on yogic philosophy, the Indian sage Patanjali defines Yoga as "that which restrains the thought process and makes the mind serene."

Yoga has been practiced in India for thousands of years, and is traditionally used by spiritual seekers as a system of self-development for purification of the body and mind. Yoga is proposed to be a preventive as well as curative system of the body, mind, and spirit. Many different schools of yoga exist and each has its own curriculum for training new teachers.

Therefore there are no commonly agreed training standards. No license is required to teach yoga and each school has its own certification process.

ENERGY - BIOENERGETIC THERAPIES

Acupuncture

Acupuncture is an ancient Oriental form of medicine practiced for millenia. Acupuncture is based on dualistic philosophy of balancing the two cosmic forces of yin and yang. Disease occurs when imbalance blocks the vital life force or qi (chi), which flows through 12 pathways in the body to the major organ areas. The aim is to restore the physical, emotional and spiritual balance of the person. It involves the insertion of small needles into the body at hundreds of points along the 14 vertical meridians and other specialized pathways. Other techniques associated with acupuncture are moxibustion and cupping. Moxibustion is the warming of acupuncture points with smoldering herbs. Cupping is the application of wood, metal or glass cups containing a partial vacuum to the acupuncture site to create blood congestion and is used in treating back pain, sprains, soft tissue injury and to relieve lung congestion.

Researchers have postulated that acupuncture works by stimulating the body to release natural pain killers such as endorphins or enkephalins. Another theory suggests that acupuncture stimulates the release of neurotransmitters such as serotonin or noradrenaline. Others have posited that the minor stimulation of acupuncture points selectively acts on impulse transmission to the central nervous system, thus closing certain neurological "gates" and blocking the transmission of pain impulses from other parts of the body. Another theory suggests that acupuncture causes the body to release vasodialators and histamines. Acupuncture has been proven successful in relieving pain and providing anesthesia.

There are currently more than 50 schools and colleges of acupuncture in the United States, most of which are accredited by the Accreditation Commission for Acupuncture and Oriental Medicine (ACAOM). The National Certification Commission for Acupuncture and Oriental Medicine (NCCAOM) certifies graduates of ACAOM accredited programs. Licensure for acupuncture is available in 35 states, including Massachusetts, where it is managed by the Massachusetts Board of Registration in Medicine. There are over 400 NCCAOM-certified acupuncturists in Massachusetts.

Qi Gong

Also originating in ancient China, Qi Gong (Chi Kung) is the practice of focused exercises to promote health and well being. All exercises or forms involve four basic elements: mind, sight, movement and breathing. As well as personal healing, some practitioners can heal others by focusing their Chi on the person who is ill.

Therapeutic and Healing Touch

Therapeutic Touch is a non-oriental practice of energetic healing. Dr. Dolores Krieger developed it in the 1970. In practicing therapeutic touch, the healer moves their hands 2 to 4 inches above the patient's body in an effort to sense the trouble spots, the blocked energy within the patient's body. The healer's hands sweep over the patient's body and act as a conduit for energies to be rebalanced to come through the healer into the patient. Healing Touch is considered very similar or even synonymous with Therapeutic Touch.

Therapeutic Touch (TT) is taught worldwide, primarily at universities, and nursing and medical schools and is still most widely utilized by the nursing profession. There is no formal licensing or certifying process for Therapeutic Touch. The scope of practice for nurses in Massachusetts covers the use of both Therapeutic Touch and Healing Touch.

Reiki (Pronounced "ray-kee")

This term can be translated from Japanese as "universal energy of life." The practice is based on methods from ancient Tibetan medicine. In the mid-1800's Professor M. Usui rediscovered and propagated this system, and in the 20th century its use reached the US. Students learn Reiki by studying with a Reiki Master. The Master initiates students through a process of energy attunement. Reiki involves the practitioner placing their hands on a number of chakras or energy points on the surface of the patient, who is typically fully clothed. Practitioners then channel this universal energy from the top of their heads down through their hands and into the patient's body.

Reiki is not currently regulated, and there is no formal licensure or common certification process. Several schools have their own certification processes based on their individual method of training. The scope of practice for nurses in Massachusetts covers the use of Reiki.

Religious and Spiritual Healing Practices

Religious/spiritual worldviews locate a person's or group's experiences in a larger, sacred framework. Religious/spiritual stories, texts, rituals, symbols, words, and actions transform the participant's experience of self and others. Many religious/spiritual teachings shape how one relates to others and to the world. A major area addressed by religion/spirituality is the question of suffering, which is often related to how illness, dying, death, and life beyond death are understood. Most religious/spiritual traditions include healing as a key aspect, whether through prayer, laying on of hands, ritual, and/or other practices. In some cases, healing refers to the expectation that the person who is sick will be fully cured. In other cases, it involves healing on a deeper level that may or may not correspond to a "cure." Indeed, in some cases, full healing may be thought to take place only after death.

Prayer and Ritual

Prayer for the sick or intercessional prayer is classified as a paranormal phenomenon. A cleric or lay person, sometimes a small group or congregation, offer prayers to a higher power in order to bring about individual healing. Western medicine has no explanation for the miraculous healing that is sometimes reported. However, this practice has become the subject of serious clinical research.

Laying on of Hands (Faith Healing)

Closely related to prayers for the sick, the laying on of hands involves the act of touching the patient while prayers for healing are offered to a higher power. The practice can be lead by a cleric who acts as an intermediary between the higher power and the patient. However, in certain groups, such as charismatic Christians, many people may lay their hands on the patient.

ALTERNATIVE SYSTEMS OF MEDICAL THOUGHT

Ayurveda

Ayurvedic medicine is the oldest system of medicine in the world, principally practiced in India. This system of medicine is named after the Sanskrit words for "Knowledge of Life". Mental, emotional and physical health based on balancing three doshas or "vital energies." This is done through diet, yoga, breathing, exercises, massage, herbal and animal remedies as well as purifying techniques. Currently, the Indian government is sponsoring research to validate Ayurvedic medicine and to integrate its practices into Western medicine.

In India the education and training requirements for Ayurvedic medicine are on a par similar to those for a medical doctor. In the United States there are a number of schools that teach Ayurvedic principles and there is no consensus as to the graduation requirements. The California College of Ayurveda (CCA), currently offers the most complete training program. Graduates receive certification from the CCA, as well as American Institute of Vedic Studies (AIV). There is no formal certifying or licensing in the United States, other than that offered by the CCA.

Homeopathy

Homeopathy is a system of medicine founded in the late eighteenth century by Samuel Hahnemann, a German physician. The science of homeopathy suggests that homeopathic remedies stimulate the body's ability to heal itself. Homeopathy is primarily based on a theory of "like cures like", where a substance causing symptoms in a healthy individual will become a cure for similar symptoms in someone who is ill. Such substances that originate from animal, plant or mineral sources are diluted multiple times to produce homeopathic remedies. Homeopathy is a popular form of medicine throughout the world. It is widely accepted in Great Britain, France, Germany, Australia, and India and is experiencing renewed interest in the United States.

The Council for Homeopathic Education in the US accredits homeopathic training programs, of which there are more than 30 in the United States. Most of the accredited training programs are post-graduate programs intended for MDs and DOs and offer didactic education as well as clinical experience. The certification process depends upon the background of the practitioner. Most physicians practice homeopathic medicine under the licensure provided by their state medical boards.. Currently, MDs and DOs are the only professions licensed to practice homeopathy in all states.

Traditional Chinese Medicine

Traditional Chinese Medicine (TCM) is based on the philosophy of balance between two cosmic forces, yin and yang and the unobstructed flow of the life force (qi). It involves several modalities such as acupuncture and Qi Gong (see above), Chinese herbology, and Asian bodywork therapies such as shiatsu.

In Chinese herbal medicine, herbs may be taken as teas, which are often bad tasting or raw. Herbs can also be packaged into pills or capsules. Herbal prescription is based on Chinese herbal lore, which matches the TCM interpretation of the symptoms of the patient with herbs, which address those conditions. The National Certification Commission for Acupuncture and Oriental Medicine (NCCAOM) certifies graduates of ACAOM accredited programs in Chinese Herbology. There are 97 NCCAOM-certified practitioners of Chinese Herbology in Massachusetts, most whom are also licensed acupuncturists.

Asian Bodywork therapy is based on the same TCM principles as acupuncture and Chinese Herbology, but instead uses manual pressure, massage, and manipulation to strengthen and enhance the flow of qi through the body. Massachusetts has over 100 professional practitioners of Asian bodywork therapies such as shiatsu (a Japanese variety) or tuina (a Chinese variety). They are commonly considered licensable as massage therapists in the municipalities where they practice.

Addressing the Challenge of Integrating Conventional and Alternative Medicine- Integrative Medicine Alliance

Is it possible to conceive of an integrative approach to healthcare—one that would bring together the best of what both conventional medicine and CAM have to offer? The great variety of alternative therapies pose equally great challenges for Boards of Health that in a responsible way wish to draw upon the resources of qualified local alternative therapists as part of a more comprehensive, integrative approach to promoting the health of their communities.

Many CAM therapies emphasize the importance of a healthy lifestyle and embrace a preventative model of healthcare that is consistent with the public health paradigm. Yet most of these therapies do not have a licensing structure in place, making the qualifications of many holistic practitioners harder to assess. While clinical trials on the effectiveness of these therapies are growing in number, and universities are beginning to undertaking more systematic research, comprehensive and definitive results are many years away.

Nonetheless, Boards of Health need to appreciate that these therapies are widespread in their communities and as such need to be acknowledged, understood, and possibly utilized.

YOGA AS EXERCISE OR ALTERNATIVE MEDICINE

Yoga as exercise or alternative medicine primarily involves hatha yoga, which focuses on physical postures. Modified versions of the physical exercises in hatha yoga have become popular as a kind of low-impact physical exercise, and are used for therapeutic purposes. "Yoga" in this sense and in common parlance refers primarily to the asanas but less commonly to pranayama. Aspects of meditation are sometimes included.

Both the meditative and the exercise components of yoga show promise for non-specific health benefits. According to an article in the Journal of Alternative and Complementary Medicine, the system of hatha yoga believes that prana, or healing "life energy" is absorbed into the body through the breath, and can treat a wide variety of illnesses and complaints.

Yoga has been studied as an intervention for many conditions, including back pain, stress, and depression.

A survey released in December 2008 by the US National Center for Complementary and Alternative Medicine found that yoga was the sixth most commonly used alternative therapy in the United States during 2007, with 6.1 percent of the population participating.

BACKGROUND AND OVERVIEW

Yoga came to the attention of an educated western public in the mid 19th century along with other topics of Hindu philosophy. The first Hindu teacher to actively advocate and disseminate aspects of yoga to a western audience was Swami Vivekananda, who toured Europe and the United States in the 1890s. However, Vivekananda did not include the physical practices of Hatha Yoga in his teachings.

The physical asana of hatha yoga have a tradition that goes back to the 15th century, but they were not widely practiced in India prior to the early 20th century. Hatha yoga was advocated by a number of late 19th to early 20th century gurus in India, including Sri Krishnamacharya in south India,

Swami Sivananda in the north, Sri Yogendra in Bombay, and Swami Kuvalyananda in Lonavala, near Bombay.

In the 1960s, western interest in Hindu spirituality reached its peak, giving rise to a great number of Neo-Hindu schools specifically advocated to a western public. Among the teachers of hatha yoga who were active in the west in this period were B.K.S. Iyengar, K. Pattabhi Jois, Swami Vishnu-devananda, and Swami Satchidananda. A second "yoga boom" followed in the 1980s, as Dean Ornish, a follower of Swami Satchidananda, connected yoga to heart health, legitimizing yoga as a purely physical system of health exercises outside of counter culture or esotericism circles, and unconnected to a religious denomination. Since then, yoga has been used as supplementary therapy for diverse conditions such as cancer, diabetes, asthma, and AIDS. The scope of medical issues where yoga is used as a complementary therapy continues to grow.

There are many different styles and disciplines and people practice yoga for a variety of reasons. One of the main goals of yoga is to improve overall well-being through teaching discipline and self-regulation. Recently, research has focused on the healing properties of yoga and how it relates to positive psychology. Researchers wonder what psychological advantages it can afford, in addition to the previously discovered physical benefits. Yoga has proven to offer different and multiple benefits for individuals ranging from consciousness of one's body and its capabilities, satisfaction from challenging oneself physically, and increased energy and mental clarity and concentration.While the topic is still somewhat new and some research is still preliminary, results have shown significant improvements in both physical and mental health among a variety of subjects in various circumstances.

The practice of yoga traditionally includes both meditation and exercise, but in the West the focus is mainly on exercise. The more classical approaches, such as Iyengar Yoga, move at a more deliberate pace, emphasize proper alignment and execution and hold asanas for a longer time. They aim to gradually improve flexibility, balance, and strength. Other approaches, such as Ashtanga or Power Yoga, shift between asanas quickly and energetically. More recently, contemporary approaches to yoga have developed (such as Vanda Scaravelli inspired, as taught by the likes of Diane Long, Sophie Hoare and Marc Woolford) inviting students to become their own authority in yoga practice by offering principle-based approaches to yoga that can be applied to any form. Nearly all types of yoga practices include asanas, pranayama (breathing exercises), and savasanas (relaxation techniques).

MAJOR THEORETICAL APPROACHES

Positive psychology

One of the most recent trends in the practice of and research about yoga as alternative therapy is how it relates to the field of positive psychology. Positive psychology is the study of that which contributes to the overall well-being of and supports the optimal functioning of individuals. As more research is released in support of yoga contributing to a better state of being, yoga becomes more in line with positive psychology's focus on developing alternate strategies for healing and bettering individuals' lives. Positive psychology refutes the concept of dualism and scientists in this field believe that the body and mind cannot be separated. This logic indicates that all physical benefits resulting from the practice of yoga are coupled with mental benefits such as development of inner consciousness, positivity, awareness, and appreciation of nature, combining to offer a whole-body therapy. Drawing from recent research on the mental and physical benefits of practicing yoga, positive psychologists have begun to look deeper into the possibilities of utilizing yoga as a positive psychology therapy.

Yoga and religion

The most historically rooted perspective taken on yoga is that of considering yoga's spiritual linkages and implications. The foundational text for yoga is a Hindu scripture named Yoga Sutra. The Yoga Sutra is a compilation of sutras, or concise, instructional writings. There remains controversy over when the writings were published. The Yoga Sutra is built on a foundation of Samkhya philosophy. The physical practices detailed in the Yoga Sutras are the manifestation of theory offered in the Samkhya philosophies. The sutras are divided into four parts, including:

- Samadhi Pada: translated: "On being absorbed in spirit." This section focuses on the "emergence of the spiritual man from the veils and meshes of the psychic nature."
- Sadhana Pada "On being immersed in spirit."
- Vibhuti Pada "On supernatural abilities and gifts."
- Kaivalya Pada "On absolute freedom." This final section discusses the "mechanism of salvation," referring to "the ideally simple working of cosmic law which brings the spiritual man to birth, growth and fullness of power, and prepares him for the splendid, toilsome further stages of his great journey home."

Evangelical Christian leader Albert Mohler is a critic of yoga, saying 'the embrace of yoga is a symptom of our postmodern spiritual confusion'.

Religious articles from a variety of views and beliefs have been published to try to show that Yoga is leading people from their previous beliefs into eastern religions. Some websites are wholly dedicated to this purpose, under names such as "Yogadangers.com"

Mindfulness

Mindfulness has been a fundamental aspect of yoga since its early documentation in the Yoga Sutra. Mindfulness is defined as "attending to relevant aspects of experience in a nonjudgmental manner". Mindfulness is attained through the practice of yoga in that one is able to maintain awareness of the present, releasing control and attachment of beliefs, thoughts and emotions. By letting go of one's thoughts and mind, allowing the mind to be calm and at peace, one is able to attain a greater sense of emotional well-being and balance. Researchers have recently begun to take interest in the healing benefits of mindfulness through yoga. Research has indicated that there are health benefits of applying mindfulness-based approaches to pain management, physical functioning, and ability to cope with stresses in everyday life.

Physical aspects of yoga

Yoga has been highly westernized in recent years, and a majority of the result of this westernization and modernization is the heightened profile of the physical aspect yoga has to offer. This physically exerting practice is typically hatha yoga, which combines asanas that exert the participant's physical self. The therapeutic healing benefits of yoga were recently discussed by van der Kolk, who posited that regulation of physical movement is a fundamental priority of the nervous system. For this reason, focusing on and developing an awareness of physical movement allows for the mind and body to connect and be in sync.

This is beneficial for humans, especially those suffering from psychological conditions such as depression and PTSD (the focus of van der Kolk's work) because the connectedness of mind and body allow for feelings of control and understanding of their "inner sensations" and state of being. The physical benefits of yoga are linked to the release of ß-endorphins and the shift caused in neurotransmitter levels linked to emotions such as dopamine and serotonin. These benefits are most likely in high-intensity practices of yoga.Lower-intensity yoga practices, which includes a majority of yoga, typically spark the "relaxation response" as defined by Dr. Herbert Benson. This response is typified by a "physiological de-activation" of tenseness and control over one's body. Benson related this release of control to the implicit dominance of the parasympathetic nervous system(PNS).

MAJOR EMPIRICAL FINDINGS

A 2010 literature review of the research on the use of yoga for treating depression said that preliminary research suggests that yoga may be effective in the management of depression. Both the exercise and the mindfulness meditation components may be helpful. However the review cautioned that "Although results from these trials are encouraging, they should be viewed as very preliminary because the trials, as a group, suffered from substantial methodological limitations." At the same time, a 2009 individual study found that the regular practice of yoga helps to decrease levels of anxiety significantly. For individuals who practiced yoga twice weekly for a period of two months, levels of state anxiety and trait anxiety decreased. People also found evidence of improved mood and increased energy after an hour-long class. Evidence also indicates that yoga has some effect on lowering levels of anxiety and stress. A study on the effects of hatha yoga showed that the emphasis on breath awareness, internal centering, relaxation, and meditation enabled participants to learn to avoid mental and emotional blockages. These strategies helped participants experience lower stress and anxiety levels in addition to higher quality of life scores.

While the healing properties of yoga help individuals with clinically diagnosed anxiety and depression problems, they also help people learn to navigate and cope with daily sources of stress. A study conducted with a group of medical school students revealed lowered stress overall in addition to less stress on the mornings of exams. Significantly fewer students in the experimental group (those who received the yoga treatment) failed their exams than in the control group. Students in the experimental group said that they had a better sense of well-being, improved concentration, self-confidence, and lower levels of irritability.

More recent studies have looked into how yoga can help participants cope with symptoms from more physical conditions, such as cancer. Learning breathing and relaxation techniques help patients manage pain, depression, anxiety, insomnia, and fatigue. The patients reported that their overall quality of life significantly improved in addition to mood, distress, sleep quality, and severity of cancer symptoms. A yoga intervention program designed for overweight women showed significantly lower instances of binge-eating and higher instances of additional physical activity both during and after the intervention. Women lost weight and most became self-motivated to participate in other forms of exercise outside of the intervention.

APPLICATIONS

Anxiety and depression

The effect of yoga on symptoms of anxiety and depression is one of the most well-studied aspects of yoga's effect on the body and mind. Although researchers are optimistic about the effectiveness of yoga in alleviating depression, a 2010 review of research says that studies to date, while suggestive, are not yet conclusive. However, some research says that regular yoga practice (at least once weekly) helps to decrease levels of depression significantly. Twice weekly yoga practice for two months showed a significant decrease in levels of depression as well as levels of both state and trait anxiety. Some studies also indicate that hatha yoga has a significant effect on lowering levels of anxiety and accompanying stress. Hatha yoga encourages an increased awareness of breath, internal centering, relaxation, and meditation. These strategies helped participants experience significantly lower stress and anxiety levels in addition to higher quality of life scores.

According to a 2009 psychology textbook, a rigorous randomized controlled trial comparing kundalini yoga with the relaxation response and mindfulness meditation in obsessive-compulsive disorder patients found a significant treatment difference, with a large effect size, in favor of kundalini yoga. Moreover, a 2005 systematic review of the research on yoga and anxiety presented encouraging results, particularly with anxiety-related disorders such as obsessive-compulsive disorder. Similarly, a 2003 study found lower scores of state anxiety and improvement in subjective well being, after a single yoga session. A similar order of improvement was observed after either a session of Feldenkrais exercise or a swimming session. Other studies have shown that yoga practices reduce anxiety and depression, all the while improving well-being.

In terms of its effects on individuals in educational institutions, recent research has found that yoga benefits students, not only in reducing basal anxiety levels, but also in attenuating further increases in anxiety as they experience stressful situations like exams. Additionally, differences in mood before and after class of college students taking different courses (swimming, body conditioning, hatha yoga, fencing exercise, and lecture) were analyzed and results suggest that courses which meet four requirements involving aerobics, noncompetitiveness, predictability, and repetitiveness may reduce stress.

Attention deficit hyperactivity disorder

A 2010 Cochrane Review concludes that there is insufficient evidence to assess the effectiveness of meditative practices such as yoga in the management or improvement ofattention deficit hyperactivity disorder (ADHD). Other research shows that there is little support for yoga as treatment for ADHD alone, but it has merit as a complementary treatment to medication.

Back pain

There is evidence that yoga may be effective in the management of chronic, but not acute, low back pain. A pilot study using a modified hatha yoga treatment showed that this was an effective treatment for chronic lower back pain, but further examination is needed specifically through studies with larger sample sizes.

Cancer

Practice of yoga may improve quality-of-life measures in cancer patients. It is unclear what aspect(s) may be beneficial or what populations should be targeted. Other studies show improvements in how participants cope with symptoms from more physical conditions, like cancer. Learning breathing and relaxation techniques help patients manage pain, depression, anxiety, insomnia, and fatigue.

The patients reported that their overall quality of life significantly improved in addition to mood, distress, sleep quality, and severity of cancer symptoms. Yoga can also help improve flexibility in cancer patients, which may allow the patients to gain confidence doing basic tasks. In a study performed by Susan DiStasio, women with breast cancer stated that they experienced lower pain on the day they practiced yoga, and men with prostate cancer said their stress decreased through yoga. The positive effects of yoga can be soothing to survivors as well and help them to deal with post-cancer distress.

Dementia

A 2008 Cochrane Review concludes that the evidence was insufficient to determine whether adding mild physical activity, such as yoga, to usual care is effective in managing or improving health outcomes in patients with dementia.

Epilepsy

A Cochrane Review found no evidence to support the use of yoga in treatment of epilepsy as of 2009.

Hernias

According to Yona Barash, some asanas can temporarily decrease pressure placed on hernias, while awaiting proper care from a physician.

Menopause

Yoga has not been shown to have any specific effect for the treatment or management of symptoms of menopause.

Pediatrics

A 2009 systematic review concludes that there is insufficient evidence to support the use of yoga for any indication in the pediatric population. No adverse events were reported, and most trials were positive but of low methodological quality.

Sport and athletics

Increasingly yoga is used to train sportspersons and athletes, to maximize performance, improve conditioning, and minimize injury. Yoga is used extensively within British soccer to minimize injury, with Manchester United star Ryan Giggs one of the most high-profile players to publicly incorporate it in his training regime. Philipp Lahm of Germany also uses yoga. This has led to increased interest in the benefits of yoga in other sports and the rise of sports-specific yoga programs linking yoga with Sports Science, such as those developed by UK-based Yoga Sports Science.

Stress

A study conducted with a group of medical school students revealed lowered stress overall in addition to less stress on the mornings of exams. Significantly fewer students in the experimental group (those who received the yoga treatment) failed their exams than in the control group. Students in the experimental group said that they had a better sense of well-being, improved concentration, self-confidence, and lower levels of irritability.

CONTROVERSY

A small percentage of yoga practitioners each year suffer physical injuries analogous to sports injuries. In regard to the practice of yoga itself, especially hatha (physically active) yoga, there are controversies over the legitimacy of "prescribing" yoga for individuals afflicted with particular conditions due to the risk of injury associated with the practice. There have been reports of yoga-related injuries and this is one reason why the practice of yoga as alternative therapy is questioned.

These include carotid artery tears, bulging intervertebral discs, rotator cuff injuries, ganglion cysts, compression of the spine (vertebral column), vertebral artery dissection, and hyperextension of the neck. According to Gary Kraftsow, author of Yoga for Transformation, many asanas aren't suitable for everyone. Orthopedic surgeon Jeffrey Halbrecht, medical director for the Institute for Arthroscopy and Sports Medicine in San Francisco, warns that both experienced and novice yoga practitioners can experience injuries.

"Yoga is marketed as such an innocuous thing," says Loren Fishman, assistant clinical professor of rehabilitation medicine at Columbia University in New York City. "But without care, injuries can absolutely happen." 'Strenuous' yoga has been connected to a form of stroke in young women. Practice of yoga has also been linked to causing hyperextension or rotation of the neck, which may be a precipitating factor in cervical artery dissection.

While much of the medical community views the results of yoga research to be significant, others argue that there were many flaws that undermine results. Much of the research on yoga has been in the form of preliminary studies or clinical trials of low methodological quality, including small sample sizes, inadequate blinding, lack of randomization, and high risk of bias. As of 2011, evidence suggests that yoga may be at least as effective at improving health outcomes as other forms of mild physical exercise when added to standard care. What is found most concerning regarding the legitimacy of yoga as a method of healing is the current lack of specificity and standardization regarding the practice of yoga. One recent study examined the difficulties of implementing yoga-based therapies and methods of healing without any detailed, standardized and vetted descriptions of the asanas promoted as being beneficial for healing. This research calls for the creation of supported intervention practices that could be distributed and applied for use in clinical practice for patients.

7

Health Benefits of Yoga

HEALTH BENEFITS OF HATHA YOGA

As we all learned on the first day of our Level One training, Hatha Yoga means "yoga for health" and is the physical aspect of the practice. It renews, invigorates, and heals the body, stretching and strengthening the muscles, joints, and spine and directing blood and oxygen to the internal organs (including the glands and organs and nerves.) Level One Manual: Section One Practitioners credit yoga for everything from improving their strength, respiration and fitness levels to "opening energy channels." While these anecdotal reports passed on through the years are real and meaningful, we must take care to assure that any benefits we express to our practitioners are more than "yogi lore" and are based on expert opinion and scientific research. Many times, a red flag goes up in a practitioner's mind when the instructor mentions that a certain pose or practice will, for example, " stimulate digestion or improve energy levels." One may wonder if this is just fable passed on through the years, backed up only by personal experience.

It has been hypothesized that yoga may benefit health through mind-body interactions. Scientific research on the effects of yoga began as early as 1924, near Bombay, India at the Kaivalyadhama Yoga Institute and about the same time at the Yoga Institute of Santa Cruz, in Bombay.Unfortunately, much of the research on yoga has been limited. Many studies have been poorly designed with lack of control groups or small sample sizes. Continued research is needed to further validate the health benefits that have been proven thus far. At this time, we can pull from current research and make some basic inferences regarding the benefits of the practice of yoga to our health. The preliminary results are promising, but should be shared with the understanding that conclusive benefits have not yet been proven. The studies which have been done have looked at various areas of benefit that one might receive from the practice of yoga. These areas include behavioral, physical, mental, physiological, personality and disease processes. We will look at the latest research findings in each of these areas, discussing their relevance to the population we instruct through the YogaFit style.

The following summary of scientific studies includes information from reviews performed by three resources which have done literature reviews of published studies on the health benefits of Hatha Yoga. The first scholar is Joan Harrington, PhD., who published a summary in the Research Bulletin of the Himalayan Institute in 1981.The second summary was done by Ralph La Forge, M.S., of Duke Lipid Disorder Training Program at Duke University Medical Center. Finally, the third review was provided by the National Standard, which is an organization that produces scientifically based reviews of complementary and alternative medicine topics. The National Standard summary was reviewed by the faculty of the Harvard Medical School and published on their website. YogaFit compiled the information from these resources to provide a comprehensive picture of current benefits of Hatha Yoga which are backed by the latest scientific research.

FITNESS

We begin our discussion looking at what is usually utmost on the minds of participants who take yoga at the local fitness facility or gym, "fitness." The population most widely served by the YogaFit style may want to know, "will doing yoga make me fit?" Before we begin, let's clarify some basic concepts.

WHAT IS FITNESS?

According to Dave Costill, PhD, Professor Emeritus at Ball State University, fitness is the "ability to live your life without feeling fatigued." An all-embracing definition from the American Council of Sports Medicine (ACSM) states that fitness is related not only to maintaining physical activity but also relating to your health, (for example, someone reducing their risk of heart disease by becoming more fit.) The ACSM describes fitness as consisting of the following: cardiorespiratory fitness, muscular fitness, flexibility and body composition. Experts have long recommended that we do at least three different types of activity to improve our fitness level. So, according to the latest studies, how does Hatha Yoga fit into today's prescription for fitness?

Does yoga increase fitness as well as other types of exercise do? The answer is yes, if done within certain parameters. For example, in a study conducted looking at physiological changes in adult women, researchers looked at the short-term effects of four weeks of intensive yoga practice in six healthy adult female volunteers measured using the maximal exercise treadmill test. Yoga practice involved daily morning and evening sessions of 90 minutes each. In this group, the maximal workout increased by 21 per cent, oxygen consumption per unit of work decreased, demonstrating an increase in cardiorespiratory efficiency. In another study, a comparison was made between the effects of yoga and the effects of physical exercise in athletes. This inquest focused on the effect of pranayama (controlled breathing). This study was a well-done investigation which lasted for two years, examining a control group and an experimental group. The results showed that the subjects who practiced pranayama could achieve higher work rates with reduced oxygen consumption per unit work than the control group, and without an increase in blood lactate levels. In a study conducted which looked at aerobic capacity and perceived exertion after practice of Hatha yogic exercises, investigators found that the practice of Hatha yogic exercises along with games helps to improve aerobic capacity like the practice of conventional exercises (PT), along with games. The yoga group practiced yoga for one hour every morning (six days a week) for six months. Interestingly, the yoga group performed better than the PT group in terms of lower ratings of perceived exertion after exhaustive exercise, bringing in the mind-body connection which is so unique to yoga.

What about the other parameters of fitness? In a study performed at the University of California at Davis, students performed eight weeks of yoga training after which muscular strength and endurance, flexibility, cardiorespiratory fitness, body composition and lung function was tested. Each week, the students attended four sessions in which they performed 10 minutes of pranayama, 15 minutes of warm-up exercises, 50 minutes of asanas, and 10 minutes of meditation. Significant improvements were noted in muscular strength (31 per cent), muscular endurance (57 per cent), flexibility (up to 188 per cent), and VO2max (7 per cent). The VO2 increase was particularly interesting as this study lasted eight weeks while the ACSM recommends that exercise research last at least 15-20 weeks, in order to see VO2 max improvements. Other studies reviewed by our resources indicated increases in respiratory efficiency and competence, cardiovascular efficiency and competence, and decreases in oxygen consumption.

So, can we tell our participants if they just do yoga, they will be "fit?" Well, that depends. As one can note by looking at the few studies described above, these positive results came only after practicing yoga according to certain guidelines. Studies have included more than an hour of practice at least two to fours days a week. The yoga sessions included pranayama work in addition to the typical yoga poses. The asanas included Sun Salutations and challenging standing and balancing poses. The good news is that the content of the yoga described in the studies is inherent in the YogaFit style of yoga. In YogaFit, we are training the body to increase physical endurance by flowing through the poses. The mind also is being trained to stay focused for the duration of the class. We also use "vinyasas," several poses linking together and flowing with the breath, in order to increase strength and endurance. Of course, the practitioner needs to practice several times a week, for at least 60 minute sessions, to incur the benefits proven so far by scientific studies. If one is able to do this, not surprisingly, the fitness benefits fall in line with the benefits achieved by other forms of exercise.

The content of the class must also be quite vigorous, again, for the YogaFit style, this is not a problem. Dee Ann Birkel, an emeritus professor at Ball State's School of Physical Education, and others point out that the Sun Salutations and other continuous linked poses increase the heart rate, making the yoga aerobically challenging. Also, the sustained isometric contractions required of the large and small muscle groups in standing poses increase strength. The concentric and eccentric work required to move in and out of poses in a controlled manner lifting our own body weight and the weight of our limbs serves also to increase our strength. Balance poses require co-activation of our core stabilizing muscles, increasing stability and strength throughout our trunk. So, we can tell our participants with confidence, that practicing yoga with the YogaFit style will increase their fitness levels, not unlike other forms of exercise as long as they practice yoga according to established fitness guidelines.

RECOMMENDATIONS FOR ENSURING IMPROVEMENTS IN FITNESS AND PREVENTING INJURY

Not only are frequency and duration of importance in improving fitness levels through the practice of yoga, but balance within each class of our yoga practice is just as important. As mentioned before, to improve muscular and cardiorespiratory fitness, one needs to incorporate salutations, flowing postures and standing poses, as well as our flexibility poses. How we perform these poses is essential in preventing injury in our participants. When choosing the postures to include in each class, we not only should choose a variety of poses (standing, seated, prone, supine), but we should ensure there is a balance in the particular areas addressed. For example, one could teach the following class which includes all the "requirements" for fitness, yet it would not be a balanced class, in terms of areas addressed, see below:

Mountain I: Sunflowers, Cat/Cow, modified ½ series, full ½ series, flowing lateral flexion,
Flowing chair/monkey

Valley I: Full Salutations either series

Mountain II Triangle, Airplane, Revolved Triangle
½ series between each side
Pyramid, Standing Straddle, Pyramid
½ series

Valley II: Dancer

Mountain III: Camel, Spinal Balance, Forward Fold, Table Top, Butterfly, Boat, Seated Straddle, Seated Spinal Twist, Supine Abdominal Work, Supine Spinal Twist

While the Mountain I and Valley I are certainly appropriate, the poses contained in the rest of the class, may present a problem. If one practices the above class, with such emphasis on forward folds and hamstring lengthening, he is benefitting from those poses certainly. However, unless that person were to come the next day and balance this class out with an emphasis on backward bending poses, he might miss out on the important benefits of strengthening the posterior muscles (through anti-gravity backbend postures) and opening of the front of the body, Only two opening poses were practiced, Camel and Table Top. Also, there were no standing lunge poses which increase strength with knee flexion. In practicing the above poses, one may open the groin area effectively with the butterfly and straddles, but what about opening the posterior hip capsule with a pose such as Pigeon? Most of our YogaFit participants are not able to anticipate what each instructor will do each day in order to "balance" their practice. It is important that we, as instructors provide a balanced class "within" each YogaFit session.

Look at the Mountain II and Mountain III described above, and consider adding counter-poses and a balanced format to the class. Change, add or delete some poses to create a more effective workout:

Mountain II: Suggested Answers: Keep Triangle, Airplane, Revolved Triangle (½ series)

May add: Extended angle, Reverse Warrior, Balancing ½ moon(½ series)

This adds some lunging standing poses, a pose which lengthens the trunk more, transitioning from Reverse Warrior to Balancing ½ Moon provides strengthening with the concentric work of knee extensors. Many other poses/sequences will be appropriate here. The main idea is that the instructor balance the poses, not so many poses with the hamstrings/adductors lengthened and the hips flexed.

Mountain III: Camel, Spinal Balance, then possibly get on their front side for some backbending antigravity poses such as the Locust, Cobra and/or Bow. Add in some posterior hip opening such as Pigeon. Also, perhaps a Seated Straddle (if not included above as Standing Straddle), Seated Forward 1Fold etc., with Spinal Twist added, all for balance within each class.

An example of practicing "unbalanced" activities and their effect on the body can be easily seen in other sports or recreation activities. For example, baseball players and swimmers frequently develop shoulder pain from repetitive practice of the same movements. Cyclists can develop low back pain from sustaining lumbar flexion for long periods of time. These participants are certainly fit in their area of performance, but can develop weakness and injuries from an imbalanced activity. Yoga is unique in that we can offer a totally balanced program, and do so effectively within each class.

Another fitness benefit which is unique to yoga is that fact that we are not only stretching muscles that have shortened, but equal emphasis is placed on correcting muscles that have lengthened. For example, we know that in forward bending, lumbar flexion can be a compensatory motion for limited hip flexion when the hamstrings are short. According to Shirley Sahrmann, PhD, PT, FAPTA; Director, Program in Movement Science at Washington University School of Medicine, the most effective intervention is to address length changes of all the muscles around a joint, not just the shortened muscles. Thus, if the lumbar spine flexes excessively (>20o) with knee extension, the back extensor muscles should be shortened along with stretching the hamstring muscle. The Seated Forward Fold with active back extension effectively addresses this issue. Our cuing to maintain an erect spine in forward bending poses is especially important as motion will occur earlier at the more flexible segment in situations where movement involves both joints. A long term consequence of continually allowing this to happen is increasing flexibility in an area which is already hyper-flexible, as well as training the lumbar spine to move into flexion whenever flexion should be occurring at the hip joint. Also, combining strengthening with flexibility ensures that we protect the joint. Dave Coulter states in Anatomy of Hatha Yoga, "if you merely stretch the connective tissue of the joint capsule without at the same time building strength in the associated muscle, the joints may become susceptible to injury."

Finally, and importantly, in order to help prevent injury in our clients, we must continue to emphasize proper alignment. The YogaFit style of yoga is extremely effective at doing this as we always offer variations of each pose in order to maintain proper alignment. Why is alignment so critical? Ideal alignment facilitates optimal movement. The better the alignment is in a pose, the less chance we have of causing micro trauma to the joints and supporting structures. Studies have shown that spinal segments subjected to the most movement are segments that show the most degenerative changes. Physical therapy is based on exercises that include repeated movements and sustained postures designed to affect tissues positively. Those expected positive results are to improve flexibility, strength and movement patterns. Yoga can accomplish a similar result, if done with proper alignment. On the other hand, the cumulative effect of repetitive movement, when movement deviates from the optimal kineseological standard for movement can be tissue damage. Most of the adult population has some limitations in flexibility or strength which keeps them from utilizing optimal movement patterns in their daily activities. Routine daily movements that are repeatedly performed incorrectly due to these limitations or dysfunctions can result in a pain syndrome. Yoga assists in improving these areas of limitation or deficit. The added benefit that yoga has is the mind-body awareness which is practiced in each session. This can assist the participant in developing an awareness of their own body and how it moves to continue moving in a more efficient manner outside the yoga class and throughout their daily activities. One could certainly hypothesize that those who perform Hatha Yoga regularly are less likely to develop pain syndromes or require physical therapy intervention.

INVERSIONS

Many practitioners have questions about the benefits of doing inversions. Inversions such as the headstand, and shoulderstand can increase the risk factors in practicing yoga if these poses are not done correctly and with care. These two poses can put compressive force on the cervical spine, especially when done by those just beginning their practice of hatha yoga. One should develop strength in the arms and shoulders to keep the weight off the head, and to avoid injury to the neck and spine, prior to attempting the headstand. For those participants who have cervical degeneration, doing these poses may cause nerve irritation. Many people do not realize they have cervical degeneration until symptoms arise. Also, one may have an old injury or mal alignment that may cause nerve irritation.

So, why bother doing inversions at all? Ralph LaForge, M.S., states that there are only two clinical trials in this country which were designed to determine the physiological benefits of inversions, and both these studies were too "statistically under-powered" to draw clear conclusions. Thus we must rely on expert opinions, case studies and educated reasoning to ascertain the benefits/effects of inversions.

The most obvious effect of inversions is to upend one's relationship to gravity. Our bodies are sensitive to the fluctuations in gravity due to the fact that we are made predominately (60 per cent) of water. David Coulter, PhD, states that after 3-5 minutes, the tissue fluids will flow more efficiently from the lower extremities and trunk, up into the abdominal and pelvic organs, creating a healthier exchange of the nutrients and wastes between cells and capillaries. In a study by Dr. DF Chandia, a lecturer on physiological and psychological effects of yoga, they found that the headstand could affect the baseline opening of blood vessels. This increases the efficiency at dilating and constricting so that the body shunts blood more quickly and efficiently to the active areas of the brain. This also may affect the cerebrospinal fluid, a fluid which flows from the brain to the spinal cord. The increased pressure on the top of the skull may increase the elasticity of cranial bones and stimulate the productions of the cerebrospinal fluid. Many times, practitioners will claim that headstands and shoulderstands improves the endocrine system. For example, these postures may assist in the metabolism by stimulating the parathyroid and thyroid glands. This has not yet been proven; however, inversions do increase blood flow to these glands, increasing their efficiency. Pat Layton, physiology teacher for the Iyengar Yoga Institute of San Francisco's Advanced Studies Program, postulates that inversions ensure healthier and more effective lung tissue. Lower lung tissue is more compressed (secondary to gravity) than the upper lung tissue. When we invert, we cause the blood to perfuse the well-ventilated upper lobes which ensures more efficient oxygen to blood exchange and healthier lung tissue

So, in summary, inversions may increase the efficiency of the cardiovascular, respiratory, lymphatic and endocrine systems, according to expert opinion. Scientific validation of these benefits has not yet been performed. We can certainly communicate to our students the benefits we believe the inversions can impart. We should always inform our students of possible risks of injury to their cervical region and thus they can weigh the benefits versus the risks themselves. There certainly are safer partial inversions which may result in similar benefits, at this time, we do not yet know. Let the research continue!

Body-mind Connection

We all know how great we feel after a yoga session, relaxed, de-stressed and invigorated. There are some variables which have been measured which help to tell us why we feel this way, other than subjective, anecdotal reports. The postures are able to assist in balancing the autonomic nervous system. This allows the body to be less "reactive" to changes in stress levels, or even vigorous exercise resulting in a calmer, less anxious physiological environment. Joan Harrington, PhD, states that based on study results, one can reasonably assume that fewer psychosomatic complaints will manifest in regular yoga practitioners. This is due to the direct manipulation of the muscles and viscera, the autonomic nerve system balance and the decreased anxiety. In fact, in a study investigating physiological changes after 3 months of training in yoga, investigators found that practicing yoga resulted in decreased autonomic arousal and more psycho physiological relaxation (heart rate and respiratory rate reduction) in the 40 subjects studied. In studies reviewed by Ralph LaForge, M.S., he found that in selected clinical trials using Hatha Yoga as therapy they found decreased resting blood pressure, increased parasympathetic tone, reduced physiological and psychological response to threat and improvement in baroreflex function/sensitivity. This are all indications of the body's improvement in regulating reactions through the autonomic nervous system. Yoga may also affect levels of brain or blood chemicals, including melatonin and stress hormones.

Through literature review of studies performed, Joan Harrington, PhD, found that studies showed that yoga can facilitate personality change. Yoga is highly effective in dealing with psychosomatic complaints and enhancing the feelings one may have of well-being. Participants are able to improve their feelings of physical health, reduce their anxiety, and enhance their self-concepts and emotional tone.

HEALTH BENEFITS

When speaking of health benefits, we are referring to benefits which relate to prevention of the onset of disease or even assistance in the treatment of disease or pathological processes. We already discussed how using proper alignment along with the hatha poses greatly affects the amount of any micro trauma to the joints and supporting structures caused by repetitive movements, even if those movements are in and out of yoga poses. What about other benefits which have been studied and validated relating to health benefits of yoga?

Asthma

Many studies in humans suggest benefits of yoga (such as the breathing exercises) when used in addition to other studies for mild-to-moderate asthma. Research has demonstrated improved lung function, overall fitness and airway sensitivity and decreased need for asthma drugs. One study at the Northern Colorado Allergy Asthma Clinic in Fort Collins, used a control group and an experimental group to look at any changes after practice of asanas, pranayama, and meditation for 16 weeks at a frequency of three times per week. While pulmonary functions did not show a significant variance between the two groups, "analysis of the data showed that the subjects in the yoga group tended to use their beta adrenergenic inhalers less Better research is needed in this area.

Cardiovascular Disease

Several studies in humans suggest that people with heart disease who practice yoga may have decreased angina (chest pain). Yoga may decrease risk factors for heart disease, including high blood pressure, cholesterol and blood sugar levels. It is not clear if yoga reduces the risk of heart attack or death or if yoga is any better than other forms of exercise. A three-month residential study treating patients with yoga, meditation and a vegetarian diet at Hanover Medical University in Germany, found a substantial reduction in risk factors including blood pressure and cholesterol in participants. In a study published in the March 2000 issue of "Stroke" magazine, it was noted that transcendental meditation (not hatha yoga) practiced for 20 minutes, two times per day was able to reduce fatty build-ups in artery walls as effectively as the drugs. It also decreased the thickness of artery walls by 1 millimeter and decreased the risk of heart attack by 11 per cent. Again, more studies are warranted in this area before strong recommendations can be made to practice yoga as a tool to help to address heart disease.

Carpal Tunnel Syndrome

Carpel Tunnel Syndrome (CTS) is a syndrome which includes inflammation of the tendons in the tight canal or "tunnel" through which the tendons and nerves must pass on their way from the forearm to the hand and fingers. The Carpal Tunnel is normally quite snug and there is just barely enough room in it for the tendons and nerves that have to pass through it. Inflammation of the tendons can occur secondary to repetitive strain injuries. Stressful hand, arm and neck positions only aggravate the potential for damage. Some sports can bring on repetitive stress injuries, rowing, golf, tennis, and downhill skiing are just a few that stress the hand and wrist joints. Injuries and ailments that cause swelling or compression of soft tissue on the nerves, such as sprains and rheumatoid arthritis, can lead to stress injuries. Yoga therapy has been studied for carpal tunnel syndrome, but it is not clear if there are beneficial effects. In one study a randomized, single-blind, controlled trial was held which compared a group of CTS sufferers who practiced yoga to a control group who simply wore wrist splints with their current treatment. The yoga intervention was specifically designed for strengthening, stretching and balancing each joint in the upper body, along with relaxation. This was given twice weekly for eight weeks. Subjects in the yoga groups had significant improvement in grip strength and pain reduction. The consensus was that the yoga-based regimen was more effective than wrist splinting or no treatment in relieving some symptoms and signs of carpal tunnel syndrome. Further research is needed before a clear recommendation can be made.

Arthritis

In a study of osteoarthritis of the hands, at the University of Pennsylvania School of Medicine, a yoga-treated group with arthritis in the hands improved significantly more than the control group in "pain during activity, tenderness, and finger range of motion." This study was published in the Journal of Rheumatology in 1994. Of course, further studies are needed to compare this with other treatments and to examine long term effects.

Other Conditions

Preliminary studies have shown that yoga therapy may help in children with mental retardation to improve IQ and social behavior. It may be beneficial when added to standard therapies for the treatment of heroin or alcohol abuse. Early studies also note that yoga may improve posture in children. Also, it has been found that yoga may reduce the intensity and frequency of tension or migraine headaches, decreasing the need for pain-relieving drugs.

Yoga has been recommended for the prevention and treatment of many medical conditions. There is some preliminary evidence that yoga can be helpful when it is practiced in addition to standard treatments for several conditions. These conditions include anxiety disorders or stress, asthma, high blood pressure, heart disease and depression. It is not clear if yoga is any more or less effective than other forms of exercise. Unfortunately, much of the research on yoga is limited with poor design. Continued research is needed to prove the above health benefits and rule out other variables. Research into yoga has had poor funding in the past, but this is slowly improving with the establishment of the Office of Alternative Medicine (1992) and the National center for Complementary and Alternative Medicine (NCCAM) in 1998. With these in place, more funding may become available to allow further research to be conducted into the benefits of yoga. The health benefits of yoga are promising, however, if we emphasize this one side of the practice, are we not missing the entire point? As Elliot S. Dacher, MD, author of Whole Healing: A Step-by-Step Program to Reclaim Your Power to Heal wrote, "Yoga is a way to get to the source of ourselves. The challenge is not to see yoga as a treatment for disease, but as an opportunity to see something deeper in the self. To reconnect with the body is one way of artfully facing the reality of pain in our life and a means for accepting and being in our lives more deeply."

YOGA BENEFITS: FLEXIBILITY

When some people think of yoga, they imagine having to stretch like a gymnast. That makes them worry that they're too old, unfit, or "tight" to do yoga. The truth is you're never too old to improve flexibility.

The series of yoga poses called asanas work by safely stretching your muscles. This releases the lactic acid that builds up with muscle use and that causes stiffness, tension, pain, and fatigue. In addition, yoga increases the range of motion in joints. It may also increase lubrication in the joints. The outcome is a sense of ease and fluidity throughout your body.

Yoga stretches not only your muscles but all of the soft tissues of your body. That includes ligaments, tendons, and the fascia sheath that surrounds your muscles. And no matter what your level of yoga, you are likely to see benefits in a very short period of time. In one study, participants had up to 35 per cent improvement in flexibility after only eight weeks of yoga. The greatest gains were in shoulder and trunk flexibility.

Yoga Benefits: Strength

Some styles of yoga, such as ashtanga and power yoga, are more vigorous than others. Practising one of these styles can help you improve muscle tone. An even less vigorous style of yoga, such as Iyengar yoga, which focuses on less movement and more precise alignment in poses, can provide strength and endurance benefits.

Many of the poses, such as downward dog, upward dog, and plank pose, build upper-body strength. This becomes crucial as people age. The standing poses, especially if you hold them for several long breaths, build strength in your hamstrings, quadriceps, and abdominal muscles. Poses that strengthen the lower back include upward dog and chair pose. When practised correctly, nearly all poses build core strength in the deep abdominal muscles.

Yoga benefits: Posture

With increased flexibility and strength comes better posture. Most standing and sitting poses develop core strength. That's because you're counting on your deep abdominals to support and maintain each pose. With a stronger core, you're more likely to sit and stand tall. Another benefit of yoga is the increased body awareness. This heightened awareness tells you more quickly when you're slouching or slumping so you can adjust your posture.

SURPRISING HEALTH BENEFITS OF YOGA

Over the past several years, yoga has experienced an upsurge in popularity in the western world among medical professionals and celebrities alike. While many associate yoga with new age mysticism or the latest fad at the gym, yoga is actually an ancient practice that connects the mind, body, and spirit through body poses, controlled breathing, and meditation. The practice of yoga has many health benefits associated with it, so read below to discover 77 benefits of incorporating yoga in to your or your patient's fitness program.

Health Benefits Within

From lowering blood pressure to increasing pain tolerance, the following health benefits can all be discovered within the body.

- Blood pressure. A consistent yoga practice decreases blood pressure through better circulation and oxygenation of the body. These two exercises can help lower blood pressure.
- Pulse rate. A slower pulse rate indicates that your heart is strong enough to pump more blood with fewer beats. Regularly practicing yoga provides a lower pulse rate.
- Circulation. Yoga improves blood circulation. By transporting nutrients and oxygen throughout your body, yoga practice provides healthier organs, skin, and brain.
- Respiratory. Like the circulatory system, a lower respiratory rate indicates that the lungs are working more efficiently. Yoga decreases the respiratory rate through a combination of controlled breathing exercises and better fitness.
- Cardiovascular endurance. A combination of lower heart rate and improved oxygenation to the body (both benefits of yoga) results in higher cardiovascular endurance.

- Organs. Yoga practice massages internal organs, thus improving the ability of the body to prevent disease. Additionally, an experienced yoga practitioner becomes better attuned to her body to know at first sign if something isn't functioning properly, thereby allowing for quicker response to head off disease.
- Gastrointestinal. Gastrointestinal functions have been shown to improve in both men and women who practice yoga.
- Immunity. Yoga practice has frequently been correlated with a stronger immune system.
- Pain. Pain tolerance is much higher among those who practice yoga regularly. In addition to pain tolerance, some instances of chronic pain, such as back pain, are lessened or eliminated through yoga (see below for more on back pain).
- Metabolism. Having a balanced metabolism results in maintaining a healthy weight and controlling hunger. Consistent yoga practice helps find the balance and creates a more efficient metabolism.

Health Benefits Without

Just as many health benefits occur within the body, there are many benefits that can actually be experienced from without the body. From better sleep to more energy and strength, this list provides several benefits found on the outside of the body.

- Aging. Yoga stimulates the detoxification process within the body. Detoxificationhas been shown to delay aging, among many other health benefits.
- Posture. The very nature of yoga teaches the practitioner how to hold and control one's body in a more healthful position. Through consistent practice, your posture will improve so that you look more confident and healthy.
- Strength. One of the premises of yoga is that you are using the weight of your own body for overall strength..
- Energy. Regular yoga practice provides consistent energy. In fact, most yogis state that when you perform your yoga correctly, you will feel energized after your yoga session rather than tired.
- Weight. The benefits of a better metabolism along with the exercise of yoga work to keep your weight in check. Additionally, the stretching of muscles longwise helps to reduce the amount of cellulite that can build around muscles.
- Sleep. Because of the many benefits to both body and mind that a yoga routine can provide, many find that their sleep is much better. Read here for more on sleep and yoga, as well as some positions for helping induce sleep.

- Balance. An integral part of the yoga practice is balance and control over your body. With a consistent practice, you will find that your overall balance will improve outside the yoga class.
- Integrated function of the body. Yoga is derived from Sanskrit and means "to join together and direct one's attention." This is exactly what happens to your body after you start practicing yoga. Yogis find that their body works together much better, resulting in more graceful and efficient body movements.
- Body Awareness: Doing yoga will give you an increased awareness of your own body. You are often called upon to make small, subtle movements to improve your alignment. Over time, this will increase your level of comfort in your own body. This can lead to improved posture and greater self-confidence.
- Core strength. With a strong body core, you receive better posture and overall body strength. A strong core helps heal and reduce injuries. This is why a lot of athletes do yoga as cross training (boxers, MMA fighters, etc). Read how this swimmeruses yoga to strengthen her core and improve her swimming.
- Sexuality. Yoga can improve your sexuality through better control, more relaxation, and more self-confidence.

Emotional Health Benefits

Due to the strong mind-body connection of yoga, there are many emotional benefits to be gained from a consistent yoga practice. Find out how yoga can help improve emotional health with this list.

- Mood. Overall well-being improves with yoga practice. The combination of creating a strong mind-body connection, creating a healthy body, and focusing inward can all lead to improvement in your mood.
- Stress Reduction. The concentration required during yoga practice tends to focus your attention on the matter at hand, thereby reducing the emphasis you may have been putting on the stress in your life.
- Anxiety. One benefit to the controlled breathing used in yoga is a reduction in anxiety. Learn more about how you can use yoga breathing to reduce your anxiety.
- Depression. Some believe the negative feelings that you may be repressing are brought to the surface during some types of yoga exercise. When this happens, the negative energy is no longer stuck within you, but released through exercise. Regularly releasing this negativity leads to a reduction of depression in many people.
- Self-acceptance. Focusing inward and realizing through your yoga practice that perfection is not the goal, self-acceptance begins to

take over. This post describes how success is not measured by perfectionism in yoga.

- Self-control. The controlled movements of yoga teach you how to translate that self-control to all aspects of your life.
- Mind-body connection. Few other exercises offer the same mind-body connection that yoga does. As you match your controlled breathing with the movements of your body, you retrain your mind to find that place of calm and peace that long-time yogis know.
- Positive outlook on life. Continued practice of yoga results in a balance of many hormones and nervous system, which brings about a more stable, positive approach to life.
- Hostility. Most yogis report a huge reduction in the amount of hostility they feel as well as a sense of control when anger flares. This calm effect is likely from the relaxation and meditation that is incorporated in their yoga practice that leads to an overall calming of the nervous system. Less hostility means lower blood pressure and stress and a healthier approach to life.
- Concentration. Researchers have shown that as little as eight weeks of yoga practice can result in better concentration and more motivation.
- Memory. Improved blood circulation to the brain as well as the reduction in stress and improved focus results in a better memory.
- Attention. The attention required in yoga to maintain the structured breathing in conjunction with yoga poses sharpens the ability to keep a sharp focus on tasks.
- Social skills. In yoga, you learn the interconnectedness of all of life. Your yoga practice soon evolves from a personal journey to one connecting to to the community at large where your social skills improve along with your yoga practice.
- Calmness. Concentrating so intently on what your body is doing has the effect of bringing calmness. Yoga also introduces you to meditation techniques, such as watching how you breathe and disengagement from your thoughts, which help calm the mind.

Body Chemistry

Several aspects of body chemistry such as glucose levels and red blood cells are affected by yoga. Learn how you can improve your body chemistry through yoga.

- Cholesterol. Yoga practice lowers cholesterol through increased blood circulation and burning fat. Yoga practice is a great tool to fight against harmful cholesterol levels.
- Lymphatic system. Your lymphatic system boosts your immunity and reduces toxins in your body. The only way to get your lymphatic system flowing well is by movement. The specific

movements involved in yoga are particularly well-suited for promoting a strong lymphatic system.

- Glucose. There is evidence to suggest that yoga may lower blood glucose levels.
- Sodium. As does any good exercise program, yoga reduces the sodium levels in your body. In today's world of processed and fast foods that are full of sodium, lessening these levels is a great idea.
- Endocrine functions. Practicing yoga helps to regulate and control hormone secretion. An improved endocrine system keeps hormones in balance and promotes better overall physical and emotional health.
- Triglycerides. Triglycerides are the chemical form of fat in the blood, and elevated levels can indicate a risk for heart disease and high blood pressure. A recent study shows that yoga can lead to "significantly lower" levels of triglycerides.
- Red blood cells. Yoga has been shown to increase the level of red blood cells in the body. Red blood cells are responsible for carrying oxygen through the blood, and too few can result in anemia and low energy.
- Vitamin C. Vitamin C helps boost immunity, helps produce collagen, and is a powerful antioxidant; and a yoga regimen can increase the vitamin C in your body.

Exercise Health Benefits

As a form of exercise, yoga offers benefits that are sometimes not easily found among other exercise regimens. Check out these reasons to include yoga in your or your patient's health program.

- Low risk of injury. Due to the low impact of yoga and the controlled aspect of the motions, there is a very low risk of injury during yoga practice compared to other forms of exercise.
- Parasympathetic Nervous System. In many forms of exercise, the sympathetic nervous system kicks in, providing you with that fight-or-flight sensation. Yoga does the opposite and stimulates the parasympathetic nervous system. The parasympathetic system lowers blood pressure and slows the pace of your breathing, which allows relaxation and healing.
- Muscle tone. Consistently practicing yoga leads to better muscle tone.
- Subcortex. Subcortical regions of brain are associated with well-being, and yoga is thought to dominate the subcortex rather than the cortex (where most exercise dominates).
- Reduced oxygen consumption. Yoga consumes less oxygen than traditional exercise routines, thereby allowing the body to work more efficiently.

- Breathing. With yoga, breathing is more natural and controlled during exercise. This type of breathing provides more oxygen-rich air for your body and also provides more energy with less fatigue.
- Balanced workout of opposing muscle groups. As with all of yoga, balance is key. If a muscle group is worked in one direction, it will also be worked in the opposite direction to maintain balance. This balance results in a better overall workout for the body.
- Non-competitive. The introspective and self-building nature of yoga removes any need of competition in the exercise regimen. With the lack of competition, the yogi is free to work slowly to avoid any undue injury as well as promote a more balanced and stress-free workout.
- Joint range of motion. A study at the University of Pennsylvania School of Medicine indicated that joint range of motion was improved by participants who practiced yoga.
- Eye-hand coordination. Without practice, eye-hand coordination diminishes. Yoga maintains and improves eye-hand coordination.
- Dexterity. The strong mind-body connection and flexibility gained from yoga leads to grace and skill.
- Reaction time. Research done in India shows that reaction time can be improved with specific yoga breathing exercises in conjunction with an already established yoga practice. The improvement was attributed to the faster rate of processing and improved concentration gained from yoga.
- Endurance. Working the entire body, yoga improves endurance and is frequently used by endurance athletes as a supplement to their sport-specific training.
- Depth perception. Becoming aware of your body and how it moves, as one does in yoga practice, leads to increased depth perception.

Disease Prevention

Doctors and nurses love yoga because studies indicate that it can help prevent the following diseases.

- Heart disease. Yoga reduces stress, lowers blood pressure, keeps off weight, and improves cardiovascular health, all of which lead to reducing your risk of heart disease.
- Osteoporosis. It is well documented that weight-bearing exercise strengthens bones and helps prevent osteoporosis. Additionally, yoga's ability to lower levels of cortisol may help keep calcium in the bones.
- Alzheimer's. A new study indicates that yoga can help elevate brain gamma-aminobutyric (GABA) levels. Low GABA levels are associated with the onset of Alzheimer's. Meditation like that

practiced in yoga has also been shown to slow the progression of Alzheimer's.

- Type II diabetes. In addition to the glucose reducing capabilities of yoga, it is also an excellent source of physical exercise and stress reduction that, along with the potential for yoga to encourage insulin production in the pancreas, can serve as an excellent preventative for type II diabetes.

Symptom Reduction or Alleviation

Medical professionals have learned that the following diseases or disorders can all be helped by maintaining a yoga practice.

- Carpal tunnel syndrome. Individuals with carpal tunnel syndrome who practiced yoga showed greater improvement than those who wore a splint or received no treatment at all. Researchers saw improved grip strength and reduction of pain in the study participants.
- Asthma. There is some evidence to show that reducing symptoms of asthma and even reduction in asthma medication are the result of regular yoga.
- Arthritis. The slow, deliberate movement of yoga poses coupled with the gentle pressure exerted on the joints provides an excellent exercise to relieve arthritis symptoms. Also, the stress relief associated with yoga loosens muscles that tighten joints.
- Multiple sclerosis. According to this chapter, "yoga is now recognized as an excellent means of MS management." Additionally, National Center for Complementary and Alternative Medicine is funding a clinical trial of yoga for treating multiple sclerosis.
- Cancer. Those fighting or recovering from cancer frequently take advantage of the benefits that yoga provides. Cancer patients who practice yoga gain strength, raise red blood cells, experience less nausea during chemotherapy, and have a better overall well-being.
- Muscular dystrophy. Using yoga in the early stages of muscular dystrophy can help return some physical functions. The practice of Pranayam yoga helped one teen regain many of his abilities lost to muscular dystrophy.
- Migraines. Regular yoga practice has been shown to reduce the number of migraines in chronic migraine sufferers. This post describes how yoga can reduce migraines.
- Scoliosis. Yoga can straighten the curvature of the spine associated with scoliosis.Find out how this yogi cured her scoliosis and continues to help others as well.
- Chronic bronchitis. Exercise that does not elevate respiration, yet increase oxygen levels in the body is ideal for treating chronic

bronchitis. Luckily, yoga can do this, as well as aerate the lungs and provide energy.

- Epilepsy. Focusing on stress reduction, breathing, and restoring overall balance in the body are the focus of how yoga can help prevent epileptic seizures.
- Sciatica. The intense pain associated with sciatica can be alleviated with specific yoga poses. Here are 10 great ones to help relieve pain.
- Obsessive Compulsive Disorder. Studies of people with OCD have shown that practicing yoga has lead to a reduction in symptoms–resulting in less medication or medication no longer needed.
- Constipation. Due to the practice of yoga and overall better posture, the digestive and elimination systems work more efficiently. If the practitioner also has a healthy diet, any constipation will be eliminated through yoga.
- Allergies. Using a neti pot to clear the sinuses is an ancient form of yoga to help reduce or eliminate allergy symptoms. Certain types of breathing can also help clear the nasal passages.
- Menopause. Yoga practice can help control some of the side effects of menopause.
- Back pain. Yoga reduces spinal compression and helps overall body alignment to reduce back pain.

8

Tools and Methods use in Health Information Systems

HEALTH INFORMATION SYSTEM?

Definitions of what constitutes a "health information system" abound and although there is no consensus around any specific formulation, it is universally accepted that health information is essential for health decision-making at all levels of the health pyramid. From the level of individual patient care, to the management of specific health programmes through to the policy level where strategic decisions are made information is an integral part of the health pyramid (4, 5, 6, 7). The health information system has been aptly described as "an integrated effort to collect, process, report and use health information and knowledge to influence policy-making, programme action and research" (8).

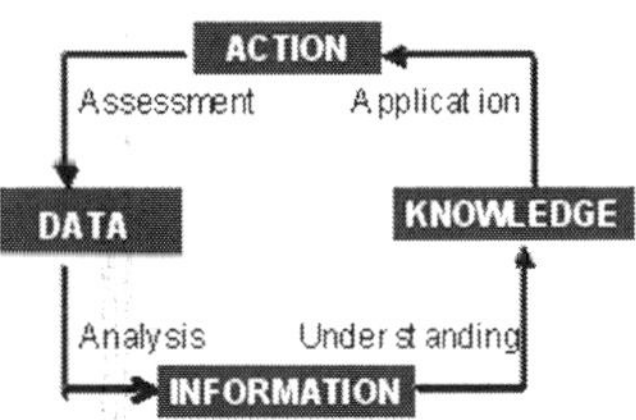

Fig. The data for action cycle

Goal of health Information Systems

What is clear is that health information is much more than the collecting of data. Data have no value in themselves – value and relevance come only when they are analysed, transformed into meaningful information, and used (FIGURE 1).

The ultimate objective of a health information system is to produce information for taking action in the health sector. Performance of such a system should therefore be measured not only on the basis of the quality of data produced, but on evidence of the continued use of these data for improving health systems operations and health status (9).

This principle applies at all levels – at the level of patient care, at the health facility, and at the community, district, national and global levels. A health information system is not a static entity but a process through which health-related data are gathered, shared, analysed, and used for decision-making – information is transformed into knowledge for action. These principles also apply to all countries, whatever the level of income and degree of sophistication of the health system.

Nor are the boundaries of a health information system confined to health – there is a strong interdependence between health information systems and information systems in other sectors. For example, higher levels of female literacy are associated with higher compliance with home treatment for diarrhoea/dehydration in infants; improved sanitation is associated with increased child survival; food and nutrition policies affect the health of children and adults alike. Making links such as these and identifying broad areas of data common to health and other sectors is properly within the responsibility of a health information system.

Within the health sector, different types of information are generated, ranging from data on the management and administration of health services to health system outputs such as coverage and quality of care. Although the health system has a particular interest in health outcomes (such as mortality rates) such data are not always generated through the health sector.

Domains of health information

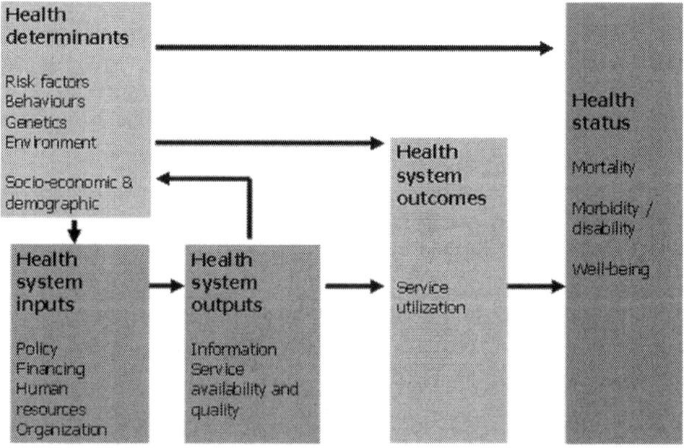

Fig. Typology of measurement domains

The domains or areas of interest that a health information system should address can be grouped into four main types:

- Health determinants – socioeconomic, environmental, behavioural, and genetic factors and the contextual environments within which the health system operates.

- Health system inputs – the structures and processes of the health system (policy and organization, health infrastructure including facilities, human and financial resources, and health information systems.
- Health system outputs – the quality, use and availability of health information and services.
- Health outcomes – mortality, morbidity, disease outbreaks, and health status.

Health information subsystems

A health information system can be considered to consist of several separate subsystems:

- Disease surveillance and outbreak notification.
- Data generated through household surveys.
- Registration of vital events and censuses (births, deaths and causes of death).
- Data collection based on patient and service records and reporting from community health workers, health workers and health facilities.
- Programme-specific monitoring and evaluation (for example for TB, HIV/AIDS, and EPI).
- Administration and resource management (including budget, personnel, and supplies).

The function of a health information system is to bring together data from all these different subsystems, to share and disseminate them to the many different audiences for health information, and to ensure that health information is used rationally, effectively and efficiently to improve health action. A strong health information system is an essential component of sound programme development and implementation, and is a prerequisite for strategic decision-making – ultimately, it provides the basis upon which improved health outcomes depend. In theory, a health information system consists of a process of gathering, sharing, analysing, and using health-related data for decision-making – information transformed into knowledge for action. In this respect the concept of a system as an entity "formed of parts placed together or adjusted into a regular and connected whole" (10) is key.

Currently however the different subsystems outlined above rarely interact or are used by disease-specific programmes in different ways (FIGURE 3). As a result different figures are available depending upon the information source used and there is no standard system for ensuring overall consistency and coherent reporting.

There is now growing acknowledgement that health information systems are not functioning as they should and an increasing awareness of widespread dissatisfaction and frustration among both the producers and users of health information. While the problems facing health information systems are most acute in resource-constrained settings, they are by no means limited to the developing world. Reviews of health information systems undertaken in a number of middle-income countries, notably in former transition economies show there are important lessons to be learned from these experiences. Peripheral health workers are frustrated by burdensome demands for data; local sectoral planners and managers are frustrated by competing demands and lack of capacity to respond; national-level planners are frustrated by lack of information relevant to policy and decision-making; and funders (both internal and external) are frustrated because they cannot effectively assess the impact of interventions. A panoply of data-collection systems exists alongside continuing unmet needs for information. There is therefore a growing receptiveness towards the development of strategies to produce more coherent and efficient systems.

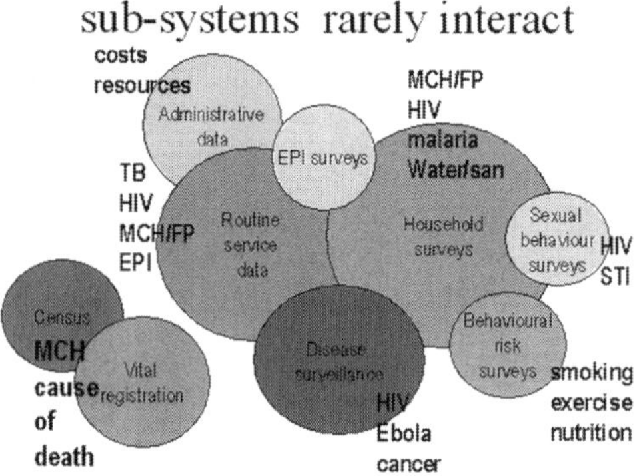

Fig. Health Information

TOOLS AND METHODS ARE USED BY HEALTH INFORMATION SYSTEMS

Data-collection methods

Just as there are different producers and users of health-related information, there are also many different tools and methodologies for its generation, including:

- Routine (service-based) health information, including medical records;
- Vital registration, births, deaths, and causes of death;
- census;
- Disease surveillance;
- Facility and household surveys;
- Modelling and estimates; and
- National health accounts.

The reach of these tools across the health pyramid varies considerably (FIGURE 5). Censuses and vital registration systems theoretically cover all levels and should provide the most basic information that a health information system needs – numbers of births and deaths, and causes of death. In practice, however, few developing countries have comprehensive vital registration systems and fewer still have ways of medically certifying causes of death. Censuses provide complete information on population numbers and location but take place only occasionally and provide only limited information on mortality patterns.

Disease surveillance systems generally cover all levels of the health pyramid, from the community or facility through to the national or, indeed, the global levels. Specified sources of data include health facility records, laboratory reports, case reports, and surveys, all of which are used to identify disease outbreaks, monitor trends in events of public health significance, identify the characteristics of those infected (such as age, sex, and location), and produce mapping of disease incidence. Whereas the reach of such surveillance systems is deep, covering all levels of the health care system, the scope is considerably narrower than that of health information systems as a whole.

Routine health information systems or service statistics, on the other hand, comprise a very broad range of health data including health system inputs, processes, and outcomes, as well as facility-based mortality, morbidity and health status. As already noted, such information is generated primarily for use in patient or facility management and much of the data collected are not intended to be used at higher levels of the system. In recent years, many countries have sought to limit the amount of data that must be transmitted up through the system from the periphery through the routine system in order to lessen the burden of reporting on hard-pressed health care workers.

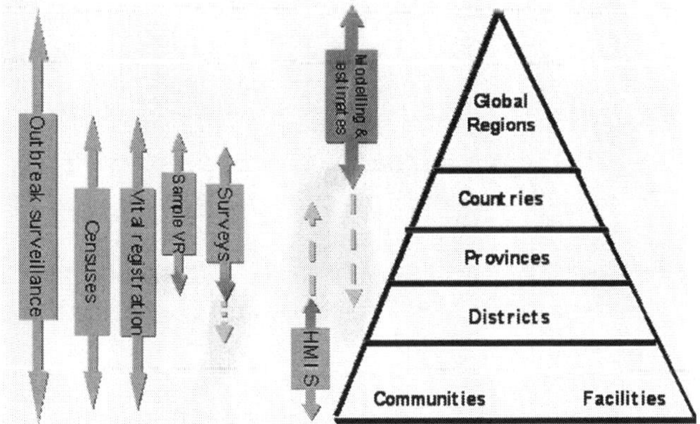

Fig. Production of health information tool coverage by level

Service-based statistics suffer from the absence of denominator data so that computation of population-based rates and ratios can be problematic. In order to address this, it is standard practice for health care planners to compute rates using population-based data generated from vital events registers, censuses and household surveys. These can be invaluable sources of information when maintained up-to-date. In general, cost considerations and sample-size restrictions limit the peripheral reach of household surveys to the provincial level, occasionally to the district level. At national level, however, surveys are used extensively for national and international databases, for modelling estimates and projections of child mortality, AIDS, malaria and other diseases, for policy-making, programme planning and evaluation, and for monitoring progress towards major international health goals. Whereas in the past, surveys have tended to focus on respondent's answers regarding health events and health-related behaviours, more recently there has been increasing interest in the potential of household surveys to generate health-outcome measures through biological and clinical data collection (health examination surveys). Concerns have been expressed that there is over-reliance on such surveys to generate data that could be produced more cost-effectively and sustainably through routine service statistics or sentinel approaches. The use of surveys is usually confined to those areas of health information that cannot be generated through alternative, cheaper mechanisms.

Many developing countries do not have comprehensive vital registration systems in place – either the coverage of vital events is incomplete (especially in rural areas) or the cause of death attribution is inadequate, or both. Clearly, the costs of setting up and maintaining functioning vital registration systems are significant, and cannot be borne by the health sector alone even though it is a key user of the information generated. In the last decade there has been an increase in the use of alternative and innovative data-collection techniques that meet key health information needs at a fraction of the costs of comprehensive vital registration systems. These methods include continuous demographic and mortality surveillance of defined geographic populations, including the use of verbal autopsies and validated income poverty measurement tools that are integrated into systems of local government (for example, the INDEPTH network). Another approach has been sentinel or sample registration. Refining demographic and mortality surveillance methods and integrating them with sample registration systems offers an opportunity to create a reliable, sustainable and cost-effective component of the information system.

Modelling

One important though under-used tool for generating health-related information is modelling. This has generally been used at the national and global levels in order to generate estimates when direct data are inadequate or missing. Models have been used to estimate life tables in areas where vital registration systems do not achieve high rates of coverage. Estimates of the incidence or prevalence of diseases are increasingly derived from modelling. Models have also been developed to estimate national burdens of disease (in DALYs by cause); to estimate healthy life expectancy (HALE) by age and sex; and for specific diseases such as HIV/AIDS, TB and malaria. Recently, there has been an increase in interest in the use of modelling approaches to provide estimates for local areas, including districts. This includes the calculation of DALYs based on subnational vital registration data, the estimation of health indicators for districts that are not included in national surveys, estimation based on incomplete data sets, and the application of spatial analysis methods. During the design of health information systems in countries the potential of and need for model-based estimates must be taken into account and integrated into the system. There is also a need to consider other issues such as the likely data requirements, the extent to which subnational estimates are possible for the different kinds of health indicators, and the required frequency of data collection.

MAIN ACTORS IN THE HEALTH INFORMATION SYSTEM?

A health information system should generate information for different uses by different health system actors. Some of these actors operate at macro-decision level (for example, strategic planning, allocation of resources, and evaluation) while others operate at micro-management level (for example, case management, programme management, administration, and deployment of human resources) as shown in FIGURE 4.

Fig. Levels of production of health information and use of health information

The kinds of information required by each type of health system actor differ in ways such as degree of reliability, levels of aggregation, levels of detail, and diversity of topics. Given the range of actors involved and the diversity of potential data items, it is imperative that the health information system has the following interlinked characteristics:

- The ability to identify detailed and disaggregated information items useful for decision-making at various levels within the health care system that are also immediately relevant at the level of data collection.
- The ability to screen and channel to central level only what is most essential and detailed enough for strategic decision-making and policy analysis.

PRODUCERS OF HEALTH INFORMATION

Health Sector

The health sector is the primary supplier of health information. It is responsible for information generated through disease surveillance and response efforts designed to provide early warning of disease outbreaks (such as polio, Ebola, and SARS); to illustrate patterns of chronic disease spread (such as HIV/AIDS or cancer); and to produce information relating individual risk behaviours to health outcomes (for example smoking and cardiovascular diseases).

Data related to the performance of health services, to the management of resources for health, and to the policy and legal framework relevant to health are also largely generated through the health sector. Information about the quantity, distribution, reach and quality of health information and service provision, on the resources needed to provide those services, and on the use of information and services by the population can be generated through routine health management information systems (HMIS).

Within the health sector, there are multiple producers of health information and while the public health authorities may be primary (particularly with regard to information for public health policy-making) information from the private for-profit and non-profit sectors is also key to an effective health information system. In many settings, health insurance systems are primary producers of data on patterns of disease and health care use. Employers too are also important potential producers of health information. Other branches of industry, such as the pharmaceutical sector, are both producers and consumers of health information. It is rarely evident that the information that can be derived in these ways is linked to the national health information system.

Other Sectors

The health sector is also a consumer of information generated by actors external to health. In many settings, the primary data producer for the ultimate health outcome (mortality) is not the health sector. Instead, data on vital events such as births, deaths and sex and age patterns of mortality, are produced through the census and the civil registration system, often under the overall responsibility of ministries of the interior or planning and national statistics offices. On the other hand, the health sector has to work closely with the civil registration authorities to generate information on patterns of causes of death because attribution of cause of death is generally the responsibility of health care professionals. Health-related information may also be produced by local and municipal authorities.

Information on resources allocated and consumed for health generally derive from departments of finance and planning, and resource flows to the health sector can be extracted from national accounts where these are available.

Surveys, Research, and Communities

In some settings departments of national statistics are primary producers of health information derived from household surveys – often the sole source of population-based information on the use of health services or health-related behaviours. Although the increasing frequency of poverty monitoring, household budget surveys and household living standards surveys can provide useful health-related data down to provincial level, they are rarely used by health information systems. Household surveys are of particular importance in settings where vital registration is incomplete (which is the case in most developing countries) and may be the sole source of population-based information on important health outcomes such as infant mortality.

Other important producers of health information are academic and research institutions, often supported by external funding. Researchers may develop new tools and methods for assessing different aspects of health and can play a major role in the evaluation of health interventions.

Frequently neglected sources of health information are communities and advocacy groups. Communities can play a major role in gathering information on disease surveillance, births and deaths, environmental issues, follow-up of patients, patterns of health-seeking behaviour and perceptions of health services. Although the information they produce may be considered non-representative or incomplete, and may be limited to qualitative information rather than quantitative statistics, it should be considered a potentially important component of the health information system. The importance of qualitative information, such as stakeholder opinions and perceptions, should not be neglected in health information systems.

USERS OF HEALTH INFORMATION

At each level of the health care system, users of health information have differing needs and use information in different ways. At the most basic level of client–health worker interactions, patient records are a vital source of information, whose utility is not confined to the individual level. Record reviews can be used to ascertain the extent of conformity with agreed norms and standards of care. Confidential enquiries and facility-based audits review provider practices in order to determine to what extent care could be improved and the degree to which deaths were avoidable and the potential policy implications of such avoidable factors.

At the facility level, managers need information on patient profiles, patterns of admissions and discharges, length of hospital stay, use of medicines and equipment, deployment of different categories of health care workers and ancillary staff, costs and income. At district level, planners and managers use this information and data on locally relevant population profiles and risk factors in decision-making regarding allocation of resources to different facilities. Within the public health sector, such information is transmitted upwards through district and provincial levels to the national level where basic resource allocation decisions are made. More problematic is the extent of such reporting by the private sector – unless there is a strong regulatory framework within which the private sector operates, it is unlikely that such information will be transmitted to the planning authorities.

Although the health information generated through the reporting of routine activities by health care facilities and health care workers provides important and useful information on the activities of the health system, this is insufficient for strategic decision-making regarding the allocation of health resources. Decision-makers need information not only about service activities and users of services, but also about those who for whatever reason do not use the services. This information is generally harder to come by than routine service statistics. Health care facilities may undertake special studies of their catchment populations in order to ascertain demand or need for information and services. More often, such information is derived from household surveys in which people are asked direct questions about their perceived need for and use of health care services. The major advantage of using household surveys for such information is that it is possible to obtain socioeconomically stratified information on use of all types of service, including the private sector (modern, private-for-profit, private, non-profit, traditional providers, social marketing outlets, pharmacies, etc.). An important disadvantage, however, is that household surveys are generally undertaken at national level and for reasons of costs, sample sizes are generally insufficient to permit detailed analysis at the district level.

When making strategic health sector decisions, national level authorities use health-related information from sources such as routine service statistics, household surveys, vital registration, census, national accounts, and education and employment data (particularly with regard to the production and availability of human resources for health). One visible manifestation of this process is the reporting at national level of progress towards national health-related goals such as reductions in child mortality or reduced disease transmission. National authorities also report health-related information to international bodies such as the United Nations. Increasing interest in the performance of national health systems has been stimulated by the goals-oriented international conferences of the 1990s, summarized in the Millennium Development Goals, endorsed by 189 heads of state and government in 2000. The progress made by countries towards these and similar goals is of interest to donor agencies and governments desirous of tracking the extent to which external assistance produces tangible results in terms of improved health.

This rapid overview of the different users of health information at different levels demonstrates three important principles:

- Different types of health-related data are needed at different levels of the health care pyramid – not all items of information need to be reported at every level.
- Those working at the periphery, closest to patient management, need more detailed information on clients seen and services provided than those working at the central level.
- In order to avoid overburdening health care workers at the peripheral level, managers and planners should consider carefully what type of data should be generated at each level, bearing in mind that to the extent possible, those collecting and transmitting data upwards through the system need to understand and appreciate why the data are required.

As discussed below, one important finding in most reviews and assessments of national health information systems is that the links between suppliers/producers, consumers and users of different types of health information are weak.

RENEWED INTEREST IN HEALTH INFORMATION

The demand for good-quality health information is growing – driven in part by the move towards performance-based resource allocation and by significant increases in the resources for health mobilized in recent years, for example through the Global Fund for HIV/AIDS, TB and Malaria (GFATM). In the context of such global initiatives, reporting requirements for countries are being stepped up, while the frequent monitoring of short-term programme outputs (such as improvements in service provision and the number of people using such services) is now required as part of performance-based disbursement systems. At the same time, enhanced reporting of health outcomes (such as improvements in the quality and length of life) is required to monitor progress towards major international goals such as the Millennium Development Goals (MDGs). However, demands for data emanating from such international and disease-specific initiatives tend to focus on particular indicators and do not necessarily translate into building systems that meet both country-level and international health information needs. The recent upsurge in demand for health information cannot be adequately met at present because there has been insufficient investment in building streamlined health information systems capable of generating data on the full array of health-related issues.

Benefits of Investing in Health Information

Investing in the development of effective health information systems would have multiple benefits and would enable decision-makers at all levels to:

- Detect and control emerging and endemic health problems; monitor progress towards health goals; and promote equity.
- Empower individuals and communities with timely and understandable health-related information; and drive improvements in quality of services.
- Strengthen the evidence base for effective health policies; permit evaluation of scale-up efforts; and enable innovation through research.
- Improve governance; mobilize new resources; and ensure accountability in their use.

The increased demand for health information and the huge potential opportunity to supply it call for an investment in building sustainable national and subnational health information systems. Countries will benefit greatly if such systems are based upon a national plan with a policy framework; core indicators; and data-collection, analysis and dissemination strategies. Such a strategic plan should be specific about how the different tools and methods will be applied and will complement each other; how health information needs will be met at the subnational, national, and global levels; and what kind of investments are needed. A national body will be required to guide and oversee the implementation of the plan with the full participation of stakeholders and users at different levels, and technical experts. International investors in health information should buy in to and support the country strategies.

Strengthening national and subnational health information systems will also require a collaborative effort at the international level. As part of this, the recently launched Health Metrics Network (HMN) described in section 7 will focus upon improving the availability and utilization of sound health information for policy-making and planning, programme monitoring and evaluation, monitoring of international goals, and measuring equity in health. Through collaboration with its many partners, HMN will work to strengthen the capacity of country health information systems to provide high-quality and timely information in a form that is useful for public health work at the national, subnational and global levels. Such a network is necessary to enhance the efficiency and effectiveness of the assistance provided by investors in health information. The standardization and enhancement of methods to assess the quality and application of health information will be invaluable in efforts to measure the real progress in achieving national and global goals in health.

REFORMING NATIONAL HEALTH INFORMATION SYSTEMS

Health information systems are in need of reform if they are to become well-functioning systems that link different components in meaningful and effective ways. They need to seen as a public good, emphasized as stewardship, and not just part of a data-collection process. The establishment of strong and cohesive health information systems would have many advantages, both in relation to evidence-based decision-making in health and in relation to the many competing demands for information made by donor agencies. Programmes and people need to be transformed from collectors of data to generators of knowledge and practitioners of using such knowledge for action. Analysis of current experience shows that few health information systems have established effective cycles of data gathering, sharing, analysis, understanding and application in decision-making in health. Even though some of these activities may be functioning more or less adequately in some settings, the full process by which data is transformed into information and knowledge for action remains elusive.

Challenges and Opportunities

The long list of health information system problems can seem overwhelming. With so much that is going wrong, is it possible to begin to make things better? This is a legitimate question especially as new challenges are now emerging stimulated by the increasing use of performance-based disbursement mechanisms associated with increased financial flows to health interventions. Greater attention to equity in health and the information needed to achieve it are also emerging as common requirements. Challenges also emanate from the need for subnational health information in the context of the decentralization of public services.

But alongside the challenges many new opportunities to reform health information systems are now emerging. These include improved tools and methods, and technological innovations such as the use of biomarkers to measure population health, information technologies and geographic information systems – all of which have the potential to significantly improve both the coverage and quality of data. Important opportunities are also emerging from the process of health system decentralization and accompanying demands for locally relevant and useful health information. It is imperative to capitalize on these movements within the health sector and to integrate health information system reform with overall health system development. Recent experience suggests that consensus on indicators can be achieved when leadership is provided and there is political will to achieve consensus among all interested parties.

There are also important opportunities to be seized outside the health sector. Efforts to build statistical capacity across all sectors in countries are under way through the PARIS 21 initiative which brings together national statistical offices, users of statistical information and donors, notably the World Bank, OECD and the European Union (13).

PRINCIPLES TO GUIDE HEALTH INFORMATION SYSTEM REFORM

Several important principles should guide health information system reform:

- Health information strengthening should be seen within the broader context of strengthening statistical capacity and should adhere to the general criteria common to all forms of information, as expressed in the Fundamental Principles of Official Statistics (14). These include impartiality, scientific soundness, professional ethics, transparency, consistency and efficiency, coordination and collaboration.
- Health information system reform should be integrated into broader efforts to improve health systems including country poverty reduction and development strategies.
- Reform of systems should start with simple and achievable objectives and should introduce further changes in a staged approach, enhancing capacity at each stage and ensuring the engagement of all partners in the process.

The value of better health information is its impact on health outcomes – better health information is the foundation for better health. Valuing health information, at all levels of the system, is associated with a culture of accountability, a desire to improve ways of working, and a realization that improving health outcomes requires not just more technical inputs but also the more effective use of available resources. Advocacy for strengthening health information systems should focus on the value of health information as a public good – it can be shared by everyone and no-one can be excluded from the benefits resulting from greater knowledge.

Reforming health information systems requires answering some of the core questions commonly raised in the reform or adaptation of any system, namely:

- Who are the key actors in collecting, using and processing information, and designing the system?
- For what purpose? – management, advocacy, strategic planning, monitoring evaluation, inventory, research?
- How can these purposes be achieved? – by using a given data-collection mode, using information technologies, using metadata standards, applying pre-established feedback and data-flow mechanisms?
- When and how frequently is information required?

Using simple questions such as these, a number of countries have recently undertaken in-depth assessments of their health information systems to clarify the essential steps needed for effective reform. Not all steps are required in sequential order in every setting – countries differ considerably in their policy, legal and administrative environments. Nonetheless, experience indicates that attention to the following issues can help to identify and address major gaps and weaknesses in existing information systems in the immediate or short term.

ELEMENTS OF HEALTH INFORMATION SYSTEM REFORM

A precondition for successful reform of health information systems is the creation of demand for good health information. A common conclusion of studies of the health information field is that whereas large amounts of data are collected at various levels of the system, relatively little is actually used for decision-making. Yet at the same time, policy-makers and planners complain that they do not have access to the kind of information they need for strategic decision-making. The need to establish a better balance between supply and demand for health information is apparent. While many attempts to strengthen health information systems tend to focus on the supply side (for example by developing better tools and methods, standardizing definitions and harmonizing approaches) it is clear that addressing the demand side is equally important. Demand for health information should come not only from the health sector but also, and perhaps more critically, from other sectors (notably finance and planning) as well as from civil society, including parliamentarians, communities, consumer groups, and nongovernmental organizations. An acknowledgement by the national authorities of the importance of basing health action on sound information is a fundamental policy statement, from which all other actions to improve health information systems flow. The development of clear policy guidance within which the health information system can function effectively and independently is the essential first step for health information reform. In the absence of explicit policy, a culture of information, evaluation and accountability will not grow and information will never be analysed or used for decision-making. Reforming health information systems inevitably affects many departments, programmes, institutions and people at all levels of the health care system. High-level direction and coordination are therefore imperative (9). High-level sponsorship will help ensure successful negotiation of the key phases of reform outlined below, namely policy analysis; strategy development; planning; and implementation, monitoring and evaluation.

Policy Analysis

- Identification of the main actors – producers and users of health information at national and subnational levels.

- Mapping of existing health information methods and products and assessment of overlaps, duplication, gaps and inconsistencies.
- Definition of a clear policy, legislative and regulatory framework supporting the health information system at all levels of the health pyramid.
- Identification of accountability mechanisms.

Strategy Development

- Development, through a broad-based consultative process, of a cohesive and inclusive strategy in the area of health-related information.
- Promotion of health information as a vehicle for strengthening health systems.
- Setting of clear goals and targets for health information systems.
- Development of guidelines for sharing data across levels and subsystems and protocols regarding health information security and confidentiality.
- Identification of criteria regarding accessibility to health-related data and information at minimal possible aggregation level.
- Development of conceptual framework for health information.
- Establishment of evaluation frameworks.

Planning

- Preparation of a detailed and costed health information plan, with defined timelines, allocation of responsibilities, and accountability.
- Assessment of costs and mobilization of financial resources for health information at all levels of the system.
- Identification of minimum data requirements and indicators at different levels and the production and dissemination of guidance for the generation of relevant indicators.
- Development of criteria and guidelines for data quality.
- Identification of processes for data transmission, analysis and feedback.
- Development of approaches for data presentation and dissemination to diverse audiences.

Implementation, Monitoring and Evaluation

- Development of human resources for health information, including recruiting, training, deploying and motivating health information officers.
- Harmonization and standardization of definitions, classifications and coding systems.
- Revision of data-collection forms and production of thematic glossaries and data dictionaries.

- Introduction of appropriate technologies (including computers) and training in their use.
- Implementation of standard criteria and guidelines regarding the use of software, databases, search engines, internet and intranet in health-related data management.
- Operationalization of monitoring and evaluation frameworks with regular review and feedback.

MOBILIZING FINANCIAL RESOURCES

Policy change provides the underpinning for resource-mobilization efforts. At present, little is known about the costs and resource flows to country health information systems – one recent review in Mexico concluded that less than 1 per cent of the total public health expenditure was allocated to health information systems. However, if we add together what is spent by donors and international agencies on monitoring and evaluation of programmes plus existing government expenditures on health data, the total sums are significant. It has been estimated that resources spent on health information in the developing world approximate to between $US 1.7–3.4 billion per year (15). However, these monies are invested in a fragmented, duplicative and uncoordinated manner with resulting serious deficiencies in the availability, quality and use of health information at all levels. Better investment of existing funds is required rather than an absolute increase in total resources.

DEVELOPING CONCEPTUAL FRAMEWORKS

A missing element from many attempts at health information system reform is an adequate conceptual framework that clearly delineates the links between health system inputs, processes, outputs, outcomes and ultimate health impacts. Not everything can or should be measured all the time and at all levels. Identifying markers that can be monitored continuously to track short-term change and monitor progress on an ongoing basis provides useful information for decision-making at different levels while liberating resources for regular but less frequent impact assessments. Policy-makers have an ongoing need to know to what extent programmes are on track and moving in the right direction. Measurement of impact and attribution of cause and effect require more in-depth and systematic evaluation.

Implementation

A clear policy, strategy and conceptual framework needs to be accompanied by explicit implementation mechanisms. This includes the establishment of a body to ensure that the various components of the existing health information system communicate effectively. This does not have to be a separate government department – for example it could consist of a focal point working with one or more permanent multidisciplinary working groups, bringing together representatives from all structures that produce, process and disseminate health-related data and information.

Defining Core Indicators

The issue of defining core indicators deserves special mention because of a rapid expansion in the range of indicators used in recent years. Every programme area has defined its so-called "minimal" lists of indicators – often at the request of external partners and donors. When added together, these can make for a formidable burden of data collection. A rational selection of core health indicators and determinant of health is therefore essential, and these indicators (to be generated at different levels of the system) must be responsive to explicit criteria including:

- Local and national priorities and measurement capacities;
- Scientific soundness including validity, reliability, specificity, sensitivity, and usefulness;
- The relevance of the indicator at the level of data collection – preferably data should only be collected that can be used for decision-making at the level of data collection or where there is a clear understanding of the need for the data at higher levels;
- The level of decentralization of health system authorities;
- the level of analysis required, including disaggregations; and
- International and global initiatives (MDGs, GFTAM, GAVI).

A parsimoniously selected set of core health indicators is a key aspect of a sound health information system. Such indicators can be viewed as the "backbone" of the system – the minimum information package needed to support macro and micro health system functions. At the same time, it is important to be aware of the natural tendency of indicators to drive programmes ("what you measure is what you do"). Therefore, all indicators should be subject to regular review and evaluation to minimize any unintended distortions.

Identifying Appropriate and Cost-Effective Data-Collection Strategies

For any given indicator there may be a wide range of data sources available. Each source should be critically reviewed to ascertain whether the indicator could be more cost-effectively generated through alternative data-collection approaches. Already established data sources and reporting systems should be used where possible, particularly where line ministries have their own statistical systems. For example, some health indicators rely heavily on surveillance systems, vital registration, and service reports. Others are generated almost entirely through household surveys. No single data source generally provides all the information needed within a health system – the challenge is to put in place the most cost-effective way of ensuring that the full range of data needs is met in a timely way. It is important to note that although the use of routine service-based health information systems may be the least costly option, they can be subject to considerable biases and to a tendency to inflate health service coverage and use. The use of household surveys may correct for the biases that are inherent in routine information systems.

Establishing a data-collection strategy requires the following steps:

- Inventory of the different data-collection modes available.
- Assessment of the overall quality of each data-collection mode in terms of the quality of information generated and cost.
- Evaluation of the extent to which existing data-collection modes are sufficient to generate all the information required by health system actors at various levels, including those required to produce core health indicators.
- Identification of key information gaps and ways of filling them, including assessment of the statistical and survey capacity at country level.
- Identification of cost-effective data-collection modes and solutions to fill the information gaps – this may include supplementing missing information through statistical modelling and statistical procedures.

DEVELOPING HUMAN RESOURCES FOR HEALTH INFORMATION

There is increasing awareness that improvements in health outcomes cannot be achieved unless attention is paid to the training, deployment, remuneration and career development of human resources. Human resources for health information are an important component that should not be neglected – too often (especially at peripheral levels) data collection and reporting are handed over to staff who see this as an unwelcome additional burden that detracts from their primary role as providers of health care. Several country assessments have shown that deploying health information officers within facilities and districts (as well as at higher levels of the health care system) results in significant improvements in the quality of data reported and in the understanding of its importance by health care workers (16).

Meeting Technology Needs

The advent of computer-based technologies has the potential to radically improve the availability, sharing and use of health-related data. Although computers are not in themselves the whole answer, they are certainly an important part of the solution. Specialized software can help reduce simple transcription errors and can provide immediate feedback in cases of data anomalies or inconsistencies in trends. Unfortunately, in many settings, computers are used as part of separate, vertical, programmes resulting in a plethora of non-compatible systems in countries. This often aggravates rather than alleviates duplication and overlap. The coherent capacity-building of human resources across all levels of the system is both more effective and more cost-efficient.

Improving Data Quality, Analysis and Feedback

Poor health information will lead inevitably to poor decision-making. Sustained efforts are therefore needed to ensure a high standard of data quality at all levels. Fundamental principles for data quality include:

- Validity – the construct measures what it purports to measure without bias;
- Reliability – measurement error is minimized;
- Comparability – over time and across populations and geographic areas; and
- Transparency – in terms of methodology and coverage.

There are, inevitably, a number of trade-offs that need to be made when setting up systems to enhance data quality. One of these is the balance between generating high-quality data and the costs associated with collecting it. An assessment of the degree of precision required in any item of data collected is important in helping to determine how much investment needs to be made. Another trade-off arises between data quantity and quality and the major impediments to data quality can be grouped under four headings:

- Technical – related to non-use of standard definitions and inappropriate data-collection instruments;
- Operational – related to poor recording and reporting, and to errors and delays in processing data and in communicating information;
- Behavioural – related to the failure to value health information (culture of evaluation), absence of feedback from data users to data producers, and failure to use health information as an accountability tool; and
- Environmental – absence of a supportive environment and supportive supervision.

Improving data quality necessitates actions on all these fronts simultaneously. All too often, it is assumed that a technological fix is the answer (such as the introduction of computers or sophisticated modelling) – in fact, the critical intervention points are environmental or behavioural (16). Nevertheless, information technology does have an important role to play in supporting efforts to enhance data quality by making it easier to identify major errors and inconsistencies and to share information among data users and producers (17).

Improving Data Presentation and Dissemination

Health information tends to be complex and difficult to interpret. It is often difficult to demonstrate real progress in short time periods and the attribution of cause and effect is not always straightforward (for example, the impact of changes in behaviour on health outcomes such as disease prevalence or mortality). The presentation of epidemiological data is frequently aimed at specialists and other experts in the topic and there is little effort to make the information palatable and understandable to the lay public or to non-health specialists. As a result, there is a widely established perception that health information is obscure, unclear and contradictory. This presents a major challenge when it comes to providing health information to decision-makers and, in particular, to funders such as ministries of planning and finance. There is a strong need to develop innovative approaches to health information that "tell the story" in ways that are simple, direct and easily comprehensible, and to report information through traditional channels such as research journals or routine annual reports.

Improving Data use

The quality, presentation and dissemination, and use of data are all closely interconnected. Data that are considered to be of poor quality do not get presented, disseminated or used by decision-makers. This in turn leads to the under-valuing of health information, thus feeding a cycle of poor quality and non-use of data (18). Even if high-quality data are produced, this does not necessarily result in their effective use in decision-making. Other factors (including behavioural, organizational and environmental) all influence the extent to which information is used (9) – entry points for improving the use of data therefore include:

- Addressing behavioural constraints, for example, through the use of incentives for data use;
- Providing a supportive organizational environment that puts a premium on the availability and use of data for decision making;
- Ensuring that data are relevant to strategic decision-making and to planning;
- Engaging all key constituencies in determining what information to collect in order to ensure wide ownership and involvement;
- Making maximum efforts to ensure confidence in the reliability and validity of data;
- Avoiding the provision of too much excessively detailed information, and making sure that important aggregations are provided;
- Providing essential disaggregations, such as health status by major measures of equity;
- Customizing data presentation to the needs of specific target audiences; and
- Ensuring the timeliness of data.

NATIONAL HEALTH INFORMATION SYSTEMS

ORGANIZATIONAL FRAMEWORK

Although there is general agreement on the broad purpose and functions of a national health information system, practices within countries vary widely. A recent review of evaluations of national health information systems (11) and reports of national experiences in several countries (12) indicate various organizational patterns of health information systems, reflecting widely different historical experiences and systems of government. In some settings, a highly centralized, rigid and unresponsive health information system collects vast quantities of data, only a small proportion of which is used to manage performance, generally through punitive measures. Elsewhere, health information systems have developed in a chaotic and unplanned way, resulting in duplication and overlap coupled with gaps in information on important health topics. In many developing countries, external donors have introduced partial health information systems designed to meet their own particular needs for accountability – the uncoordinated manner in which such donor-driven information systems have evolved for different programmes resulting in duplication of data collection and data sets.

The burgeoning interest in monitoring and evaluation has had a positive impact on the perception of the need for a clear policy and organizational framework for health information. However, countries with an articulated government policy on health information systems are in the minority, and in most countries such systems do not exist as a clearly defined entity but as highly fragmented and uncoordinated parallel subsystems (FIGURE 6). As indicated by the arrows, information flow is generally exclusively upwards (from the periphery to the centre). In addition, the information channels in different parts of the system (such as statistics departments, public and private health sectors, and other sectors) are generally weak, as indicated by the dotted lines. Finally, there is little horizontal transmission of information between actors and consumers at the same level of the system, for example between communities and facilities, or between different programmes.

Such fragmented and often disease-specific reporting flows inevitably lead to further problems. For example, separate data flows may exist in parallel for general ministry of health reports, for surveillance and epidemiological reporting, for monitoring of specific disease-focused programmes, and for reporting by statistical agencies. One unfortunate result of the predominantly upward flow of information through several channels (with long time lags between data generation and data reporting) is that by the time data reach decision-makers, they are often out of date or too aggregated for useful feedback to peripheral levels. The advent of information technology and the use of electronic data transmission are often presented as a solution to this problem but their reach is currently restricted in most developing countries to the district level and higher. Within health care facilities themselves, computers are not generally available or connected.

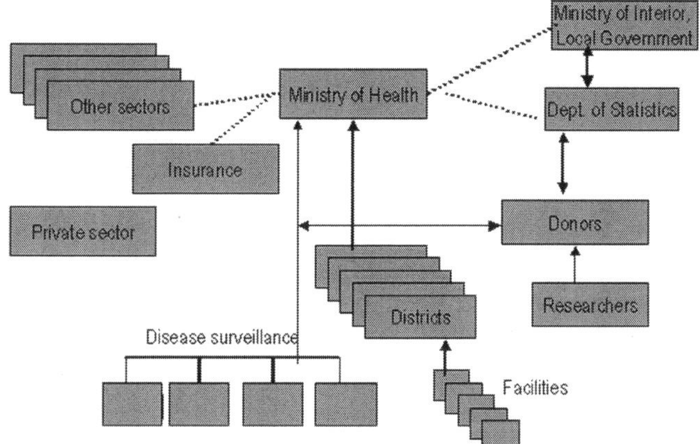

Fig. Typical organization structure of the Health Information System

Information System Processes

Too often, government policies are weak and donors tend to dominate – while demanding more and better data for their for their own reporting purposes. Such data are seldom relevant or used at the national level. Several donors operate their own monitoring systems because of constraints in the national systems. Health care workers find themselves having to report similar information to several different donors or programmes, though generally in different formats. This results in a lack of clarity and accountability regarding available resources, both human and financial.

Even within ministries of health, there is poor sharing and coordination of data and information from and between different departments, and duplication of data-generation efforts often due to external pressures. The efforts of different units involved in the production of health information are uncoordinated and unlinked and mandates are weak or non-existent. Inevitably, as a consequence, there is little attention given to meeting the human-resource needs in the form of suitably skilled and motivated health information officers. Much of the health information system relies on the inputs of primary providers of health care who often feel that the burdensome reporting requirements distract them from their primary responsibility of patient care. The health information staff that are available often receive low remuneration and experience poor employment and promotion conditions, with inadequate access to training. Even at higher levels of the system, health planners and managers receive little or no training in statistics, epidemiology or the use of information for planning and management. On the other hand, there is evidence that a shortage of financial resources for health information is not always a major bottleneck, though this is less related to the availability of core funding than to the interest of donors. However, the level of external donor funding varies between countries and over time, creating problems of sustainability.

In recent years there has been a significant increase in the availability of computers for storing, transmitting and presenting health information. However, although computers exist and function well at the district and national levels, they are seldom used systematically to analyse data or for electronic communication. In addition, some countries have adopted technology-driven systems that they cannot afford to maintain and do not have the expertise to manage. One important finding from several studies is that the introduction of technology is not necessarily the answer to a weak health information system. Where the will and capacity to manage paper-based systems exists, the introduction of computers is likely to be well managed and fruitful. In the absence of such a supportive environment, computers alone do not provide the solution.

Data Quantity and Quality

In addition to the above-mentioned organizational fragmentation (see FIGURE 6) and poorly coordinated processes there is also an absence of guidance on what data items should be included in health information systems and where responsibility lies for producing them. Few countries have undertaken systematic reviews, involving all stakeholders, of their health information needs and minimum data requirements. There is little standardization of the indicators, targets or tools to be used, too much information is collected, and it is poorly analysed, not easily comparable and often not used. There is data overload, especially at peripheral levels, and major problems with the quality and use of information for decision-making. Those tasked with collecting and reporting data often cite a lack of relevance of the multitude of data collected, the limited capacity of facility and district staff in data collection and analysis, and the often limited decision-making power at district level. There are too many forms to fill in at the facility or district level, with the same person often reporting similar information to several recipients but in slightly different formats. Ironically, juxtaposed with this information overload is an almost total absence of information from some key players in health, notably the private sector. The huge volumes of data collected also impinge upon data quality and reliability. It is a common complaint that data are inaccurate because of poor diagnostic tools, inaccurate classification and coding of diseases, and inadequate validation procedures.

As also outlined above, the upward flow of information appears to be associated with an absence of data analysis and use, particularly at the lower levels where the data originate. Data are provided by the lower levels of the system and most often analysed at the top of the pyramid – if analysed at all. The information system seems to stop at the stage of data production – diligent recording and reporting of health data is associated with weak analysis and comments on the findings. This is most striking in the context of decentralization which increases the demand for data for decision-making at the district level but which has not been accompanied by an increase in the capacity to analyse and use information effectively. Indeed, in some settings, decentralization has resulted in the weakening of the health information system due to lack of central guidance and monitoring.

The lack of analytical capacity is matched by weaknesses in the presentation of information to different constituencies. And this links to a major constraint identified in most settings, namely the lack of use of collected data and information. The reasons for this are manifold but seldom clearly identified. Although information is only one component of the decision-making process, it should be seen as fundamental to the decision-making process but currently it seems to take second or third place to political and other non-informational factors.

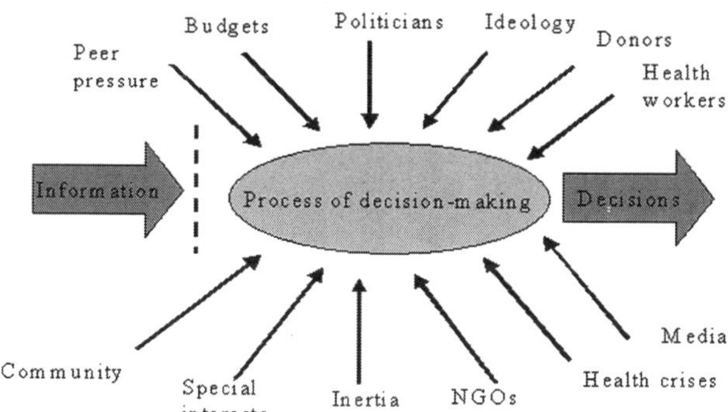

Fig. Factors Iinfluencing Decision-making

HEALTH INFORMATION AND HEALTH REFORM

Recent health sector reform has not generally been accompanied by serious efforts to strengthen health information systems. As a result, the health information field finds itself facing new challenges which it is ill-equipped to deal with. For example, the decentralization of decision-making to the district level has rarely led to enhancements in the capacity to generate and use data at that level. Little guidance has been provided on how to reconcile information generated through integrated interventions such as Integrated Management of Childhood Illnesses (IMCI) with syndromic diagnoses. Nor can growing demands for data to permit analysis of inequities be met. There is little known about how to generate good data for decision-making with regard to marginalized populations or in areas of conflict or mass migration. Little is also known about the costs of generating health information so that it is almost impossible to take evidence-based decisions on which kinds of data-collection tools are most appropriate in different circumstances.

An interesting finding from the many assessments and evaluations of health information systems that have been undertaken over the past few years is that all the problems afflicting health information systems outlined above are well known, commonly shared across countries and regions, and have not changed significantly over time. However, the recommendations of such evaluations have rarely been implemented.

9

Yoga Techniques in Implications for Stress Management and Health

YOGA PRACTICE

The basic mode of respiration used in many yoga practices and recommended for normal daily activities is slow, smooth breathing using the diaphragm rather than the respiratory muscles of the chest (Christensen, 1987, p. 136; Samskrti & Veda, 1985, p. 10). This breathing pattern is sometimes referred to as abdominal breathing, although, as noted below, the abdominal muscles may play a minor role. Breathing is through the nose rather than the mouth.

Scientific Information

The diaphragm is the dominant respiratory muscle for quiet breathing in awake healthy adults, but increased use of chest muscles and increased breathing rate are common results of stress and may become habitual. Slow diaphragmatic breathing appears to reduce adverse effects of stress and promote parasympathetic cardiovascular dominance. The opposite effects are induced by more rapid breathing using the chest muscles. Before discussing the available data, a brief review of the respiratory process may clarify the nature of these modes of breathing and the methodological issues in their investigation.

The Respiratory Process

Three muscle groups can be used in breathing: (a) the diaphragm, (b) the muscles of the rib cage, and (c) the abdominal muscles. This summary of the roles of these muscles is based on Collett, Roussos, and Macklem (1988); Grassio & Goldman (1986); Guyton (1986); and Troyer and Loring (1986).

The diaphragm is the most important muscle for inhalation. It is a thin sheet of muscle separating the chest and abdominal cavities. When relaxed the diaphragm forms an open-bottomed cylinder that extends up into the lower part of the rib cage along the sides of the rib cage, and forms a dome on top. Diaphragm contraction shortens the cylindrical portion and pulls the dome down. This movement expands the lungs by pulling them down, which creates a partial vacuum that causes inhalation if the airway is open. When the diaphragm relaxes, the elastic recoil of the lungs pulls it upward, causing exhalation. The downward pressure on the abdominal viscera from contraction of the diaphragm forces the abdominal wall to extend forward and/or the lower rib cage to expand to the sides. The term abdominal breathing derives from this easily observed movement of the abdominal wall, but can also refer to the use of abdominal muscles described below.

Although upper chest movement is relatively inconspicuous in quiet breathing for a relaxed person, some thoracic muscles play a role. The external and parasternal intercostals (joining adjacent ribs) and the scaleni (connecting the shoulder area and spine) are activated during inspiration to hold the ribs in an expanded position that compliments the force of the diaphragm. However, the exact roles of each of the muscles are not yet resolved. The minimal chest movement combined with the fact that some chest displacement could be a result of diaphragmatic action have contributed to the difficulty in resolving this question. The internal intercostals may sometimes play a role in exhalation.

The abdominal muscles are the most powerful and important muscles for forced exhalation, but are normally not used in quiet breathing. Contraction puts inward pressure on the abdominal viscera, which then push the diaphragm up and reduce lung volume. In addition, these muscles may assist expiration by pulling down and deflating the lower rib cage. The important abdominal muscles for respiration are the rectus abdominous, the transverse abdominous, and the external and internal obloquies.

Abdominal muscles can contribute significantly to inhalation by pushing the relaxed diaphragm farther into the rib cage. This action (a) places the diaphragmatic muscle fibers on a more favorable part of their length-tension curve, and (b) converts some of the respiratory system expiratory elasticity to inspiratory forces.

Only about 10 percent of total respiratory capacity is used on each breath in quiet breathing. The volume of each exhalation or tidal volume is about 500 ml for a quiet adult male. Most of this tidal volume goes to lung areas that exchange oxygen and carbon dioxide with blood, but about 150 ml is dead space from passages that cannot contribute to gas exchange. Dead space volume is relatively constant whereas tidal volume varies greatly with physical exercise, breathing pattern, and other factors. Thus, larger tidal volumes have a smaller proportion of dead space. Dead space can increase significantly with lung disorders. During normal quiet breathing, exhalation is driven by the elastic forces of the lung. Muscles used for inhalation contract to slow and control the rate of exhalation. The position of the relaxed diaphragm and corresponding lung volume after exhalation depend on a balance between the elastic forces collapsing the lungs inward and the elastic forces expanding the chest outward. This lung volume at the end of relaxed expiration is called the functional residual capacity (FRC).

About one fourth of the respiratory capacity not used with quiet breathing can be accessed with additional exhalation and three fourths with additional inhalation. If abdominal muscles force maximum reduction of lung volume, the expiratory reserve volume of about 1100 ml of air below FRC for an average male is expired. This combines with the tidal volume (500 ml) and the inspiratory reserve volume of about 3000 ml to give a vital capacity of 4600 ml. In addition, a residual capacity of about 1200 ml of air remains in the lung after maximum exhalation. These values are typical for a young adult male. The volumes are about 25 percent less for an average female, and vary with body size, posture, and physical condition.

Adequate air flow or ventilation of the lungs can be achieved with slow breathing rate and large tidal volume or fast rate and small tidal volume. The ventilation rate is normally set to provide oxygen and remove carbon dioxide in accordance with metabolic needs. The abdominal and chest muscles also have important functions for posture, locomotion, and verbalization that must be integrated with and may modify respiratory functions.

COMPLETE BREATH

YOGA PRACTICE

The complete breath technique, also called three part breathing, slowly fills and empties the entire lung capacity (Christensen, 1987, p. 137; Samskrti & Veda, 1985, p. 173; Satchidananda, 1970, p. 142). A smooth maximum inhalation is accomplished by first expanding the abdomen and lower rib cage, then expanding the middle rib cage, and finally expanding the upper rib cage. The abdomen naturally withdraws as the chest is fully expanded. The arms are sometimes slowly raised overhead to help expand the chest. A slow maximum exhalation follows in the reverse order—sinking the upper chest, then the middle chest, and finally pulling in the abdomen. The complete breath may be done in either a sitting or a standing position. The mind is focused on the breath and the release of tension during breathing.

This technique is often done three to five times at the beginning of hatha yoga sessions or at the beginning of the yoga breathing practices. Yoga texts recommend this technique at other times to counter stress and refresh the mind and body.

Scientific Information and Further Research

The summary of scientific information and suggestions for further research are combined because very little relevant scientific work has been done on this technique. (As discussed below, the technique has been used in studies that combined various breathing and physical relaxation practices.)

Autonomic Effects

Because the complete breath is the extreme case of slow deep breathing, the psychophysiological effects discussed for diaphragmatic breathing may possibly be extrapolated to this technique. However, such an extrapolation would go beyond the range of available data as no studies were found that used this specific sequence for full breathing capacity. For example, Hirsch and Bishop (1981) found that respiratory sinus arrythmia (a good index of parasympathetic tone) consistently increased as tidal volume increased, but, the maximum tidal volume studied was only half vital capacity and the sequence of breathing was not specified.

The complete breath passes through a range of changing autonomic reflexes so the net effects are difficult to predict. Lung volume or stretch reflexes, for example, decrease parasympathetic activity at moderate lung inflations, which in turn causes increased heart rate due to increased sympathetic dominance. At large lung volumes, however, autonomic reflexes cause decreased heart rate (Daly, 1986). Basic research on the psychophysiological effects of the complete breath remains to be carried out.

Physical Effects

The complete breath gently contracts and stretches all respiratory muscles. This presumably is beneficial, particularly for sedentary persons who may not otherwise exercise some respiratory muscles. Research on release of muscle tension accumulated during stressful activities might be fruitful.

The full inhalation of the complete breath should provide maximum opening of the collapsed lower airways, which may be of particular value to older persons and those with lung impairment. However, the full exhalation will also provide maximum collapsing of airways. For maximum airway opening, the complete breath practice should end after an inhalation, rather than after a full exhalation.

BREATH HOLDING

YOGA PRACTICE

During intermediate and advanced practice of rapid breathing and alternate nostril breathing techniques, the breath is held after full inhalation (Rama, 1986; Satchidananda, 1970). With rapid breathing, the breath is held between groups of rapid breaths for just a few seconds initially and, after more practice, for as long as comfortable. With alternate nostril breathing, each completed inhalation is held for a few seconds initially and gradually extended to a period four times as long as the inhalation time—the time ratios for inhalation, breath hold, and exhalation being 1:4:2 in the final stage. In more advanced practices, the breath may also be suspended after exhalation. The mind is focused inward during breath holding and may concentrate on a particular area of the body such as the heart or forehead regions.

During breath suspension, the head is bent forward with the chin pressing against the hollow of the throat, and the anal sphincter muscles are usually contracted. These techniques are called the chin lock (Jalandhra Bandha) and root lock (Moola Bandha) respectively.

The abdominal lock (Uddiyana Bandha) is applied in more advanced breath holding, but is performed as an independent practice first. In the initial practice, the person stands, bending forward slightly with the arms resting on slightly bent knees. As air is exhaled, the abdominal muscles are drawn back and up toward the spine, creating a hollow in the abdomen. After maximum exhalation, the chin lock is applied and the chest is expanded, creating inhalation pressure against the closed air way, which further draws the abdominal region upward. When used with other breathing practices, the abdominal lock is initially used with exhalation. Later, chest expansion and abdominal muscle contraction are applied with breath holding after full inhalation, although inhalation pressure, of course, reduces as lung inflation increases.

Most yoga instructions give stern warning that prolonged breath suspension (kumbhaka) should be done only by experienced practitioners under the guidance of a knowledgeable teacher (e.g., Rama, Ballentine & Hymes, pp. 117-118, 122; Satchidananda, 1970, p. 144). Breath holding is commonly introduced gradually and without strain in yoga training.

Scientific Information

As discussed below, breath holding can initiate powerful parasympathetic and sympathetic reflexes. The net psychophysiological effects depend greatly on various physical and apparently psychological parameters during the breath hold. The limited available data suggests that the yoga locks during breath hold minimize stimulation of these potentially strong reflexes in beginning and intermediate students. Large oscillations of heart rate and blood pressure have been reported during yoga breathing techniques after several years of advanced practice.

Cardiovascular Effects of Breath Holding

Increased blood carbon dioxide concentrations from breath holding cause opening of the nasal airways as noted under alternate nostril breathing. Other effects of breath holding depend strongly on interactions among concomitant autonomic reflexes.

Heart rate for an inactive person (a) commonly decreases by roughly ten percent if the breath is held after maximum inhalation (summary in Lin, 1982, p. 274), (b) has little change if breath suspension is after normal exhalation (i.e., at FRC), and (c) increases or has little change if suspension is after maximum exhalation (Angelone & Coulter, 1965; Kawakami, Natelson, & DuBois, 1967; Openshaw & Woodroof, 1978; Song, Lee, Chung, & Hong, 1969). This research is characterized by significant variability of results among subjects and among studies. These and other studies also verify that the breath can be held much longer after inhalation than after exhalation (Lin, 1982, p. 286).

Exhalation pressure against the closed airway during breath holding increases heart rate whereas inhalation pressure can reduce heart rate (Craig, 1963; Paulev, 1968; Paulev et al., 1988; Sharpey-Schafer, 1965; Song, Lee, Chung, & Hong, 1969). Strong exhalation pressure (positive intrapulmonary pressure) can increase heart rate by over 30 percent above the baseline rate. Heart rate effects from negative intrapulmonary pressure are usually of smaller magnitude and lower consistency than the effects of positive pressure. Lack of control of lung inflation and intrapulmonary pressure in many studies of heart rate during breath holding probably contributes to the variability of experimental results. Control of pressure in the lungs requires deliberate effort because respiratory system elasticity leads to exhalation pressure if the respiratory muscles are relaxed after inhalation. Thus, heart rate slowing from breath holding can be canceled unless tension is maintained in the respiratory muscles.

Breath holding also causes vasoconstriction and decreased blood flow to the limbs, presumably with well maintained flow to the brain and heart (Brick, 1966; Elsner, Franklin, Van Citters & Kenny, 1966; Heistad, Abboud, & Eckstein, 1968). The reduced peripheral blood flow is accentuated by exhalation pressure during breath holding (Paulev, 1969, pp. 83-99).

Breath holding combined with stimulation of receptors on the face or in the nose initiates the dive response. This response greatly enhances (a) heart rate slowing, and (b) blood flow to the brain and heart muscle at the expense of the periphery (reviewed in Daly, 1986; Elsner & Gooden, 1983). The response also reduces the drive to breath and often increases blood pressure. Heart rate reductions of 20 to 35 percent are common for an inactive person (Lin, 1982, p. 274). The dive response may override the normal cardiovascular response to exercise and may even be intensified by exercise (Elsner & Gooden, 1983, p. 50).

The nature of facial stimulation appears to be important, but is not well understood. Water or some types of mechanical stimulation on the face, eyes, or nasal lining can initiate the dive response (Daly & Angell-James, 1979; Elsner & Gooden, 1983, pp. 92-96; Jackson, 1976; Widdicombe, 1986). One uniform finding is that cold water on the face enhances the response. Stimulation of the receptors without concurrent breath holding appears to cause the same types of cardiovascular responses, but to a lesser degree (Brick, 1966; Heistad & Wheeler, 1970; Whayne, & Killip, 1967). However, better understanding of these receptors and possible interactions with lung volume and intrapulmonary pressure is needed before these effects can be discussed with confidence.

Breath holding and the dive response can initiate both parasympathetic and sympathetic cardiovascular responses. Heart rate slowing is apparently mediated by the parasympathetic system whereas the reduced peripheral blood flow presumably results from increased peripheral sympathetic activity (Elsner & Gooden, 1983, p. 101; Paulev, 1969, p. 94). For comparison, meditation and related relaxation procedures often tend to increase peripheral blood flow (Levander, Benson, Wheeler, & Wallace, 1972; Luthe, 1963; Rieckert, 1967), as does mental stress (Bennett, Hosking, & Hampton, 1976). Various mechanisms may mediate the cardiovascular responses. For example, the altered heart rate during positive or negative intrapulmonary pressure may be, in part, a response to altered venus return to the heart due to intrapleural pressure changes (Craig, 1963; Paulev, 1969, p. 71).

Psychological factors can override or possibly enhance the autonomic responses to breath holding. Mental distraction or preoccupation during breath holding or the dive response can attenuate or eliminate the cardiovascular responses (Ross & Steptoe, 1980; Wolf, 1978; Wolf, Schneider, & Groover, 1965). Wolf et al. (1965) also reported that subjects who were rushed or harassed with a multitude of instructions failed to show a dive response, but the response normally occurred in quiet test conditions. They also reported that with repeated testing, the dive response became more pronounced and became a conditioned response—the cardiovascular responses began at the signal for facial immersion prior to immersion. Fear appeared to enhance the dive response (Wolf, 1978; Wolf et al. 1965). In a few subjects, the stress of arterial puncture for the experiment induced striking heart rate slowing and peripheral vasoconstriction prior to the breath holding procedure.

These psychological factors may contribute to the wide variability in the results of experiments on breath holding.

Chin and Abdominal Locks

Given the importance of factors such as intrapulmonary pressure, the chin and abdominal locks may have decisive influence on the cardiovascular response to yogic breath holding.

The available data indicate that heart rate for relatively inexperienced subjects increases slightly or shows no change during breath holding with chin and abdominal locks. Average heart rate increased about 8 percent during full inhalation breath holding with the chin lock (but no abdominal lock) compared to the average baseline rate (Bhole, 1979). The six subjects had only about seven weeks experience with the lock. Average heart rate showed no change from the baseline rate during abdominal locks in a study with 39 subjects with apparently less than eight months training (Oak & Bhole, 1984). Average heart rate increased by about 10 percent in another study with 28 subjects (Gopal, Anantharaman, Balachander & Nishith, 1973). This study included the root lock and found similar heart rate responses in subjects with no previous experience and in subjects with at least six months training. Likewise, heart rate responses were similar for breath holding after full inhalation or exhalation.

However, certain individuals may show a striking heart rate decrease during yogic breath holding. The heart rate of a healthy 21 year old male slowed to 34 beats per minute while doing the abdominal lock after three weeks practice (Monjo, Gharote, & Bhagwat, 1984). Heart rate was normal before and after the maneuver.

Radiological and direct observation indicated that the expanded chest of the combined chin, abdominal, and root locks avoided physical pressure on the heart and blood vessels, and maintained blood flow to and from the head (Gopal & Lakshmanan, 1972). The authors also reported that the shape of the heart indicated good venous return. This latter result is not surprising because contraction of the abdominal muscles greatly increases venous return and cardiac output (Guyton, 1986, p. 277). Similarly, Lamb et al. (1958) noted that pilots discovered early in aviation that "undesirable effects of G forces could be alleviated in part by tightening of the stomach muscles and taking a deep breath, thus enhancing venous return to the heart" (p. 570). Yogic writers have also noted that the chin lock can help maintain a closed air way during breath holding (e.g., Rama Ballentine, & Hymes, 1979, p. 124).

Advanced Breath Holding

Schmidt (1983) observed large rhythmic swings in heart rate and blood pressure during advanced yoga breathing practices by a subject with over five years experience. Heart rate during alternate nostril breathing increased to about 120 beats per minute during breath holding and quickly decreased to about 60 bpm during the slow exhalation. Blood pressure in the left brachial artery decreased to about 55/30 mm hg (systolic/diastolic) during breath holding and quickly increased to about 150/65 mm hg during the slow exhalation. The subject's baseline resting heart rate was about 70 bpm and blood pressure about 105/50 mm hg. The time ratios for inhalation, breath hold, and exhalation were 1:4:2, with about one breath per minute. Similar large swings were observed for two other slow full volume yoga breathing techniques and for two other advanced practioners.

The subjects reported that the experience of enhanced energy, mental and physical balance, calmness, and mental clarity associated with the breathing practices increased greatly after several years of practice. The author noted (with out providing data) that beginners following the same techniques did not show such strong physiological changes. According to the advanced subjects, more successful practice and prolonged breath holding depend on increased concentration and relaxation during practice.

Schmidt noted that these cardiovascular responses presumably cause large oscillations in blood flow to various organs, which could possibly be related to the mental effects. However, he also noted that further research is needed to determine the mechanisms and details of these striking cardiovascular effects. Positive intrapulmonary pressure may contribute to these effects. The valsalva maneuver (sharp exhalation pressure against a closed airway) produces increased heart rate and reduced blood pressure, which is followed by reduced heart rate and increased blood pressure after cessation of the maneuver (Daly, 1986, p. 569).

Cardiac Arrhythmias

Breath holding and the dive response can induce a variety of cardiac arrhythmias (Lamb, Dermksian, & Sarnoff, 1958; Olsen, Fanestil, & Scholander, 1962; Wayne & Killip, 1967), but these appear to be a health threat only for people with significant pre-existing heart abnormalities (Paulev, 1969, p. 72). The strong parasympathetic cardiac stimulation from the dive response has been successfully and safely used as a means of halting paroxysmal atrial tachycardia, but requires extreme caution in patients susceptible to ventricular abnormalities because dangerous arrhythmias can be induced (Mathew, 1978; Wildenthal & Atkins, 1979; Wildenthal, Leshin, Atkins, & Skelton, 1975). Efforts to minimize fear and distractions that could possibly enhance or neutralize the dive response are recommended with this treatment (Wildenthal, Leshin, Atkins, & Skelton, 1975).

In case studies of two patients reporting heart rhythm abnormalities at rest, the abdominal lock exacerbated a nodal cardiac arrhythmia in one case and induced premature ventricular beats in the other (Monjo, Gharote, & Bhagwat, 1984).

Thus, the yogic cautions that breath holding techniques should be introduced gradually and only with proper guidance and experience appear to be reasonable, particularly in the absence of a thorough heart examination. The techniques appear to pose no threat when done properly and introduced gradually for normal subjects. The implications of the reported large swings in heart rate and blood pressure during advanced breath holding practices need further study.

Physical Effects

The very limited data on oxygen consumption during rapid breathing with breath suspension are within the range discussed above for rapid breathing without breath holding (Karambelkar, Deshpande, & Bhole, 1983;

1984b; Miles, 1964). This limited data provides no evidence that yogic breath holding causes either an extreme increase or an extreme decrease in oxygen consumption.

Further Research

Psychophysiological effects.The elevated carbon dioxide levels from breath holding may have psychophysiological effects similar to those discussed for diaphragmatic breathing. Substantial blood carbon dioxide concentrations appear to contribute to the beneficial effects of slow deep breathing. Further research on the psychophysiological effects of the yogic breath holding techniques is needed, particularly when combined with rapid breathing and alternate nostril breathing. The evidence that advanced practices produce effects that are different from the beginning practices must be considered in planning research.

Psychological factors. Mutual interactions between autonomic responses to breath holding and psychological factors such as distraction, stress, fear, etc. may provide important information on the relation between the autonomic and central nervous systems as well as on useful breathing techniques.

Carotid sinus stimulation. Some yogic writers suggest that after extensive practice, the chin lock stimulates the parasympathetic carotid sinus pressure receptors in the neck and alters the practioner's state of consciousness (e.g., Kuvalayananda, 1966, p. 28; Rama, Ballentine, & Hymes, 1979, p. 124). Although the available data show little evidence of strong parasympathetic stimulation (heart rate slowing) during the chin lock for most subjects, the topic needs further study as minor modifications of the technique could easily have major effects. Stimulation of the carotid sinuses while holding the breath may pose significant cardiac threats (Daly, 1986, p. 577).

ALTERNATE NOSTRIL BREATHING

Yoga Practice

Alternate nostril breathing consists of slow deep quiet breaths using one nostril at a time (Samskrti & Franks, 1978, pp. 159-161; Satchidananda, 1970, pp. 143 & 149). The thumb or ring finger are used to close off the other nostril. Three variations exit, depending on when the nostrils are switched. In one variation, the active nostril is switched after each inhalation. In the second variation, exhalation is through one nostril and inhalation through the other. After a few cycles, the inhalation and exhalation nostrils are reversed. The third variation switches nostrils after several breaths. For all three techniques, each breath is as slow as comfortable using full lung capacity as in the complete breath. A sitting position is used.

Beginners attempt to make the duration of inhalation and exhalation equal and do only about six single nostril breaths between rests. With practice, the duration of exhalation is slowly extended to twice the duration of inhalation and the practice is continued for several minutes. The mind is focused on the slow deep breathing in a manner similar to meditation. The advanced practice continues for 10 to 20 minutes or longer with the breath held after inhalation and/or exhalation. Yoga writings use a variety of terms for alternate nostril breathing, including nadi shodhanam, nadi suddhi and sukha purvaka.

Scientific Information

Existing research efforts have focused on understanding the psychophysiology of nasal functioning. This work is important background for understanding the potential effects and significance of the alternate nostril breathing technique, but basic direct research on the technique remains to be done. As discussed below, research has verified the yoga claims that nasal air flow is usually greater in one side of the nose than the other, and that the open side switches every few hours. The available data relevant to the yogic claim that this asymmetric nasal air flow is related to lateral brain functioning are inconsistent and difficult to interpret.

Autonomic Effects

Average heart rate increased from 71 to 78 beats per minute and blood oxygen, carbon dioxide, and pH did not change significantly after ten minutes of alternate nostril breathing (Pratap, Berrettini, & Smith, 1978). The ten subjects had two to five years experience with the technique. Average respiration rate was 2.7 breaths per minute during the last minute of alternate nostril breathing. The breath was not held except very briefly to move the hands while switching closed nostrils. (Data from an investigation of advanced alternate nostril breathing is presented in the later section on breath holding.)

Background on Nasal Dominance

According to yoga tradition, alternate nostril breathing improves the functioning, coordination and balance for two modes of cognitive activity that are reasonably similar to current concepts of right and left hemispheric brain functioning (Rama, Ballentine & Ajaya, 1976). Ancient yoga writings claim that the modes of mental activity are related to which nostril is dominant or most open to air flow. Mental capabilities corresponding the left hemisphere dominate when the right nostril is more open. Likewise, right hemispheric mental capabilities dominate when the left nostril dominates. Equal air flow through both nostrils represents a balance of the two mental modes.

Yoga tradition also claims that nostril dominance and corresponding cognitive mode alternate approximately every one (Bhole & Karambelkar, 1968) or two hours (Rama 1986, p.89). According to these writings, the cycle becomes erratic with emotional disturbance, irregular eating or sleeping habits, and various other life style factors.

Nasal Airway Resistance

The airways of the nose are lined with erectile tissue that swells when engorged with blood. The swelling increases congestion and resistance to air flow, which enhances humidifying and warming of inhaled air (Cole, 1982, 1988) and may be an efficient passive mechanism for braking the respiratory system elasticity during periods of low ventilation (Hairfield, Warren, Hinton, & Seaton, 1987; Jackson, 1976; McCaffrey and Kern, 1979a; 1979b).

Nasal airway resistance changes in response to changing air flow or air conditioning needs. Nasal congestion (a) decreases (vasoconstriction) with exercise or with elevated carbon dioxide levels from breathing carbon dioxide, rebreathing with a bag, or holding the breath, and (b) increases (vasodilation) with hyperventilation or breathing cold air (Cole, Forsyth, & Haight, 1983; Cole, Haight, Love, & Oprysk, 1985; Dallimore & Eccles, 1977; Forsyth, Cole, & Shephard, 1983; Hasegawa & Kern, 1978; McCaffrey & Kern, 1979b; Richerson & Seebohm, 1968; Takagi, Proctor, Salman, & Evering, 1969; Tatum, 1923). Nasal resistance can vary greatly among subjects and over time (Holmes, Goodell, Wolf, & Wolff, 1950; Takagi et al., 1969).

Psychological factors such as stress, fear, and frustration can apparently affect nasal resistance. Eccles (1982) noted that adrenaline, which is released during stress, causes decreased nasal resistance. Clinical observations of patients with chronic or recurrent nasal congestion found that congestion increased during periods of anxiety or conflict with frustration, resentment and guilt (Holmes et al., 1950; O'Neill & Malcomson, 1954; Wolff, 1950), but decreased during fear and panic (Holmes et al., 1950, pp. 58 & 114). Holmes et al. (1950, p. 140) suggested that increased nasal congestion was associated with a passive, withdrawing response to stressors, whereas decreased congestion occurred in preparation for heightened respiration of an active fight or flight response.

Sympathetic nerves control nasal congestion whereas parasympathetic nerves control nasal secretion with some associated influence on blood flow and congestion (reviewed in Eccles, 1982). Reduced nasal sympathetic vasoconstrictor tone causes congestion, whereas increased sympathetic activity causes decongestion. Reduced parasympathetic tone causes reduced nasal secretion and reduced congestion, whereas increased parasympathetic tone causes increased nasal secretion and increased congestion. These conclusions are supported directly by experiments with animals and are consistent with the effects of surgical and chemical nerve blockade in humans (e.g., Chandra, 1969; Golding-Wood, 1973; Haight & Cole, 1986; Millonig, Harris, & Gardner, 1950; Richerson & Seebohn, 1968).

Nasal Dominance

Numerous studies consistently show that one side of the nose usually has higher airway resistance in most people and that the asymmetric resistance switches sides after a few hours (e.g., Clarke, 1980; Eccles, 1978; Gilbert & Rosenwasser, 1987; Hasegawa & Kern, 1977; Heetderks, 1927; Keuning, 1968; Stoksted, 1952, 1953).

However, the widely used term nasal cycle may not be technically correct because there is little evidence that the changes in nasal resistance have reasonably constant periods. As noted by Gilbert and Rosenwasser (1987), most nasal cycle studies have observed subjects for only a few hours on one day whereas much longer or repeated study periods are needed for relevant time series statistical analysis. Changes of nasal dominance during these short periods cannot be assumed to be a continuing cyclic (i.e., fixed period) process. In one of the few studies to attempt replicate testing, Hasegawa and Kern (1977) noted "of the five subjects who had second studies, none had reproducible findings" (p. 33). Likewise, failure to observe nasal resistance alternations in these short study periods does not mean they do not routinely occur in a subject.

Longer studies have given mixed evidence for regular cycles. Obvious regular shifts about every three hours were found for one subject examined for 18 hours (Principato & Ozenberger, 1970). Regular shifts about every one to two and half hours were found for two subjects examined for seven days (Eccles, 1978). However, for eight subjects studied for one month, the alternations in nostril dominance did not have regular periodicities, except for some very weak daily patterns found by averaging over the month (Clarke, 1980; Funk & Clarke, 1980). Most subjects in these latter studies also had one side dominant more often than the other.

Factors Affecting Nasal Dominance

Asymmetric or unilateral pressure on the chest, shoulders, trunk or buttocks can shift nasal dominance. The pressure triggers vasomotor reflexes that increase nasal resistance on the side of the pressure and decrease it on the other side (Bhole & Karambelkar, 1968; Cole & Haight, 1984, 1986; Davies & Eccles, 1985; Haight & Cole, 1984, 1986; Rao & Potdar, 1970; Singh, 1987; Takagi & Kobayasi, 1955). These reflexes cause (a) the readily observed congestion in the lower nostril and decongestion in the upper nostril when people lie on their sides, (b) the ancient yoga observation that placing a crutch or yoga-danda under one arm while upright leads to ipsilateral nasal congestion and contralateral decongestion, and (c) in at least some persons, nasal dominance shifts due to asymmetrical weight distribution while seated (Haight & Cole, 1986). The widely varying time periods between nasal dominance shifts are not surprising if asymmetrical weight distribution can cause the shifts. Haight and Cole (1989) report that 37 of 42 subjects showed a nasal response to unilateral pressure.

Increased ventilation demands can also alter nasal dominance. Nasal resistance can become low and nearly symmetric during exercise, rebreathing with a bag, and probably breath holding (Dallimore & Eccles, 1977; also supported by the example in Ohki, Hasegawa, Kurita, & Watanabe, 1987). The amplitude of nasal resistance fluctuations is less while standing compared to sitting (Cole & Haight, 1986).

The hypothesis that anxiety and other life style factors cause shifts in nasal dominance is conceptually consistent with the evidence noted above that psychological factors affect nasal resistance, but specific studies of psychological factors and nasal dominance have not been reported. Eccles (1978) suggested that uncontrolled environmental factors may normally obscure the regular nasal cycles observed in his seven day laboratory study.

The neural mechanisms controlling nasal resistance are primarily ipsilateral, but some evidence suggests possible contralateral effects in some people. Unilateral sympathetic efferent severance or blockade in humans caused pronounced ipsilateral nasal congestion, and no apparent effect on contralateral nasal resistance and responses in several studies (Fowler, 1943; Haight & Cole, 1986; Holmes, et al., 1950, pp. 113-119). However, during unilateral sympathetic blockade, slight increases in contralateral resistance that may have been related to the blockade occurred in one study (Stoksted & Thomsen, 1953) and reduced contralateral nasal responses to exercise occurred in another study (Richardson & Seebohm, 1968). Unilateral parasympathetic severance has resulted in less secretion and less congestion on the side of severance in several hundred patients surgically treated for excessive nasal secretion (Golding-Wood, 1973; Jarvis, Marais, & Milner, 1970; Millonig, Harris, & Gardner, 1950). The immediate unilateral effects were followed by contralateral effects about two weeks after surgery in about one third of the cases. The factors causing the unpredictable contralateral effects in a minority of the patients are not known.

Ultradian Rhythms

Shannahoff-Khalsa with various others have suggested that the nasal dominance alternations reflect an underlying endogenous cycle of shifting right-left dominance in the brain and autonomic system. They report lateral changes in brain wave activity (Werntz, Bickford, Bloom & Shannahoff-Khalsa, 1983) and peripheral catecholamines (Kennedy, Ziegler, & Shannahoff-Khalsa, 1986) tightly coupled with nasal dominance. In addition, they cite a variety of studies suggesting ultradian (less than a day) cycles in psychophysiology and performance with periods of about 80 to 150 minutes. In particular, the report by Klein and Armitage (1979) of 90 to 100 minute cycles in verbal and spatial performance that were 180 degrees out of phase supports the hypothesis of alternating lateral processing. These cycles are proposed to be an extension of alternating lateral dominance in rapid eye movement and nonrapid eye movement sleep stages.

Unfortunately, there are few noncontroversial findings in ultradian-laterality rhythm research. Replication of the Klein and Armitage (1979) study failed to find cycles of lateral cognitive processing (Kripke, Fleck, Mullaney & Levy, 1983). Some recent writers have strong arguments for doubting the basic hypothesis that rapid eye movement/nonrapid eye movement sleep cycles reflect reciprocal shifts in lateral brain activity (e.g., Antrobus, 1987; Armitage, Hoffman, Loewy, & Moffit, 1989). The integrated total EEG measure used by Werntz et al. (1983) and in several previous studies of lateral brain activity primarily reflects alpha activity, whereas lower amplitude higher frequency activity may be more important indicators of lateral cognitive processing (Armitage, 1989; Ray & Cole, 1985). The situation is compounded because Werntz et al. used the opposite interpretation than is traditional for this measure (i.e., they hypothesized that higher amplitude EEG [i.e., alpha activity] indicated more mental activity instead of less).

Convincing conclusions about rhythms of lateral physiological functioning will probably require extensive further research. This is a very difficult research area—the number of potentially important variables and methodological details are vast, as are the speculations about inconsistent findings.

Single Nostril Breathing and Brain Laterality

A recent experiment found evidence that performance on left hemispheric (verbal) and right hemispheric (spatial) tasks were affected by single nostril breathing, but the results provided little support for the specific predictions from yoga (Block, Arnott, Quigley, & Lynch, 1989). The results were contrary to the yoga predictions for males, and in the predicted direction for females on only the spatial task. For the spatial task, males performed significantly better during right nostril breathing than during left nostril breathing, whereas females had the opposite result. For the verbal task, males performed significantly better during left nostril breathing than during right nostril breathing, whereas females showed no difference in performance. Nasal air flow was not measured in this study. Single nostril breathing began five minutes before the tasks.

Two earlier experiments found that breathing through one nostril did not significantly affect performance on verbal and spatial tasks, but males and females were not analyzed separately (Klein, Pilon, Posser & Shannahoff-Khalsa, 1986). In one study, performance was measured before, during, and after 15 minutes of single nostril breathing. In the other study, performance was measured before and after 30 minutes of single nostril breathing.

The Klein et al. (1986) experiments also included measurement of asymmetric nasal air flow and reported equivocal results correlating air flow with performance on the tasks. Post hoc analyses combining both experiments correlated the difference between task scores with the degree of asymmetric nasal air flow. The correlation for the data collected before the single nostril breathing period gave a suggestive result ($p < .05$, uncorrected for multiple post hoc analyses) in the direction of yoga predictions, but explained less than four percent of the variance for 114 subjects. A similar result was obtained for the data collected after single nostril breathing. These results were due primarily to performance on the spatial task. Unfortunately, males and females were not analyzed separately. The initial subject pool was 56 percent female, but some subjects of unspecified sex were excluded. The effect of single nostril breathing on lateral nasal airflow was not reported.

Another study reported single nostril breathing caused relatively larger total integrated EEG activity contralateral to the open nostril (Werntz, Bickford, & Shannahoff-Khalsa, 1987). The results for the one male and four female subjects were all in the same direction. As noted above, the traditional interpretation for this finding would be relatively more mental activity on the same side as the open nostril, which is counter to the predictions from yoga. After citing a study (Ray & Cole, 1985) suggesting that alpha activity, and by implication total integrated EEG, does not reflect lateral cognitive processing, the authors considered the results ambiguous.

Several physiological studies on animals and humans indicate that nasal air flow receptors stimulate electrical discharges predominantly to the same side of the brain as the receptor (Kristof, Servit & Manas, 1981; Servit, Kristof, & Kolinova, 1977; Servit & Strejckova, 1976; Ueki & Domino, 1959). Although the studies show that unilateral nasal hyperventilation can trigger ipsilateral, and to a lesser extent contralateral, epileptic EEG activity in susceptible subjects, the overall implications are not clear. Of course, the very slow air flow rates of the alternate nostril breathing technique should minimize stimulation of the nasal airflow receptors indicated by these and other studies (Widdicombe, 1986).

Taken together, these studies provide little evidence for the specific cognitive effects of single nostril breathing that have been hypothesized based on yoga tradition. However, the specific yogic alternate nostril breathing techniques apparently were not used in any of these studies. In addition, any conclusions appear premature until basic questions about methodology and interpretation are resolved, and until further replications and explorations are carried out.

VARIATIONS AND OTHER TECHNIQUES

In addition to the basic yoga breathing techniques described above, several variations and other techniques are described in yoga manuals. For example, rapid breathing may be done through one nostril at a time (Samskrti & Franks, 1978, p. 158). Because yoga practice focuses on the basic techniques described in earlier sections and virtually no research has been carried out on these other techniques, they will not be discussed here. However, the Ujjayi technique should be mentioned as it is considered a fundamental technique in some yoga schools, though not as widely practiced in the Unites States as in some other countries. This technique has also been the topic of research. Ujjayi consists of very slow smooth maximum inhalation, followed by slow smooth maximum exhalation. Air flow is restricted by keeping the glottis in the throat partially closed, which results in a soft uniform low hissing sound. During inhalation, the abdominal muscles are kept slightly contracted, resulting in increased emphasis on maximum chest expansion. The technique is continued for a few minutes initially. In more advanced practice the breath is held after inhalation and sometimes after exhalation. The ratio of inhalation, breath holding, and exhalation in the advanced practice is 1:4:2. The mind is focused on breathing, particularly the low hissing sound.

Ujjayi was one of the techniques that induced the large oscillations of heart rate and blood pressure reported by Schmidt (1983). The pattern of cardiovascular fluctuations was similar to that described above for alternate nostril breathing. Studies investigating oxygen consumption during Ujjayi have found varying results. Rao (1968) reported that oxygen consumption for one inexperienced subject during Ujjayi increased above resting rates by about 8 percent at low altitude and about 10 percent at high altitude. Miles (1964) reported oxygen consumption for one experienced subject (who smoked cigarettes regularly) increased by an average of 19 percent during Ujjayi. Karambelkar, Deshapande, and Bhole (1984b) reported that average oxygen consumption during Ujjayi was slightly below the average resting rate for three subjects with over one year experience. Breath holding was done in all studies.

IMPLEMENTATION PRINCIPLES FOR MENTAL HEALTH TRAINING

Serving in the military is mentally challenging. Military life, training, deployments and combat places tremendous demands on the mental health of service members. Military organisations are challenged with establishing conditions to ameliorate the negative impact of these demands on service members as well as enhance the adaptation and performance of service members. Mental health resilience training has the potential to teach and/or increase skills and self-confidence to ensure service members can handle stress, grow and thrive in the face of challenges in the military and bounce back from adversity.

Mental health resilience training should systematically prepare service members for the mental challenges they will confront throughout their military careers. The objective of mental health resilience training is to enable service members to identify the realities of challenging environments, to develop skills to thrive and be resilient in the face of these realities, and to know how to use these skills to help themselves, fellow service members, and those they lead.

When mental health training content is being developed and validated, how the training will be implemented should be considered. While distinct, the training content and the implementation strategy dramatically influence each other.

One of the objectives of the NATO HFM-203/RTG 'Mental Health Training' is identifying considerations for training implementation. In this paper we discuss the fundamental principles of mental health training and implementation.

The paper is based on a (none published) paper 'Military Mental Health Training: Building Resilience' by Castro and Adler (Castro, C. A., & Adler, A. B., 2009) which was discussed within the RTG.

FUNDAMENTAL PRINCIPLES OF MENTAL HEALTH TRAINING AND IMPLEMENTATION

All good training, regardless of the topic or domain, rest on several fundamental principles (see Table 1 for an overview). This is not different for an effective mental health training program in the military. Explicitly stating these principles can guide the development of new modules, thus contributing to the coherency of an integrated training system. Furthermore, without these specific principles, one or more of them may be more likely to be overlooked or violated in the attempt to develop mental health training. In the following sections, each of these principles is discussed.

Table 1. Fundamental Principles of Mental Health Training and Implementation (Castro, C. A., & Adler, A. B., 2009)

Fundamental Principles of Mental Health Training and Implementation	
Mental Health Training	**Implementation**
Relevant Purpose and Content	Appropriately Timed
Experience-based	Quality Control
Explanatory	Train-the-Trainer Program
Team-based	Exportable and Scalable
Action Focused	Training Guidelines
Developmental	Refresher Training
Comprehensive, Integrated	Mobile Training Teams
User Acceptability	Sustainable
Evidence-based and Validated	Program Improvement
	Policy
	Leader Supported
	Verifiable Claims
	Packaging and Multi-media
	Ownership

FUNDAMENTAL PRINCIPLES OF MENTAL HEALTH TRAINING

Strength-Based

Effective mental health training should build on skills and strengths that soldiers already possess. A strength-based approach explicitly rejects a deficit or medical model. Practically, being strength-based means providing a positive approach that sets the expectation of success for the individual, and does not reinforce stereotypes that individuals are weak or will become sick as a result of some stressful experience like deployment.

The strength-based approach also explicitly builds on existing skills and abilities. New skills tap into these existing skills. For example, mental health training can emphasize the importance of building relationships back home. The individuals are reminded that they already have the skills to build relationships as evidenced by the strong bonds they have formed with their buddies. Existing strengths and skills provide a scaffold by which new skills and information can contribute to the resilience of an individual. In addition, since a medical model is rejected, mental health training does not need to include a list of mental health symptoms or include a discussion of mental health diagnosis, as is found in many military mental health training programs.

There is a fine line, however, between avoiding a medical model in which symptoms are prescribed or at least elucidated and providing individuals enough information about typical reactions so that they know what's normal and what might be a sign that professional help is warranted. This balance must be maintained throughout the training and continually re-examined. One way to maintain this balance is to obtain feedback from participants about their perception of the training message and to ensure that the training addresses how existing strengths and new skills can be applied and that there is sufficient time to practice those skills before they are needed.

Relevant Purpose and Content

All training should have a clear purpose or objective, and all the training content should support that purpose. Consistent with this principle, the content for mental health training should be based on documented needs. Rather than making assumptions about what soldiers experience, or what they need to know, the training must evolve out of an on-going systematic needs assessment. Feedback from this research is important for the (continuous) development of the content of each training module. By using this kind of rigorous approach, the training can avoid being the product of a trainer's idiosyncratic experience, which can lead to a training program of limited value.

Relevance refers not only to content but to the timing of the training so that the training matches the needs of the group at that time.

Experience-Based

Good mental health training should also include scenarios and situational training that reinforces the information and skills being trained (Thompson & McCreary, 2006). For every skill or educational point addressed in the training, there should be a real-world example that can be used to reinforce that point. Examples should be used that the soldiers and/or families can relate to and that use the language of the military. These examples should be based on experiences of soldiers, not on the experiences of the trainer. When trainers are mental health professionals, their personal examples may undermine their credibility. The trainers may appear misguided if they appear to think that their experience of deployment or stress mirrors the experience of a junior soldier on patrol, an NCO in logistics, or an officer in command of a combat arms unit. To overcome this problem the mental health trainer needs to have detailed speaker notes that contain numerous real-world examples from experienced soldiers.

Explanatory

Good mental health training is explanatory; it highlights conflicted or misunderstood reactions that service members might experience. For instance, while soldiers are happy to be home from a long combat deployment, they also often report being angry and on edge. The training normalizes this dual experience and explains that while many soldiers report being happy to see their family and friends, they are often angry about being deployed for a year or angry about how they were treated during the deployment. Providing soldiers with the words to understand this mixed reaction can help them to understand and normalize it. The development of explanations for such complex and conflicted reactions requires professional expertise in behavioral health.

Team-Based

The military organization is fundamentally based on teams, on leadership, and on unit cohesion. Any mental health training with the military needs to integrate these fundamental components of the organization. Military mental health training should take advantage of the natural camaraderie and hierarchy that exists within all military cultures. Unit cohesion and buddy support are core elements of all military training. Mental health training should teach participants how to look after other unit members and use this buddy-focus as a way to increase self-awareness as well. Specific training modules for leadership can highlight the role of leaders and the leaders' responsibilities for ensuring that their subordinates get the mental health care they need. By providing the training in a unit context, unit members will comment to one another and point out particular reactions that relate to a unit member, interacting in a way that enhances the relevance of the material.

Action Focused

Mental health training should be more than a theoretical description of stress responses. The training should address specific actions individuals can take. In keeping with the team-based approach mentioned above, these actions include behaviors that soldiers can take to help themselves, buddies, and those they lead.

One of the key components to teaching action-based strategies is the need for flexible and adaptive coping in response to a myriad of potential stressors. The training needs to specifically advance the idea that there are different types of stressors and which coping mechanism is best depends on how much direct control the individual has over the stressor. For many military personnel, significant stressors are outside of their direct control and so they need to practice action-based strategies that are not "action" in the sense of getting rid of the stressor. The action may involve a change in cognitive coping, a reduction in physiological arousal, seeking social support, or acceptance. Redefining action as incorporating each of these kinds of skills, and emphasizing the need to match the appropriate coping response to the situation, is a key part of an integrated mental health training system.

Developmental

Effective training builds on prior training or upon existing strengths and skills and progressively adds new concepts and skills. Ideally, we believe that a mental health training system should strive to develop skills of increasing complexity, beginning with simple concepts. For example, the training can introduce a simple approach to cognitive restructuring in managing the stressors of basic combat training while waiting until later in the career of a soldier to teach how cognitive restructuring can be used to manage a high-stress environment like a combat deployment. Another example of the developmental approach is to introduce the concepts of posttraumatic stress disorder (PTSD) without detailing the complexities of the diagnostic criteria. The initial training could include an overall appreciation for how PTSD-related reactions can interfere with getting along with friends, family and at work without discussing the disorder itself. This approach avoids the temptation of presenting PTSD criteria in an oversimplified manner which might inadvertently lead soldiers to think that they have PTSD if they have only a few PTSD symptoms. In subsequent courses for certain personnel such as leaders or medics, more information could be presented about symptoms, symptom clusters, and time course. Such information underscore the need for content to be informed by experts in mental health, as will be discussed under implementation principles.

Comprehensive, Integrated

Mental health training needs to be more than a one-session event. Mental health training should not be one-off training that occurs only once a year or only when the service member gets ready to deploy or only when the service member returns from deployment. Mental health training should be integrated with and focused on the service member's military career phase and point in the deployment cycle. By conceptualizing mental health training as an integrated system, the lesson plans can build on one another and can reinforce the points of each training module. It needs to provide the target population with an integrated and comprehensive system that builds skills, reinforces concepts, and targets areas of relevance to the group at the right time.

In a wider perspective mental health training should be part of an overall comprehensive and integrated paradigm for maintaining health, well-being, readiness and performance.

User Acceptability

Mental health training must be perceived to be useful by those being trained in order for the training to become accepted into the organizational culture. Even if the training is efficacious, if the training is not face valid, the audience does not accept it, and the trainers do not support it, then the training quality is likely to deteriorate or drift and resentment may preclude the training from helpful.

However, while user acceptability is necessary, it is not sufficient for establishing good mental health training (Iversen et al., 2008; McKibben et al., 2009; Sharpley et al., 2007). In order to demonstrate that mental health training improves mental fitness, randomized controlled studies must be conducted.

Evidence-based and validated

What does it mean to say "evidence-based"? As mentioned previously, the material in the training needs to be based on research evidence. In addition, the training itself needs to be validated. This validation extends beyond satisfaction ratings or demonstration of changes from pre- to post-training. The standard needed for demonstrating mental health training efficacy is a randomized controlled trial. This approach can be difficult, time-consuming, and complex statistically but the end result is evidence assessing the training's effectiveness. Exactly what these studies assess as markers of effectiveness depends on the goal of the training.

There are many possible markers of a successful mental health training program. Typically, in order to assess a program's effectiveness, the outcomes should match the intent of the program. For our purposes, military mental health training outcomes should include measures of (1) attitude, (2) skill attainment, (3) mental health fitness, (4) training satisfaction, (5) unit climate and leadership.

First, in terms of attitudes, mental health training should target stigma associated with seeking mental health care. Seeking care should be regarded as a sign of strength and readiness, not as a sign of weakness. Second, in terms of skill sets, outcomes should address the specific skills and knowledge addressed in the training. For example, training may address knowledge about when to seek professional care or skills associated with anxiety management. These skills should be assessed as part of mental health training. Third, in terms of mental health fitness, outcome indicators should include measures of distress that go beyond traditional PTSD symptoms. Outcomes of relevance to the organization should be included such as aggression, sleep problems, relationship conflict, and risk-taking behaviors. If the aim of the mental health training is to enhance well-being, then assessment of positive psychological health is also merited. Fourth, as mentioned previously, measures of training satisfaction and user acceptability should be included. Fifth, measures of unit climate should be included because the training can have an impact on the way the unit climate is perceived and because the training can have an impact on the leadership itself. Thus, these measures should address the degree to which mental health training may have had an impact on cohesion and leadership quality. Similarly, the training should also assess the degree to which leaders support the mental health skills and training provided by the organization. Without support from the leadership, the training will likely be less effective.

PRINCIPLES OF IMPLEMENTATION FOR MENTAL HEALTH TRAINING

Below is a description of key implementation principles (see Table 1 for an overview) regarding mental health training in organizations that must be kept in mind as the mental health training is being developed. While this is not an exhaustive list of all the implementation issues that need to be considered when developing mental health training, it does represent the common issues that arise when implementing mental health training.

Integrated into Organizational Culture

Military mental health training must be integrated into the organization's culture (Thomas & Castro, 2003). Ideally mental health and resilience training should be integrated with and focused on the service member's military career phase and point in the deployment cycle. Whether the program is seen as an education or as training depends largely on the timing and the place where it is delivered. In the context of a military academy, the terminology may need to emphasize "education" rather than "training." In general all mental health training contains educational material and involves skill strengthening or skill development. The two concepts can also be regarded as sequential. Thus the first phase of the program has to be termed "education" and the second phase in which the skills are practiced is termed "training". The larger issue is that the language used to describe and promote the program needs to make sense within the organizational context.

Mental health training should also be conducted within existing units, preferably at the platoon or company level in order to optimize the impact of small group dynamics and leadership. Conducting mental health training in small, pre-existing groups ensures group members will have the opportunity to share their experiences with each and that group members will feel comfortable enough to share their experiences. Training conducted in large groups in an auditorium or gymnasium runs the risk of being too impersonal, and too large for focused skill development to occur. In general, mental health training conducted in large groups is likely to become educational or didactic in nature, with little interaction or sharing of the group members' personal experiences.

The degree to which group size actually influences the efficacy of the training remains unclear. Indeed, Thomas et al. (2007) compared the small and large group Battlemind Training and did not find reliable differences between the two types of training.

Appropriately Timed

Mental health training should be relevant to the phase of the deployment cycle or the service members' level of professional development. This point has been made earlier but it deserves repeating. For instance, mental health training designed to be given prior to deploying shouldn't be given during the deployment, nor should mental health training designed to be given at post-deployment be given during the deployment or prior to deploying. Since the content of mental health training should vary depending on the phase of the deployment it stands to reason that the training cannot be used interchangeably.

Creating a one-size-fits-all approach to the training cycle is not likely to meet the needs of service members as their needs change depending on the phase of the deployment. Proponents and/or developers of such global approaches to mental health training fail to recognize the organizational context and may not have ensured that the needs of the service members are adequately addressed.

Quality Control

Any standardized training program requires a robust quality control program to ensure that the training is being conducted as intended. Constant vigilance is required to ensure that the content of the mental health training is maintained; the content should not be altered nor should additional material be inserted into the training modules. Further, the mental health training needs to be conducted using the procedures that have been validated. A mental health training quality control program should systematically ensure that trainers are prepared to conduct the training, that the training materials and lesson plans are clear and detailed, and that the training conducted remains consistent. Maintaining quality training can be difficult in a large organization like the military. Mechanisms such as refresher courses, team teaching, training evaluation, and spot checking by a mobile team responsible for training quality can facilitate quality sustainment over time.

Train-the-Trainer Program

The first step in preventing drift in the content and implementation is to develop a train-the-trainer program in which each mental health trainer receives formal training and certification that documents they are capable of delivering the training program to standard. At a minimum, a train-the-trainer program should include the training material, a detailed course syllabus, and detailed speaker notes. A train-the-trainer course should also include practice for the individuals who are being certified as trainers and an evaluation of their training performance. Only after the individual being trained has shown competence in giving the mental health training and in answering anticipated questions regarding the training should they be certified. A train-the-trainer program, however, does not preclude the need for a quality control program as drift in training can still occur.

Obviously during the development of a mental health training program it must be decided who will be conducting the training. For example, will the mental health training be conducted by behavioral health care providers, chaplains, experienced combat arms service members or some other group? This decision needs to be addressed early in the training development process because the decision regarding who conducts the training is likely to shape the content of the training material. Regardless of what decision is made regarding who conducts the mental health training, it should be noted that although individuals may have a personal preference for one type of trainer, the training material itself needs to be the key ingredient rather than a trainer's personal style. Personal style cannot be dictated in a set of lesson plan instructions. Regardless of who these trainers are, they will need to acknowledge what they are not. If they are not experts in mental health, they can talk about how the material has been developed by mental health professionals experienced in working with the military. If they have not been deployed, they can talk about how the material has been developed based on what soldiers have said is important to know. Even if the trainer has deployment experience, this experience can be misleading – establishing a link to the service members that is not really there. For example, most trainers with deployment experience are not likely to have been a junior enlisted combat arms soldier out on patrol every day. The train-the-trainer course needs to underscore the reality that the trainers can not be everything to all people. The trainers can acknowledge what they do bring to training in terms of their expertise, but most importantly they can bring their level of commitment, their enthusiasm, and their professionalism.

Exportable and Scalable

Regardless of who conducts the mental health training, a mental health training program must be designed with the average trainer in mind, not the ideal trainer. Whatever the mental health training program, it must be exportable and scalable. For example, a mental health training program will be of little utility to large organizations such as the military if only a handful of people in the world are capable of conducting the training or if it takes years to train others to conduct the training.

Training Guidelines

Another means to ensure that mental health training is conducted consistently across military installations and over time is to develop clear guidelines as to how the training is to be conducted. In military language, this approach to training is known as establishing "task, condition, and standard." Task, conditions and standards are applied to every form of training conducted in the military, regardless of the type of training. The "task" component of this approach specifies exactly what needs to be accomplished. The "conditions" specify the context or the variables in a situation that may affect performance. Finally, the "standards" delineate the markers of success. Thus, a "task, condition, standard" approach to mental health training details the exact training that is to be conducted, who is to be trained, who is to conduct the training, the environment in which the training is conducted, and the means for assessing the effectiveness of the training. This standardized approach to mental health training will also facilitate a rigorous quality control program that can evaluate if the training is being conducted as intended.

Refresher Training

Like most effective training, mental health training should contain refresher training modules. Service members should not be repeatedly subjected to the exact same mental health training material because the training will inevitably become stale, which will likely blunt its effectiveness. Off course, various modules provided over time and over the course of the deployment cycle serve to reinforce the key principles but refresher modules could certainly also be developed.

Mobile Training Teams

Implementing mental health training on a large scale can be facilitated through the use of mobile training teams. These teams can train service members directly but, more importantly, they can conduct train-the-trainer courses to certify other trainers.

Sustainable

Whatever mental health training program is adopted, it must be sustainable and supportable. The importance of the trainer and standardization has already been discussed in some detail. Equally important is how long the training needs to be in order for it to be effective in increasing mental fitness. In the military context, training time is a valuable commodity that must compete with a myriad of other demands. Whatever system results, it must remain cognizant of the issue of time as well as other resources such as personnel, equipment, and coordination. If too many resources are required, then in the long run, the training program may not be sustainable.

Program Improvement

Along with ensuring that the training program can be sustained in terms of implementation, there also needs to be a vigorous system for continually assessing whether the mental health training program is achieving its stated goals and to identify how the program can be improved. Unfortunately, military leaders may be reluctant to commit resources for program assessment and improvement. Without such a program in place, however, there will be no systematic, on-going analyses to ensure that the mental health needs of service members and families are still being met. These program improvement efforts are not only important for ensuring the program remains effective, but these efforts are another way to ensure that service members do not become bored by the same material.

Policy

Even the most effective mental health training cannot be successful without a parallel effort on the part of the organization to institutionalize its implementation (Thomas & Castro, 2003). In the case of the military, policy must be developed that supports and directs that mental health training be conducted. There must also be guidance issued that describes how the training will be implemented. In short, orders must be given that mandate that the military mental health training occur. Otherwise, such training will be left up to the discretion of each commander, usually with the result that the training is not conducted to the standard that has been shown to be effective, or it will not be conducted at all.

Leader Supported

Whether the training is mandated or not, leaders are critical for the successful implementation of mental health training. Leaders at all levels play an important role in service member mental health both directly and indirectly. The findings of an international military leaders' survey on operational stress show that leaders themselves state that it are the commanding officers who should be responsible for the psychological readiness of unit members (Adler et al., 2008). Consequently, their explicit and implicit support for a program can mean the difference between a supportive training environment and one in which the training is conducted as a way to "check the block" that simply meets a specific organizational requirement. Leaders can demonstrate their support for mental health training by attending the training themselves, by emphasizing the importance of the mental health training to their subordinates, and by ensuring that the training is a priority on the unit calendar. Research evidence demonstrating the efficacy of mental health training can directly impact the leader's endorsement of the program. If scientific findings can be provided to leaders showing them that mental health training is effective in increasing the mental fitness of their unit then the leaders are more likely to support the training. Obtaining high profile endorsements from senior enlisted service members and officers can also enhance the acceptability of mental health training.

Verifiable Claims

Credibility requires that any claims made regarding mental health training be consistent with verifiable facts that are based on scientific. Leaders need to be provided with realistic expectations about what mental health training will achieve and what it won't, the organization needs to make decisions based on science in order to differentiate between effective training and another good idea, and professionals need to uphold the integrity of the field.

Packaging and Multi-media

Effective mental health training needs good packaging. While this implementation principle may sound superficial it is critical because it ultimately means that the information will be presented in such a way that the organization and the individual service member will be more likely to accept it. Furthermore, good packaging through catchy slogans or the use of easy-to-remember acronyms, enhance the degree to which individuals are likely to remember the training content. The use of humor can also make mental health training more engaging. Still, care must be exercised that the training does not become so slick that the trainees are put off by the training or that the style distracts from the training objective or message.

Wherever possible, multi-media (e.g., interactive computer simulations, video scenarios, music, gaming technology) should be considered in developing a mental health training program. While there is no clear evidence that mental health training is more effective if it employs multi-media, the training is likely to be more engaging which increases the likelihood that individuals will attend to the training content. Appropriately incorporated, multi-media training can also enhance standardization of training. Multi-media approaches also help to underscore a central tenet of training: training should be conducted to engage the three fundamental types of learners. Visual learners prefer to be able to see the point written out, or visually depicted in a diagram. Auditory learners prefer to listen and discuss the information. Finally, experiential learners prefer to practice a concept and grapple with some task related to the concept.

Ownership

The final implementation principle reviewed here is ownership: who actually controls the content of the training program and retains the right to revise it. Mental health and mental fitness issues facing service members and their families are complex and varied. How to build resilience and increase mental fitness in order to help these folks meet the demands of combat and deployment are equally complex and nuanced. Thus, the content of the mental health training program needs to belong to military behavioral health care experts. The content of mental health training must be determined by behavioral health experts. They are the subject matter experts - not the commander, not the chaplains, not the policy makers or others who are interested in helping service members. Obviously, these individuals are expert in their own areas and their input is invaluable for ensuring that the training material addresses issues in a way that is relevant to the audience. In fact, the training development process should actively solicit input from a variety of domains such as operational leadership, the chaplaincy, military families and soldiers themselves. However, caring about service member mental health or having been deployed to a combat environment does not make one an expert in mental health training; the behavioral care experts should own the content of the training.

10

Transformation of the Health Purchasing Marketplace

In the 1990s, physicians and the AMA abandoned their unsuccessful resistance to group practice and agreed to support the Health Maintenance Organization (HMO) concept. While HMOs had provided coverage for less than 10 percent of individuals in various geographic areas for many years, HMO enrollments greatly expanded in the 1980's. In some parts of the country, like Minneapolis and Northern California, HMO coverage exceeded 50 percent. The $300-billion insurance industry saw important opportunities for cost containment and began to transform itself, and many companies allied with a variety of physician groups so that the payment or insurance function was linked to the physicians who provided individual care. Insurance companies like Prudential, CIGNA,

Aetna, Metropolitan Life, Travelers and the nonprofit "Blue" plans evolved into HMOs and turned away from the more traditional indemnity type of insurance. The purpose of a health insurance company is to sell insurance policies by keeping its premiums low. The best way it has to control expenses is to reduce its policyholder use of health care services (utilization). Conversely, health care providers want to give their patients the best and most of everything, under conditions convenient to the providers and thereby maximizing their patients' welfare and to their own benefit.

The health purchasing marketplace had been transforming itself from the unstructured fee-for-service system of several years ago to one with varying amounts of what is generally called Managed Care. Under the old open-ended system of "indemnity insurance, " physicians prescribed pretty much what they wished and the insurance company paid the bill. Open-ended opportunities, with the consumers of health care relatively insensitive to costs because their employers paid their insurance premiums in pretax dollars, led to spiraling health care costs. Managed care is the antithesis of unmanaged care or the present system - attempts to make certain that patients receive the care they need at an affordable price. Unfortunately, the use of discounted fees and the employment of thousands of new people to watch the doctors at work - and additional hundreds to watch the watchers - have destabilized the health care system. Several hundred insurers write insurance in most states and the paperwork they generate is so intense that most physicians and many nurses spend up to 30 percent of their time away from their patients completing forms. Each insurance company seems to have its variety of forms to be completed. They frequently have different fee schedules and they often use different techniques to "manage" physicians to keep their costs to a minimum. American physicians have become so frustrated that many have indicated that they might accept a nationalized or Canadian-type system if it were accompanied by a predictable income and a major reduction in paperwork.

Socialized medicine, a frightening phrase to many physicians and one often used to defeat any new approach to health care policy, is quite simple in concept. In socialized medicine, the central government budgets funds needed for health care. All physicians and hospitals are paid at the same rate. A central board defines the services available to each citizen. The cost is paid from tax revenues so that there is little paperwork or billing effort required. Opponents have often orchestrated campaigns against such alternatives, warning Americans about the long waiting lines and inadequate care of the British or Canadian systems, which are based on socialized medicine. (See Foreign Health Plans) Most experts agree that because Americans place such high value on "free choice" and rapid response in medical care, socialized medicine (or a "single-payer" system) will never be accepted politically. Indeed, the death of the Clinton health care plan indicates that these assumptions are probably correct.

Critics charge that the American health care system was designed to be expensive so that those in control, such as physicians, hospitals, and insurers, could maximize their financial return. They describe the system as a guild controlled mainly by the professionals providing services. Unlike other guilds, however, there was a readily available source of funds to meet the self - determined requirements of members of the guild. Buttressed by laws and regulatory mandates, this fee - for-service or indemnity system guaranteed free choice of physicians by patients and free choice of treatment by physicians.

There is direct negotiation over fees between physician and patient with the third party payer-the readily available source of funds-excluded from the table. Solo practitioners until recently dominated the scene, further inflating prices since controls on the kinds of consultants were not allowed. Hospitals and employers were prohibited by state insurance regulations and by Title XVIII of the Social Security Act from contracting with health maintenance organizations or group practices; anti-trust legislation emphasized competition that kept physicians' fees steadily increasing.

DEFINITIONS OF MANAGED CARE

Because the costs of medical care rose so rapidly and dramatically, practically choking employee benefit plans, it became apparent that cost must be managed and at the same time, control the rising costs of medical care. Therefore, medical care costs must be "Managed" and at the same time, the patients must continue to receive appropriate medical care. The techniques developed to provide these services were proclaimed as "Managed Care." Or to put it another way, Managed Care is the system in which quality medical care can be delivered at a reasonable cost.

The term "Managed Care" is very often used to describe a structured health care system such as a Health Maintenance Organization, or a Preferred Provider Organization. These two types of structured organizations are better known to the general public and receive the majority of the publicity. Other programs that contain cost-management or cost-containment features, such as a "Wellness" program by an employer, can be constructed to be Managed Care even though technically there is no actual "care" involved. With the variations of health insurance programs today, such as Point of Service plans, Care Manager plans, etc., they are generally all considered as part of Managed Care. Indeed, they were created to fill a particular void in the Managed Care technique system.

WHY MANAGED CARE?

The magic words " Managed Care" seem to be mentioned at least daily in some fashion and usually in uncomplimentary terms. It would be interesting to know how many television reporters and journalists actually know what that term means. To most people, it simply means an HMO that is taking away one of their precious rights, that of being able to choose their own doctors and hospitals. Politicians use it frequently and in most cases, they are "against it", regardless of the situation.

One statistic that gives them pause, is that in 1995 the average monthly premium of an HMO for a family was $447, while the average monthly premium for a family under a traditional health insurance plan (indemnity insurance) was $493, almost 10% lower. Also, in the United States, Health-care expenditures rose an inflation-adjusted 1.9% in 1996, the slowest rate of growth in nearly four decades. These figures were produced by a team of government researchers, and not from the Managed Care industry.

In late 1997 and early 1998, several newspapers and other publications reported the results of various studies, both government and private. These newspaper and news magazine articles were a result of many anecdotal reports from unhappy HMO members for the most part. But the report, the broadest annual accounting of the nation's health costs, appeared during a period of time when there was growing concerns - especially among the nation's employers - that a rash of troubles in the Managed Care industry jeopardizes a five-year period in which medical bills were coming under control as a result of Managed Care.

The journal "Health Affairs" found that the "total health-care tab in the U.S. topped $1 trillion for the first time in 1996, the latest year for which figures are available, despite the low rate of growth. That amounted to 13.6% of the gross domestic product, a percentage that has remained steady since 1993."

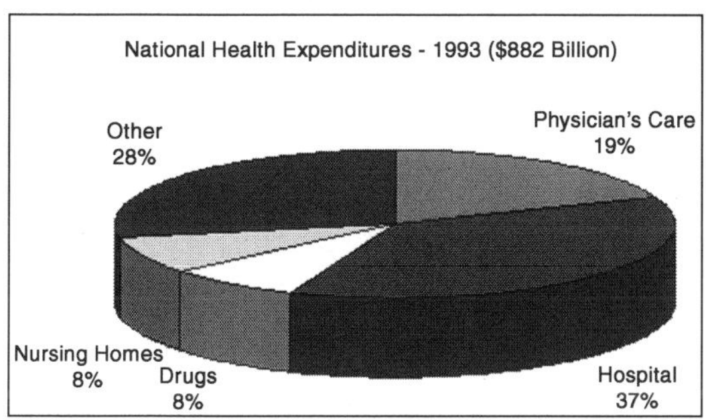

Regardless of what many construe to be a "Pollyannish" outlook, there continues to be increased friction between the public and private sectors as to who will bear most of the cost of anticipated growing medical inflation in the future. It is very significant that these sources report that spending on publicly financed health-care services, including Medicare and Medicaid program, "rose at an annual average rate of 9.7% between 1989 and 1996, while private-sector spending, largely through employer-sponsored benefits plans, increased an average of just 5.8% a year over the same period." The big difference in the growth rates may narrow significantly or even reverse itself in the near future. The new federal budget has provisions for Medicare costs to increase just 2.5% for each enrollee in 1998. However, Medicare in particular is an extremely delicate political problem, so many Washington insiders see many changes before cost predictions can be used with any degree of accuracy.

Of primary importance to those in the health insurance industry, the fact is that we are now seeing increases above 5% in the private sector for the first time since the early 1990s. The federal governments own employee health-care plan is reporting an increase averaging 8.5% for 1998. Benefits consultants believe that large employers expect health costs to rise about 4% in 1998 and even more in 1999. One important factor in these increases is a profit crunch at major managed-care companies. This has caused some retirements, mergers and acquisitions among health care systems heavily involved in Managed Care.

During the 1990s, higher rates of Medicare spending gave providers "something of a safety cushion" as they lost income in the face of pressure from Managed Care. However, since Medicare spending growth is slowing, health providers are trying to find ways to raise rates again in the private sector. It can be expected that growth in overall expenditures, both in health care and in administration, may begin to rise. A return to the double-digit increases of the 1980s is not expected. It was also reported that national health expenditures in 1996 rose 4.4% before inflation to $1.04 trillion, or $3,759 a person. In 1995, the nation spent $991.4 billion, or $3,633 for every American.

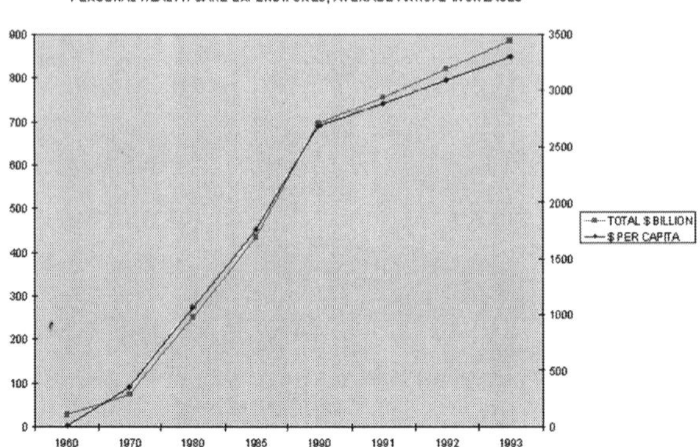

Credit for the declining growth rate was attributed to the growth of Managed Care, plus the fact that expensive hospital and doctor services are playing a smaller role in the health care economy. Even though doctors and hospitals are still the predominant players in health care, it was reported that the combined share of national health-care spending allotted to doctors and hospitals fell to 54.1% in 1996 from 57.6% in 1990.

Prescription drugs muddy the statistics to some degree. Costs for prescription drugs rose by 9.2% in 1996. However, experts attribute a lot of this increase to 2 factors (1) managed-care plans have succeeded in reducing hospital stays, with the results that many patients are now getting drugs from their own pharmacy instead of getting them during the hospital stay, and (2) private insurance covered 45% of prescriptions filled in 1996 compared with 34% in 1990. Indeed, a Prescription Drug Card is often taken for granted by those covered under private insurance. Private health insurance premiums accounted for $337.1 billion of health expenditures in 1996, of which $316.4 billion came from employer-based health benefits programs. Many companies have passed on an increasing share of health costs to the workers. Employers paid 83.4% of the health insurance premiums, compared to 94.5% in 1990, a 1.1 percentage-point difference. While 1.1% doesn't sound like much, it actually shows a shift in employee cost of $3.6 billion in 1996 alone!

FOREIGN HEALTH PLANS

Most of the industrial nations have some type of government sponsored health care, in most cases, some form of socialized medicine. In discussions of Managed Care, it is almost inevitable that the health care systems of others countries will be references and used by some as examples of how Managed Care should be accomplished. Basically, European and Canadian systems practice Managed Care taken to the extreme, and cannot be called anything other than "rationed care." They do not make massive investments in medical research, they do not purchase the latest in medical technology and they do not furnish medical treatment to elderly people who need this technology. For example, in the United Kingdom, those over age 60 are not eligible for heart transplants although they continue to pay taxes that support such a system. Therefore those that fall in this category must either pay for the transplant out of their own pocket, or simply die.

Canadian procedures are performed three times as much in the United States as in Canada. In Canada, those over age 75 and women received proportionately fewer cardiac procedures in Canada than in the United States. The Canadians also wait longer for treatment. For those with left main coronary artery disease; in the United States they were operated on within 7 days, but in Canada 70% of the Canadians waited for 31 to 60 days. A study revealed that for breast cancer the median waiting time between diagnosis and postoperative radio therapy was 61.4 days. Generally, according to specialists, in 81% of cases awaiting surgery, the times are longer than they consider reasonable, and they feel that 45% of all patients are waiting in pain.

Canadians have contracted with U.S. hospitals to provide technical services such as MRIs and brain injury care. From 1991 to 1993, 10% of those needing cancer therapy in British Columbia were served in the United States. It appears that Canadians can afford to ration health care because they have the underused U.S. system just across the border if the shortages of specialists or treatment centers becomes too severe.

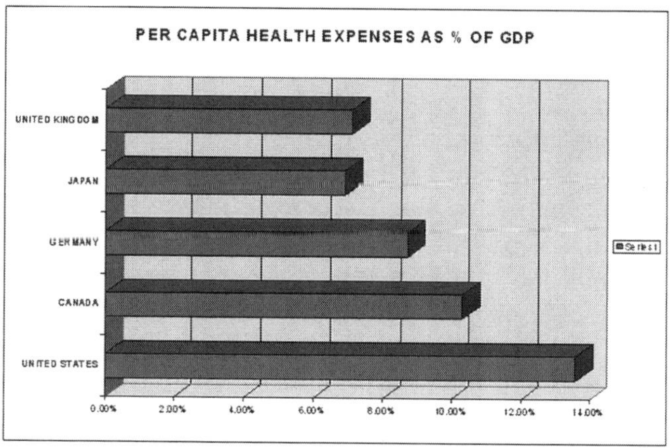

There is no doubt that Americans have the best technology, and our system, with its readily available medical technology and specialists, enables all Americans to enjoy a better quality of life.

WHO PAYS THE BILL FOR INCREASED MEDICAL COSTS?

According to the latest government figures, patients pay 20% of their own medical bills. Funds for this expense comes directly from the income and savings on those to receive the medical services. Government programs pay for the largest part of the overall medical costs, 42%. Of course, this includes Medicare and Medicaid, plus medical care for service personnel and their dependents, and government workers and their families. Insurers, including some self-funded organizations and third-party administrators, pay for 33% of the medical services. Included in this category are HMO's and variations of Managed Care, while not technically "Insurers", do provide insurer-like services. Other private sources, many of which are trusts organized under Federal Law, medical personnel who receive "free" services, etc., pay approximately 5%.

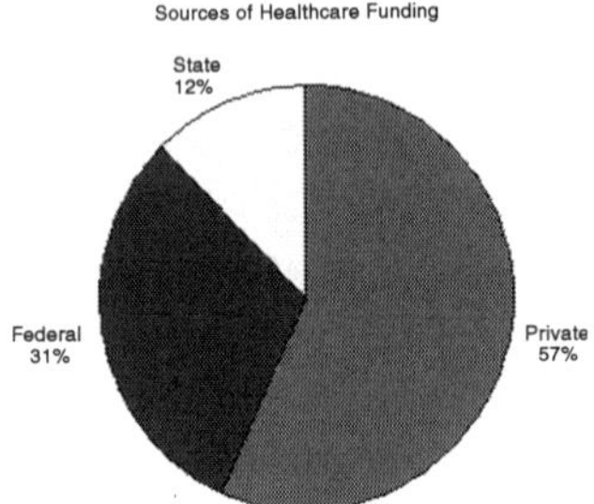

Businesses pay a substantial portion of the nation's medical costs through Workers Compensation (5%) and employee group health benefits, 10%. Because businesses pay taxes that, in turn, fund government spending on medical care programs, plus business taxes, payroll taxes - in some cases such benefits and taxes exceed the after-tax profits of the business - it is commonly held that business actually pays for the health services and suffers the most when medical costs increase dramatically. Although this is a widely held belief, the sad truth is that the consumer and only the consumer, ends up paying for the health services, either directly or indirectly. The government does not "make" money (it prints "money" but does not "earn" money). It survives on the largesse of the governed in the form of taxes from a wide variety of sources, but ultimately all taxes come from individuals.

While businesses pay taxes, in actual practice the cost of increased taxes and increased cost of benefits is passed on to the consumer, either in the form of increased cost, decreased products or benefits, and/or less earning for the owners and/or stockholders. In 1980, the cost of employee health care was equal to 24% of the corporate profits of U.S. businesses. In 1990 it reached 100% of the corporate profits. That means that employers were paying as much for employee health costs as they were making in profit. Or, to state it another way, if employers didn't have to pay for employee health care, their profits would double. (Actually, this would probably never happen, as employers could afford to be more competitive, so they would lower their profit in order to gain more market share, and thereby reducing their profit. But the point of the total cost to the employers of employee benefits is well made with this illustration). Many individuals receive benefits from their employer, sometimes with the employer paying for all of the benefits, or a portion thereof. However, where does the employer get the money to pay for benefits? Again, from its customers and from the individuals that support the business.

Not only is there considerable benefits savings in health insurance with large employers, but they also report considerable savings in Workers Compensation costs, after they have contracted with a Managed Care firm or established a Managed Care program. Overall, Employee benefits costs have increased at substantially lower rates after implementing a Managed Care program. For example, S.W. Bell went from an average increase of 36% to 12% in 1996. In 1993, a year that showed the largest decline in the increase in health cost, the average employer increase was 14%, while increases for employers with Managed Care plans increased only 8.4%.

MEDICAL CARE CONTINUE TO RISE TECHNOLOGY

New medical technology adds about $30 billion to the nation's medical care bill each year. (CAT scans and MRI can easily cost more than $1,000).

Certain annual surveys rate goods and services used on a daily basis as the best value for consumers' money. In 1989, 1992 and 1994, contrary to what you might guess, poultry was rated number one (above cars and TV's) as the best value for the money. The same surveys in the same years also agreed on the worse value. Again, contrary to popular believes, it wasn't lawyers (next to last), but it was hospital charges. Health insurance and doctors' charges were also rated quite low. The reason that poultry is rated so high and hospitals so low is because of technology. Even though technology has made chickens and health care better and cheaper, medical technology is overbought and helps to increase the hospital costs, which registers negatively with the consumers.

Medical technology differs from other technologies in cars, chickens and computers in the impact on consumers because many new medical technologies have been purchased by health care institutions, and many of the institutions use the new technology very little. The health care industry does not compete primarily on the basis of price. In 1940, if a person had a gall-bladder operation, the surgeon would charge about $1,000, and the hospital would charge anywhere between $2,000 and $4,000. While this may not seem expensive today, $5,000 was about a fourth of the median income of Americans at that time. Not only was surgery expensive, but the lengthy hospital stays were costly and patients were out of work in a recovery mode, with a reduced or loss of income for many.

Even though American technology obviously improves the quality of life, Americans think that hospitals spend too much money. U.S. hospitals are too big, with too many beds, too much technology and the expenses to go along with it. In 1995, the occupancy rate of American hospitals was only 59.7%. A

Holiday Inn with that occupancy rate could not survive for long, so one can imagine the losses that a hospital must incur if 40% of its beds are not filled on a constant basis. And with the new technology, new drugs and procedures are continually being developed that will eliminate even more need for hospital beds.

But do not weep for the poor hospitals, as they continue to hold their own. In 1992 while the length of stay in a hospital dropped drastically, the average number of beds in the hospitals remained fairly constant, and the number of hospital personnel actually increased from 3.1 million in 1983 to 3.6 million in 1992. But while inflation rose by 2.3%, salaries rose by 5.5%. In 1993, on the average, the CEOs of hospital systems made $400,000 in compensation, and CEOs of individual hospitals made $243,000. However, they seemed to be worth it, as they maintained a profit of 5.4% for the for-profit hospitals.

Another important factor in the low esteem of medical services is related to who pays the bills. For example, in 1994 it is estimated that hospitals were 97.5% compensated by third parties (not the patients). Doctors, who also rate low, were 85% compensated by third parties. On the other hand, pharmaceuticals (34%) and vision-wear compensated only 41% by third parties were rated quite high. The most effective new technology, according to many experts in the medical field, was developed after plastic was invented. Previously, exploratory operations were quite common, as that was the only way that the surgeons could actually see the patient's condition. Now surgeons can view almost any part of the human anatomy with fiberoptic light sources that illuminate the surgical site for miniature cameras. A surgeon can operate and watch the procedure on a screen, never actually viewing his surgery except on the screen.

Computer technology automated the tiny camera and it also developed other instruments that diagnose and monitor the body without invasive surgery. The most well known is the computerized axial tomography (CAT) scanners, and the magnetic image resonators (MRIs). In addition, recent advances in anesthesia now allow various areas of the body to be anesthetized so that only the affected area will not feel pain, thereby reducing many problems than have arisen when larger amounts of the body were so deadened against pain. New technologies allow many surgical procedures to be performed outside of the in-patient section of a hospital. It is estimated that 65% of the estimated 29 million surgeries in 1994, were performed outside of the hospital. These surgeries included cataract removals, inguinal hernia repair and knee arthoscopy for those on Medicare.

INCREASING SALARIES OF MEDICAL PROVIDERS

Salaries of medical providers has risen at double-digit rates, 3 times faster than inflation of the rate of average non-medical salaries. Three/fourth of medical school graduates go into specialized care, and 2/3 of all physicians are specialists. Please note, however, that the impact of Managed Care has affected the incomes of physicians, not only specialists, but the independent doctors also. In 1990 median income for family practitioners was $93,000, surgeons and radiologists averaged over $200,000. The median net income of private practice office-based physicians went from $153,620 in 1992, to $148,890 in 1994. Gross revenues (the amount billed to patients) of all physicians fell even more during this period of time. Specialists and those in larger offices have compensated for this decrease in gross revenue by implementing cost-control features in their own practices.

Managed care also affects the incomes of health providers by promoting the use of Primary Care Physicians (PCPs) who perform more medical services through gate keeping activities of referring patients to specialists only when necessary. In most cases, the PCP has a tendency to treat the patient if he feels comfortable in doing so, instead of sending the patient (and the fee) to a specialist, even though in the past, referral was a typical procedure. This gatekeeper feature is dominant in Managed Care, especially in HMOs, and was one of the major complaints in the early years of Managed Care. However, the Managed Care procedures now provide for evaluation of PCP's on a regular basis and the area of specialist referral is a key item under scrutiny.

Some doctors feel that "if you can't beat them, join them," and negotiate the discounts of doctor's fees in return for bringing them into a network. The networks are aware that most doctors have a substantial patient list, and if they join a particular network, they will bring many of their patients with them. Therefore, in many cases, the joining of a network is to the benefit of both the physicians and the network. While the payment of a capitation fee - paying physicians a set fee for each patient enrolled in the system, regardless of how much or little each enrollee uses the medical services - has also come under criticism by consumers, it actually increases a physician's income. The money that he receives for those who do not require medical services, frees him up to treat those who do require medical services. It also helps to level the provider's income by providing a steady flow of income, thereby allowing more effective business planning for his practice.

IS THE TREATMENT NECESSARY?

Consumer magazines, industry publications, and actuarial studies have estimated that nearly a third of all professional medical care, including tests, surgery and drugs, is unnecessary. While it is agreed that some of the statistics can be rather subjective, depending upon the organization doing the study and estimation, these statistics have been widely reported.

- One/fourth of hospital patients do not have to be admitted to a hospital.
- Half of the pacemakers installed every year are unnecessary.

- More than half of all hospital stays are not necessary. In view of vacant hospital beds the situation is more desperate for hospitals than many think. However, more and more medical procedures are conducted in clinics or on an outpatient basis.
- People still go to a doctor when they don't have to, estimate as much as 15% of office visits are unnecessary. Some of this can be contributed to the advent of the "co-payment" provisions in HMO and insurance contracts. Many consumers don't mind spending $10-$15 to go to the doctor for a minor complaint. It can be noted that the copayment provisions has increased recently, and the average is now estimated to be approaching $25.
- Approximately half of the coronary bypass operations, of which some 130,000 are performed each year, really aren't necessary. While this is highly subjective and cardio-vascular surgeons may disagree with these studies, even assuming only one-fourth are unnecessary, this amounts to millions of dollars that didn't need to be spent.
- While studies show that 60% of preoperative laboratory screening tests are not needed, it should also be stated that many doctors use some tests strictly on a precautionary basis, even if results and the present condition doesn't seemingly warrant such tests. Some of this overusage is thought to be caused by malpractice concerns.
- Several magazines and Television programs have discussed the amount of hysterectomies performed in this country. More than one-fourth of these operations are considered as unnecessary.
- A recent medical problem that has developed due to the increasing use of computer keyboards, is carpal tunnel syndrome. This requires an operation to alleviate the pain, however for a while it became almost a "fad" operation, and surveys indicate that approximately 17% were determined to be unnecessary.
- 16% of tonsillectomies are considered unnecessary. Many parents who have had their tonsils removed when they were young, have the same procedure performed on their children, whether they really need it or not.
- Chronic back pain is frequently due to herniated discs, and many surgeons perform operations to remove the disc, instead of prescribing lifestyle changes which in many cases can alleviate the pain. It is estimated that 14% of laminectomies could be eliminated.
- Many people have suffered through a "GI" (gastrointestinal) X-ray studies, generally to determine if there is an ulcer or other problem with the digestive system. In particular, the upper GI series appears to be overused, as 30% of the studies are believed to be unnecessary.
- One of the more startling discoveries was that half of all cesarean deliveries are not necessary. Some of this can be attributed to modern parents who want their children delivered at the time most

convenient to them, but it must also be recognized that a cesarean is a much more expensive procedure, with the added cost of surgery and a longer stay in the hospital.

- Quality waste, i.e. fix what should have been done right the first time, has been estimated to consume as much as 35% of health care expenditures.

  It must be recognized that these abuses are generally not the fault of the providers, but much of the blame can be placed on the patients who demand the very best and who seek more treatment and at a higher level than is needed. Hospital admissions is a good case in point. Many insurers have allowed hospital admissions without question, but in recent months, hospital admission pre-certification has become almost a standard procedure. Managed care helps to reduce the unnecessary treatments and hospitalizations, by reviewing the reasons for the treatments, the appropriateness of the treatment, and restricting what they consider as excesses.

Too Many Providers

A real conundrum exists regarding how hospitals with nearly a million beds, can continue to operate with about a third of them empty. No successful hotel or motel chain can operate with such a high vacancy rate. In any other business, an oversupply would drive down the prices in an effort to obtain more customers. But this does not seem to apply to hospitals.

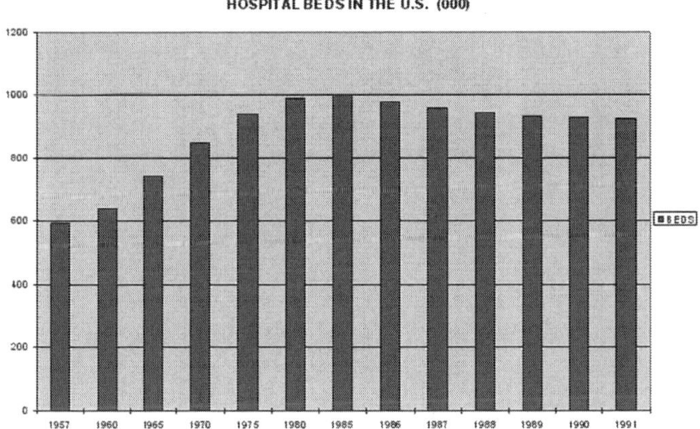

One answer to the puzzle would appear to be that in situations where the customer pays directly, normal business rules in regards to oversupply applies. But with hospitals and other similar medical providers, the bills are paid to the facilities by Workers Compensation companies, employee benefits providers, or similar insurance providers. The patient (customer) seldom pays any attention to what is being charged, and in many cases, could care less. Since the customer is insulated from the effects of pricing, the oversupply does not cause a reduction in cost. Another aspect is that many of the empty beds occur in hospitals located in heavily populated areas. A study by the University of California of 5,732 hospitals nationally, illustrated that hospital costs are higher by as much as 26% in areas where hospitals had more than 9 competitors within a 15 mile radius. One of the most positive effects of Managed Care, is that it is allows the direct payers for medical care, such as insurance companies and self-insured businesses, to direct patients to the most cost effective providers. In respect to physicians, in 1972 there were 153 doctors for every 100,000 of population in the U.S., in 1992 it was 220.

UNBUNDLING COSTS THROUGH CREATING BILLING

For over a period of several years, the medical profession has developed a system that allows for proper billing of services provided, using a coding system. Every medical procedure is provided with a code and fees are based upon the code. With the advent of Medicare and the reporting to the federal government, a coding system was an absolute necessity, as described elsewhere in this text. In 1991, the government reported that fraudulent health care billing amounted to overcharging $50 to $100 Billion.

While coding is necessary, it gave rise to an overbilling practice, described as "unbundling" or "fragmentation." This is accomplished by fragmenting (breaking down) a medical procedure into its very basic components, and then billing for each "fragment" individually. Almost any operation, by fragmenting, can increase the cost from double to six or eight times by adding together each little facet of the procedure, even though the overall operation may have its own code. In the same vein, adding another (often-fictitious) element into a simple procedure can increase the bill dramatically. As an example: carpal tunnel syndrome surgery can be accomplished by one surgeon, however by adding a bill for an assistant surgeon, the cost of the operation increases considerably.

One of the functions of Managed Care is to review the bills from the doctors and hospitals in order to avoid any of these abuses. They can also provide an audit to avoid duplicate billings, and inappropriate billings, whether fraudulent or by mistake. Complex billing programs by providers is required to comply with local, state and federal laws, and the complexity leads to a lot of erroneous billings. This review function care is one of the most financially rewarding aspects of Managed Care.

Present Results of Managed Care

The purpose of Managed Care as it is practiced today, should never be forgotten: "Managed Care is the system in which quality medical care can be delivered at a reasonable cost." Has Managed Care performed as anticipated? The answer to that question may not be resolved for many years, or within a few years, but the trend is that so far, so good. There are criticisms of Managed

Care, particularly in the operation of the HMOs, but these criticisms are taken seriously by the industry and many of them are solved rapidly, and some criticisms will be with us for some time. At the time this text was being composed, data on health care spending is being released by the government and the news media. The following information indicates that at least some of the goals have been obtained.

HEALTH MAINTENANCE ORGANIZATIONS (HMOS)

HMO's are often considered as synonymous with Managed Care in many people's mind. Even Managed Care "experts" will define Managed Care as HMOs. However, HMOs are only one part of Managed Care, arguably the most important part, and is actually a method of providing Managed Care. HMOs differ from other health care organizations in several primary respects.

- Medical care is provided on a pre-paid basis, as opposed to the typical indemnity agreement offered by insurance companies, that pays for medical services after they have been received.
- Persons that belong to an HMO plan (members) pay a monthly fee, regardless of how much medical care or medical services they receive that month.
- In most situations, an HMO provides all types of medical service, including physicians, specialists, surgeons, hospitalization, laboratory work, clinics, and in many cases, even prescription drugs.
- A significant feature of HMOs is that preventative care is often included, such as routine physical examinations.
- HMO's are noted (or notorious) for tight operational control. With the exceptions of emergencies, that occur outside of the HMO's service area, or for treatment not provided by the HMO, HMO members are required to obtain any medical care through the HMO network. This is accomplished, in most cases, by first consulting a Primary Care Physician (PCP), who will then refer the member to a specialist if the PCP feels it is necessary.

If one factor could be determined as the primary reason that HMO's have been successful in holding down medical costs, it is the extremely tight utilization rules. As with any other medical provider, it must be determined as to the type of care that the network is designed to provide. If an HMO is designed as a "Medicare" HMO, specialists in geriatrics and other age-related diseases must be on the network. If the HMO is designed as an employee benefit plan, then family doctors, pediatricians, Gynecologists, etc., must be available. For Workers Compensation Managed Care, physicians specializing in trauma and those experienced in Workers Compensation claims should be available as PCP's, or at the very least, on the specialist list for referrals.

TYPES OF HMOS

Because of the changes in the structure of Health Maintenance Organizations, it has become necessary to categorize HMOs into major sections, or "Models." As the HMO concept matures, subtle changes in the way that Managed Care is provided will create additional types, but at this time these types of HMOs are evident. The variations that have occurred from these models are of such importance that the industry has given them separate names and descriptions, as discussed later.

The principal differences between these Models are as follows:

- The amount of control over the health care providers in the organization.
- How the providers are compensated.
- Do they treat only HMO members.

The industry has categorized HMOs into four primary "Models" as follows:

- Staff Model
- Group Model
- Network Model
- Individual or Independent, Practice Association (IPA) model

Staff Model HMO

A Staff model HMO can be classified as a "classic" HMO, or the "original" HMO, as this was the type of HMO first introduced by Kaiser Permanente. The health care provider uses the physical facilities that are provided by the HMO. Hospitals may be owned or leased by the HMO, and include hospital equipment and supplies. Physicians and other healthcare providers are paid a salary by the HMO, and the salaries are not contingent upon how many patients are treated. Most of the physicians are Primary Care Physicians, but also includes specialists. The number of physicians and specialists depends upon the size of the HMO and the number of members. Only HMO members are treated in the Staff Model HMO.

These HMO's exercise tight control over the healthcare providers, and therefore are the most effective in managing costs. The providers have no incentive to over treat patients as all providers are salaried, and their treatment programs can be closely monitored for efficiency in cost and medical treatment results. Staff Model HMO's range in size, as large as a multi-state HMO (such as Kaiser) or they can also be located in one building, or even in a hospital. However, the Congressional Budget Office reports that a Staff Model HMO reduces the use of resources by nearly 20 percent, while the less restrictive models barely reduces the use of resources at all.

Group Model HMO

The Group Model HMO resulted primarily from reaction by providers, who saw the Staff Model HMO as a threat to their livelihood, and to the medical profession as a whole. As a defensive measure, providers organized into large professional associations ("P.A.'s"). This allowed them to negotiate their fees and services with the HMO on a basis of strength in numbers. The Group Model HMO is usually a corporation that performs all of the duties of an HMO with one important exception; it cannot actually practice medicine. The HMO must, therefore, negotiate with these large professional groups, what medical services will be required, and the fees that they will pay for these services. The contract with members of its organization to provide the number and type of physician necessary to provide the types of services needed and contracted for with the HMO. They provide the necessary hospital services, they pay their providers, and they provide facilities for the contract physicians. In effect, the professional groups become the service-rendering arm of the HMO, and the HMO performs the marketing and some of the administration.

Whey would these groups need and HMO? The HMO provides all (or at least most) of the patients for the providers. They can negotiate for payment amounts and for various operational procedures necessary for the success of the HMO. An HMO is usually not limited to a contract with only one group practice, and may contract with several such organizations. However, they always contract with large multi-specialty practices so that more services can be offered to its members. The Staff and Group Model HMOs continue to lose market shares, and the Group Model shares most of the patient criticisms of the Staff Model.

Network HMOS

Network Model HMOs contract for all of their services, both hospital and physician groups. Similar to Group Model HMO's, they contract with physicians to provide healthcare services, however they will contract with physician groups of all sizes, including one-doctor offices. The providers continue to operate out of their own office or that of the group to which they belong, and they are allowed to continue with their private practice. Many provider groups will contract with more than one HMO, and still continue their fee-for-service practices. Hospital services for their members are handled on a contractual basis with local hospitals. Even though the control exercised by the Staff and Group Models is not present with the Network HMOs, in many respects the Network Model has been just as successful. Some of the larger health insurance companies have elected to form a Network HMO with allows them to compete with older and more established Staff or Group HMO and to do so with a minimum of organization time.

MEDICARE HMO

"Medicare HMO" is simply an HMO that accepts only persons on

Medicare, both those age 65 and older, and those under 65 receiving Medicare because of disabilities. It may be any of the Models listed above, but it also has its own peculiarities.

If a Medicare Beneficiary enrolls in an HMO, the Beneficiary is no longer on Medicare. To be approved by Medicare, the IB40 must furnish all of the medical services provided by Medicare, plus those services provided by a Medicare Supplemental policy. The HMO may provide additional services, and many do; for instance many provide routine checkups that would not be covered under Medicare. In some states the Medicare HMO provided prescription drugs that would not be provided under Medicare, or under most Medicare Supplement policies. In most Medicare HMO's the Medicare beneficiary does not pay a premium to the HMO, but continues to pay the Part B Medicare premium as he would have paid had he remained on Medicare. The IM40 is paid a contracted sum for each Medicare beneficiary that changes to the BA40. The sum paid can vary from $300 a month, to twice that amount or more, depending upon the geographical location and availability of medical care.

In today's market, the HMO is rapidly taking over the need for Medicare Supplements, to the point that in some geographical areas, the HMO "owns" the supplemental market. In some locations, the IB40s organize Senior Clubs, sponsor outings, provide club houses for social functions and become heavily involved in the social life of the Beneficiaries. In many retirement areas, HMOs have become popular because of the lack of out of-pocket expense (no need to purchase a supplement), and they provide some prescription drug programs where there is none available otherwise. Many observers are positive that in the not too distant future, Medicare will be available only in some form of HMO.

INTEGRATED DELIVERY SYSTEMS

The Integrated Delivery System refers to the merging of the methods of paying for health care, and can be used when referring to several different organizations. The delivery of medical services is integrated by uniting groups of doctors and a (or several) hospital(s) into one cohesive unit, or one organization. A Staff Model HMO which owns its own hospital and employs its own physicians, is an example of such an integrated delivery system.

Staff model IB40s are considered fully integrated, both vertically and horizontally. Vertical refers to the ownership of the hospital and (employee) the physicians. Horizontal means all of the services that they offer and the financial risk that they assume, i.e. vertical means the entity owns the hospitals and employers the physicians. Full horizontal integration would mean complete range of medical and claims services managed intensively through utilization management, gate keeping, data management, and assumes full financial risk by providing both physician and hospital care for a tee per person (capitation fee). Kaiser Permanente is an example of a fully vertical and horizontal integrated delivery system. A Group Model HMO that does not own its own hospital would not be a fully vertical delivery system.

PROFIT AND EXPENSE COMPARISONS - HMO & TRADITIONAL

Traditional insurers have a lower expense ratio, 6.9% compared to HMOs average of 10%. HMOs earn 8.3% profit on every dollar or premiums, indemnity insurers earn only 3.7% profit margin on their premium dollar. Managed care organizations spend proportionately less on providing medical care per premium dollar than do indemnity insurance payers. A 1995 CBO study concluded that Managed Care organizations reduce use of health care services by 8% when compared with a typical indemnity plan.

HMO members generally experience lower hospital admission rates and lengths of stay, than indemnity plan policyowners. HMOs use fewer expensive procedures, e.g. average Managed Care patient spent 2 fewer days in intensive care and 5 less days in the hospital, with financial differences approximately $4,000 for average patient. National Cancer institute found that a study of breast cancer surgery results found that survival rates were "significantly worse at HMO hospitals than at large or small community hospitals."

HMOs do provide as much diagnostic and preventive care, if not more than, indemnity programs. A 1996 report found that significantly higher dissatisfaction among sick members of Managed Care plans as opposed to fee-for-service plans in the wait for appointment and the doctors interest in the case. Many doctors feel that "Managed care and rationed care are synonymous." (Dr. Warren Francis, Letters to the Editor, New York Times, Feb. 26, 1995.)

Younger and healthier people have more interest in HMOs as they have no particular relationship with a family doctor and they like the preventative care and the reduced premiums. This has left the fee-for-service and indemnity companies with those who are older and of poorer health.

PREFERRED PROVIDER ORGANIZATIONS (PPO'S)

The basic similarity of HMOs and PPOs is that they both consist of healthcare networks. However, with a PPO the providers are paid for the medical services they actually provide, as if they were in a fee-for-service system. The principal difference between the PPO and the fee-for-service (FFS) system is that the providers cannot charge whatever they wish, as they have contracted with the PPO to accept a pre-determined fee for the services rendered. In most cases, the fees are discounted from what they would normally charge for the service. In addition, providers usually agree to certain Managed Care procedures imposed by the PPO. The employee benefits plans or individual contracts utilizing PPOs have a financial incentive to use the network. The coinsurance payment required by the plan will be markedly reduced if non-network providers are used. As an example a traditional plan will offer 80% coverage for medical bills (after a deductible, or without a deductible, depending upon the plan) if network providers are used. If non-network providers are used, then the plan will only pay a reduced amount, such as 60%. This would provide sufficient inducement to receive treatment only from the network providers.

An additional incentive frequently arises as the network providers have all contracted for the amount that they will charge for the medical procedure. A non-network provider has no such contract, and can, and frequently will, charge more than the plan allows. The user of the plan is responsible for the amount charged by the provider and that was not paid by the plan.

With the pre-determined fees and the Managed Care procedures imposed on the PPO providers, PPO medical care costs have remained lower than the FFS costs. The HMO's experience a lower cost for medical care than do PPOs, however the PPO users are generally much more satisfied with their plan than those covered under HMOs. The principal attraction appears to be the fact that the PPO member can choose a provider from a large number of providers, and they can also choose their own specialist, regardless of what their doctor wants. The amount of "freedom of choice" that a PPO user loses when they leave a fee-for-service plan, appears to be acceptable in these situations.

PPOs can be sponsored by a wide variety of businesses and organizations. Most of the PPOs are sponsored by insurance companies, but there is a rapidly growing group of independent investors who own PPOs. Also, hospitals, doctor groups (or an arrangement between both), HMO's, or Third Party Administrators (TPAs) own PPO's. In some cases, smaller PPO organizations band together to form a larger PPO that can offer more services.

Most PPOs attempt to offer the broadest range of medical care possible, including hospitals, laboratory and x-ray facilities, and even mental, vision and dental care. By offering all of these services, there are fewer incentives for patients to go outside of the network and the easier it is to control costs.

Originally, PPO providers were paid on a contractual pre-negotiated discount system. However, some providers would raise their rates until the actual amount they received was equal to (or more than) the fee before the discount. Obviously this was counterproductive, so a system of fees, pre-negotiated, was developed based on the numeric codes used by physicians to describe the medical procedures they provide to their patients. There are two code systems, the Current Procedural Terminology (CPT), which described the procedure, such as suturing, injections, etc., and the International Classification of Diseases, 9th Edition (ICD-9), describing the diagnosis.

A price is assigned to each code, and this price is the amount that is paid to the provider. Medicare with its ever-increasing amount of paperwork, adopted the RBRVS (resource based relative value scale) in 1992 as a method of compensating physicians. Because of the growing number of Medicare recipient's providers are familiar with the system. One advantage of the RBRVS system is that it takes into consideration services other than treatments, such as consultation, examinations, etc. This was appreciated by those in general or family practices as they spend more time with their patients than do the specialists. Hospitals obviously use different systems, as their billing procedures are much different. Originally they used a negotiated discount, but have now adopted one of the following systems:

- Per Diem: A set fee is paid for each day a patient stays in the hospital, thereby eliminating any reason to raise fees to compensate for any discount.
- Tiered Per Diem: A set fee is paid for each day a patient stays in the hospital, but the fees vary according to specialty area within the hospital. It may also upon the number of PPO patients in the hospital.
- Per Care (Diagnosis Related Group): Medicare introduced the DRG method in 1983, and it has been adopted by many private hospitals. The amount of care that is necessary to treat each patient is determined, and the hospital is then paid on that diagnosis instead of being paid for the actual amount of care that was received. This led to the "sicker and quicker" concept of getting patients out of the hospital before they are completely cured. In turn, this produced a rash of regulations and the problem appears to have been mostly solved. Providers are sensitive to any adverse publicity as a result of being discharged too quickly while under the provider's care.

MANAGED CARE MANAGEMENT FOR PPO'S

PPO providers must contract for and agree to utilization management controls. These controls pertain to practice patterns, outpatient procedures, hospital care, and specialized areas such as chiropractic care, physical therapy and mental health. These utilization procedures consist of analyzing treatment patterns, and if the pattern falls outside of the norm for the same or similar medical situation, this information is provided to the participating providers. This allows the providers to compare their treatment of a specific condition, and the results thereof, with that of their contemporaries in their geographical region or in their area of specialty.

POINT - OF SERVICE PLANS

For the user, it can be difficult to differentiate between PPOs and Point-of-Service (POS) plans, as they are actually HMOs. POS plans can provide for out-of-network coverage with a penalizing reimbursement differential so as to direct patients to their network. Providers may be compensated on a variety of systems, either per-patient capita system, or under some contractual fee arrangement. Points-of-Service name arises because members can access medical care at a point of service other than their PCP. Since the choice of physician restriction posed a major barrier to acceptance of HMO's by the members and by the general public, POS plans have grown to be very popular and most of the recent growth in HMO enrollment is from Point of Service plans. And importantly, they have contained healthcare costs as well as HMO's.

PHO'S - PHYSICIAN-HOSPITAL ORGANIZATIONS.

The PHOs meld a variety of providers to provide health care services for insurance companies and employers. In 1996, 10 percent of all medical groups with more than 50 doctors were owned by hospitals. Also, 69% of physician groups, 62% of home health agencies, 55% of Managed Care organizations and 46% of skilled nursing facilities were involved in these integrated health systems. Some provider groups have decided to go directly to employers and offer their services, thereby bypassing the HMOs. This way they will be rewarded for keeping costs down, while if they were with an HMO, the HMO would keep the savings for themselves. Hospitals have formed subsidiaries that are designed to bring the physicians into a closer business relationship with the hospital without making them employees.

The Physician-Hospital Organization (PHO) brings physicians and hospitals together in a joint business enterprise. Frequently, a PHO consists of one hospital and many doctors that contract with the hospital to accept their Managed Care patients. By physicians and hospitals working together, large numbers of patients can be channeled to certain providers. By forming a PHO, both hospitals and physicians can create a more powerful contracting entity. A feature of the PHO that can have powerful influence on Managed Care in the future, is their ability to advance both vertically and horizontally, and as they evolve, they can be substantial competitors with HMOs and PPOs in the health care market. Physician groups that "capitate" and act as insurers, can eliminate the "gatekeeper" function of the Primary Care Physician. The gatekeeper function was found during a survey to be of significant concern to 68% of American consumers. There is little data available as this is a relatively new arrangement, but it appears that these groups do not increase the cost of care, but may even decrease the cost because of the elimination of the gatekeeper function.

Carve - Outs

"Carve-Outs" refers to a plan that is taken from a larger plan providing more benefits, and provides services only to a special or particular area. Many such medical services can be "carved-out", including mental health, dental or vision benefits, chiropractic, physical therapy, prescription drugs, etc. Usually they consist of healthcare providers who contract with insurers or

HMOs to provide certain specialized benefits and at a fixed price. These providers are usually part of a loosely organized provider network. One example is a network of cardiologists and heart surgeons, with over 500 members located all over the United States. In order to qualify each physician must perform at least 150 heart bypasses or similar operations, and to do so in hospitals that do at least 500 or more of such procedures each year. They are subject to strict peer review and their mortality rate must be very low in order to participate. A PPO or HMO that specialized in a particular type of care may be more successful at controlling costs for that type of care than a general purpose medical care network. Prescription drugs are the most familiar "carve-out", as prescription drugs appear to be approaching 25% of the total medical care costs. In order to contain these costs, certain options for prescription drugs are available.

Card Plans

Card plans are the most popular plan. The customers are issued cards to be presented to a pharmacy (that is part of the network) which has agreed to furnish drugs at a predetermined discount. Since this is done electronically, administrative costs are lower and paperwork is reduced dramatically. Some card plans require a co-payment only, frequently differing from generic and standard brand drugs, and the plan paying the remainder of the cost. Some plans provide for drug utilization review, which reviews the drugs and its application, and uses a "formulary". (A formulary is list of drugs that covers all, or most of drug therapy that might be used to cover the treatment offered by the plan. An "open" formulary allows for drugs not listed, wherein a "closed" formulary restricts drugs to only those on the provider list.)

Mail - Orderplans

A mail-order plan allows customers to order drugs through the mail. These drugs are primarily for maintenance, such as high-blood pressure, allergies, etc. as obviously they cannot be obtained quickly for medical emergencies. This provides considerable savings as they can usually be obtained in a larger supply than normal and the pharmacies supplying these drugs furnish the prescriptions at substantial discounts. Some firms offer a managed prescription drug plan wherein they contract with a large number of employees and furnish the prescription drugs at a negotiated price.

MENTAL HEALTH AND SUBSTANCE ABUSE

Another Carve-out program is for Mental Health and Substance Abuse. It is necessary to carve-out these plans because either (a) the benefits provided by the general healthcare plan are too limited, such as being restricted by the provisions of an HMO; or (b) the employer wants to keep the inpatient benefit for mental health or substance abuse from being overutilized. An employer may also wish to offer expanded mental health and substance abuse benefits and at the same time keep control of the costs. The carve-out allows this.

BUSINESS SPONSORED WELLNESS PROGRAMS

Nearly twenty percent of the illnesses that can be related to lifestyle, it is estimated, costs over $171 billion dollars per year. One of the most easily identifiable lifestyle illness, heart attacks, are reported to cost employers an average of about $80,000 in hospital costs, and over $15,000 in disability benefits. In addition to the costs related directly to medical care and disability, lost productivity is very expensive. There are approximately 200,000 employees - ages 45 to 65 - each year disabled by heart problems and which cost employers more than $700 million to replace these employees. Obviously, it is in everyone's benefit to reduce the financial toll that lifestyle illnesses bring to employers.

When a business has healthier employees, the business will make more money, be more successful, and can afford to expand a wellness program. Many businesses work with local health clubs to promote wellness programs. The health club industry has developed statistics that show productivity (and profit) can be increased by as much as 20% with an active and professional wellness program. Absenteeism due to illnesses and injury is reduced dramatically for those participating in such a program. A well-designed wellness program is an attractive recruiting tool and soon becomes known as an employee benefit. For those employees that use the program on a regular basis, it becomes a social as well as fitness aid. Productivity increases as the employees are able to see the results of the program and they start to feel better about themselves.

Coors Brewing Company was mentioned in particular, at a recent IRSA (Association of Health Club owners) meeting as they have had a wellness program installed for several months. A cardiac rehabilitation program at this brewery has shortened the length of time that an employee lost due to heart problems, from 7 months to just 5 weeks, and with excellent results with no negative effects. Medical claims for Coors employees who regularly use (two or more times a week) its wellness center are 13% lower than those for non-users. Coors' wellness program includes a program designed to help temporarily disabled employees get back to work as soon as possible. In addition, they offer nutrition counseling and smoking cessation classes. Coors attributes cost savings in excess of $4 million for a recent year.

Typically, a corporate wellness program will return in excess of $3 for every dollar invested, and can have a measurable value to the company.

While typically a Wellness Program is provided or installed by a local health club, in some situations it will include preventive screenings, and non-medical programs designed for behavioral changes such as stress management and smoking cessation.

PROGRAMS FOR THE PREVENTION OF INDUSTRIAL ACCIDENTS

Managed care is not restricted to reducing employee benefit and health insurance premiums, but also can be used for the prevention of accidents in the workplace. Since over 10,000 workers are killed on the job each year, and 6 million are injured, this is of prime importance to all employers. The prevention of illnesses and accidents in the workplace is primarily designed to reduce Workers Compensation costs but it also affects employee benefit costs. Employees, who are taught to recognize workplace hazards, and how to respond to such hazards, generally continue with these practices even while not on the job.

EMPLOYEE ASSISTANCE PROGRAMS

Employees are human beings, and all humans have problems serious enough to affect their job performance at some time or other. When these problems arise, many will go away without any professional intervention. However, those that do not will probably continue to worsen and will be reflected by a decline in work habits and product quality. Inevitably, absenteeism, injuries on the job, and increasing medical costs will arise.

Originally, these types of programs were designed to help those with alcohol problems. In the 1940's, many returning servicemen had alcohol problems so many employers instituted formal programs to assist those to overcome their problems and to better assimilate into society. These programs have grown to encompass counseling and referral services, financial and legal counseling, marital counseling, childcare issues, chemical dependency and psychological problems. Large companies offer plans like this today and are quite popular, with an estimated 80% of large employers participating

If employees will use such a program, a recent study shows that medical claims averaged 30% less than for employees who did not use the program. Another study found that early intervention in chemical dependency could reduce medical costs by up to 69%, reduce the number of employee sick days by 47%, and lower accident benefits by 48%.

Index